THE FREEDOM AGENDA

★★★★★★★★★★★★★★★★★★★★★★★★
★★★★★★★★★★★★★★★★★★★★★★★★

THE FREEDOM AGENDA

WHY AMERICA MUST SPREAD DEMOCRACY

(JUST NOT THE WAY GEORGE BUSH DID)

JAMES TRAUB

FARRAR, STRAUS AND GIROUX   NEW YORK

★★★★★★★★★★★★★★★★★★★★★★★★
★★★★★★★★★★★★★★★★★★★★★★★★

Farrar, Straus and Giroux
18 West 18th Street, New York 10011

Distributed in Canada by Douglas & McIntyre Ltd.
Printed in the United States of America
First edition, 2008

Library of Congress Cataloging-in-Publication Data
Traub, James.
    The freedom agenda : why America must spread democracy (just not the
way George Bush did) / James Traub.—1st ed.
        p.   cm.
    Includes bibliographical references and index.
    ISBN-13: 978-0-374-15847-7 (hardcover : alk. paper)
    ISBN-10: 0-374-15847-9 (hardcover : alk. paper)
    1. United States—Foreign relations—2001–   2. United States—Foreign
relations—20th century.   3. Democracy—United States—Government
policy—United States.   I. Title.

JZ1480.T73 2008
327.73—dc22

                                                                2008021492

Designed by Jonathan D. Lippincott

www.fsgbooks.com

1   3   5   7   9   10   8   6   4   2

To the men and women who stand up for
democratic change in the Islamic world—
undaunted, even when overmatched

Contents

THE FREEDOM AGENDA

Introduction

In his second inaugural address, in January 2005, President George W. Bush declared, "The survival of liberty in our land increasingly depends on the success of liberty in other lands." This was the most succinct possible statement of the post-9/11 doctrine that came to be known as the Freedom Agenda. Of course it was an arguable proposition: Perhaps our liberty depended more on the success of something else in other lands—economic growth, the rule of law, simple justice. But all that was, in a sense, detail. For if the deeply repressive political cultures of Saudi Arabia or Egypt had helped produce the foot soldiers and the leadership cadre of Al Qaeda, and if the chaos of Afghanistan had served as the petri dish for the Taliban, then it was plain that our safety depended on the internal conditions, and not just the foreign policy, of other states. As Secretary of State Condoleezza Rice put it with a bit more intellectual finesse: "The fundamental character of regimes now matters more than the international distribution of power."

The Freedom Agenda was a restatement, in far more urgent terms, of a venerable American axiom. From the time of the founding of the republic, Americans had believed that Providence had singled them out to offer a world living in darkness the great blessings of liberty—to serve as "a standing monument and example for the aim and imitation of people of other countries," as Thomas Jefferson wrote. We hold that the principles upon which our country is founded are not peculiar to us but, rather, constitute timeless and universal truths. The Declaration of Independence, Abraham Lincoln said, gave "liberty, not alone to the people of this country, but hope to the world for all future time." And as our reach became global in the twentieth century, we would not only testify to the glories of democracy, but actively seek to propagate them across the globe. To this day we describe this policy as "Wilsonian," after Woodrow Wilson, the first president to explicitly seek to spread democracy abroad.

Our pursuit of these ideals has led us to make choices that would not have been dictated by a strict calculation of national interest: building the foundations of democracy in the Philippines in the first years of the twentieth century; defending the right of self-determination of colonized peoples; establishing after World War II a network of multilateral institutions that constrained our own power; rebuilding Germany and Japan as well as our wartime allies; assailing not just our adversaries but our friends for the abuse of human rights; undertaking a humanitarian intervention in Kosovo; and in recent years, supporting the solitary voices calling for reform in the Middle East. But there's a reason the term *Wilsonian* conjures up naïveté and recklessness as much as it does moral commitment. As the political theorist Hans Morgenthau wrote soon after World War II, "The missionary conception of the relationship between our domestic situation and our foreign policy" blends inevitably into a crusading one, in which "the American example is transformed into a formula for universal salvation by which right-thinking nations voluntarily abide and to which the others must be compelled to submit"—"with fire and sword, if necessary."

And this brings us back to President Bush. Democracy has always been our national credo, and the ambition to spread it abroad, our missionary impulse. The terrorist attacks of 2001 reconfigured this act of cultural self-affirmation into a matter of national security. The assault might well have persuaded a President Al Gore—or John McCain—that our liberty depended on the success of liberty in other lands. But the language that the Bush administration used to express this new principle had a self-righteous and theological flavor; and the policies with which it pursued this goal were heavy-handed and often bellicose. In Iraq, the president tried to bring liberty to the Middle East by fire and sword. America's own past experience, and the history of the Arab world, offered all the lessons he could have needed in the difficulty and perhaps the futility, and certainly the hubris, of this exercise. Iraq was meant to be a demonstration model, and it has been—but not in the way the administration intended. Iraq is now taken as proof of the folly, and indeed the hypocrisy, of America's idealistic adventures abroad; of a brute doctrine of transformation by warfare; of the hollowness of *democracy* as uttered by our leaders; and of the absurdity of imagining that the United States can promote its values abroad, whatever they are.

And it's not only in Iraq that America has been seen to discredit its own professed principles. At the very moment when officials were trying to repair the damage done to our image by decades of steadfast support for Arab dictators, the worldwide media were dominated by stories of American torture at the Abu Ghraib prison, perpetual imprisonment without judicial recourse at Guantánamo Bay, the clandestine smuggling of detainees to third world countries with scant regard for human rights. America had tried to promote democracy abroad while showing contempt for it at home. Is it any wonder that in a recent poll, only 29 percent of respondents in eighteen countries thought that the United States was having a "mainly positive" effect on the world, while 52 percent considered the effect "mainly negative"? In Turkey, America's chief ally in the Muslim world, the number of respondents who expressed a "favorable view of the U.S."—a phrase that usually elicits a much more positive response—had fallen from 52 percent in 1999–2000 to 9 percent in 2007. How can you seek to universalize your values in places where ordinary citizens think you stand for something deplorable?

The Bush administration first codified the core principles of the post-9/11 world in the National Security Strategy of 2002. The document posited that we must be prepared to act preemptively, as well as unilaterally, to prevent terrorists from acquiring, or of course using, weapons of mass destruction; that we must be willing to overthrow a regime that threatens us and the international order, as we had in Afghanistan; that we must retain unrivaled military supremacy; and that we must remove the conditions that foster terrorism by making "freedom and the development of democratic institutions key themes in our bilateral relations." We can now say, in retrospect, that the Iraq war, and the larger war on terrorism, have discredited the doctrines in whose name they have been fought. This is, in effect, the intellectual wreckage left behind by the political and diplomatic fiasco of the last eight years.

We have had only one foreign policy since 9/11. And that policy has been shaped by the fear and anger and sense of vulnerability provoked by that horror, and by the ways in which President Bush and his team have responded to, and exploited, that national mood. As I write these words, the Bush era is drawing to an end. We will soon have another president, and thus another way of understanding our place in the world. We will have, in effect, a post-post-9/11 policy. And in shaping such a policy, we need to ask what, if anything, we should rescue from the rubble of President Bush's national security strategy. We will, of course, continue to reserve the right to act preemptively and unilaterally under certain circumstances, to act against state sponsors of terrorism, to retain our military superiority. We have done so in the past—but without elevating these principles to the status of core doctrine. And as the world has become so much more dangerous, at least compared to a decade ago, we need to be unambiguous about our willingness to use force.

But since 9/11 we have defined ourselves almost exclusively by our heightened awareness of danger, and our heightened willingness to respond with a show of military might. We have made ourselves awesome, and frightening. Or rather, to give both principal moods of the Bush White House their due, we have bristled with terrible force, and beckoned to an almost magical realm of possibility—with Vice President Dick Cheney in charge of bristling, and President Bush urging the people of Iraq, and of Palestine and of Egypt, to somehow claim the universal birthright of freedom. We need to learn once again to speak to the world with hope—but a hopefulness tempered by a sense of the possible. And this requires clearing away the wreckage of recent years.

If we accept that the character of many regimes now affects us more than the way in which they project power abroad, and thus that our own security depends on the progress of liberty—or of something—among those regimes, then we must, in fact, find a way to revitalize, and rethink, the Freedom Agenda. What would this mean? Perhaps, for example, it's not liberty—or freedom, or democracy—that we should seek to support abroad. Assailing the bipartisan faith in "Democratism," Anatol Lieven and John Hulsman, the authors of *Ethical Realism*, a scathing critique of Bush administration policy, propose instead that we seek to fashion "The Great Capitalist Peace," incorporating nations into the global economy. Others argue that infant democracies are actually more turbulent and dangerous than authoritarian regimes. In *Electing to Fight: Why Emerging Democracies Go to War*, Edward D. Mansfield and Jack Snyder insist that we should forestall elections until countries develop the liberal institutions that will permit a more stable transition.

There's a lot to be said for this view. Nations such as Poland and Hungary, which had lived under Soviet domination, made a swift and relatively pain-free transition to democracy when the Russians pulled out, because they had a long tradition of liberal values and institutions. In Africa, where no such tradition exists, the arrival of democracy has often done nothing to mitigate, and at times has even exacerbated, corruption, poverty, and warlord rule. And we cannot simply assume that democracy is an unmitigated good for citizens, or a bulwark against terrorism. The link between democracy and development is tenuous, if broadly positive; Asia furnishes any number of examples of dynamic autocracies. And it is blithe to imagine that democratic states do not foster terrorism. The democratic Philippines produces far more terrorists than does authoritarian China. And many of the jihadists who have murdered civilians in Europe were born and raised in the democratic, cosmopolitan West.

Democracy does not cure all ills. And yet people want it. What's more, the era when you could tell people to wait until they were "ready" is long since over. In recent years, citizens in both Ukraine and Nigeria have clamored for genuinely democratic rule. Ukraine is a largely middle-class European nation with decent democratic prospects; Nigeria is a giant, chaotic, impoverished African country with a tradition of tyranny and corruption. Should we have supported the Ukrainians and told the Nigerians to hang on? We didn't; but it wouldn't have made much difference if we had. Democracy has become a near universal aspiration about which we cannot choose to be agnostic. And you cannot spend time in even the most wretchedly impoverished democracies without learning that people everywhere care about having a voice in their own affairs, and having recourse in the face of abusive treatment.

But what can we actually *do* to help the democratic cause? At critical moments in a nation's history, when an authoritarian leader refuses to step down, or when the military overthrows a democratically elected figure, or when an election pits democratic against autocratic forces, outsiders can play a crucial role, as the United States has over the years in Chile, the Dominican Republic, the Philippines, and Soviet Georgia, among other places. Otherwise, however, outsiders can only nurture. Democracy cannot be "exported," much less imposed, as of course autocracy can be; outsiders can help only where the wish for democracy already exists (as it did not in Iraq). And even where a seed has already sprouted, outsiders can only help coax it out of the ground and into the air. "Democracy promotion" is too aggressive by half, and its history over the last century counsels modest expectations.

Perhaps outsiders can make a difference; but what if the outsider is the United States? How, today, can we promote anything, much less democracy? The American project in the Middle East is now associated, fairly or not, with regime change and global aggression. It may be that the very word *democracy* has become so tainted that we will have to put it away until the toxins have leached out. And even a new and more charitably regarded president would confront the same strategic issue that this White House has faced: We rely on autocrats such as Hosni Mubarak of Egypt to play a moderate role among neighbors, just as in the cold war we relied on anticommunist dictators in Latin America and elsewhere. They need us, but we need them; and they know it. How do we respond when a Mubarak, or a Pervez Musharraf of Pakistan, claims that opposition forces are destabilizing their regime? Can we call their bluff? What if the opposition forces are Islamist? Should we be willing to support "moderate Islamists"? Is there such a thing?

Democracy promotion presents a series of hard choices about our behavior abroad; but it also demands that we think about the principles we apply to ourselves. We have called insistently for democracy elsewhere, and yet rarely, if ever, in our history has the United States itself been seen as so poor a model of democracy. We seem to be trapped in a paradox: The same threats that have prompted us to try to shape more liberal outcomes beyond our shores have persuaded us, or at least the current occupants of the White House, that we can no longer afford to be the open society we were before 9/11. Thus we reserve for ourselves the right to torture prisoners because the stakes of the war on terrorism are so high. And yet it's precisely at such moments when a nation's commitment to its principles are tested.

We cannot escape the accusations of hypocrisy. We cannot hide the facts from those others to whom we wish to preach, any more than from ourselves. We live in a transparent world, and we must treat transparency as our great advantage, not a threat to our security. Bill Clinton recently remarked that when he convened Israeli and Palestinian officials in a last-ditch effort to make peace at the end of his tenure, he didn't know if he would succeed, but "I was going to get caught trying." Clinton was right in thinking that the effort itself would help our standing in the Middle East, no matter what the outcome. And the principle applies in general: Just as we can get caught trying to ship "enemy combatants" to secret interrogation camps, so we can get caught trying to sustain the forces of democracy in authoritarian countries, overmatched though they are. We can get caught engaging with moderate Islamists who believe in free speech and the rule of law. We can get caught offering a democratic alternative to African countries beguiled by the Chinese model of top-down, autocratic development. We can get caught, in short, behaving in conformity with our deepest principles.

1

An Education in Self-Government

In Which We Teach the Filipinos, and They Teach Us

American foreign policy throughout the nineteenth century was largely governed by the principle that President John Quincy Adams famously laid out in his 1824 inaugural address: "America does not go abroad in search of monsters to destroy." With our own continent still to explore, and an apparently bottomless supply of natural resources, we had little need of foreign markets or foreign products, and we deprecated the European scramble for colonial dominion as unworthy of a democratic nation. But by the end of the century we had exhausted our frontier, we had become a global trading power, and we had surpassed much of Europe as an industrial and financial force. Our long era of self-absorption ended with a bang when Adm. George Dewey sank much of the Spanish fleet in Manila Harbor on May 1, 1898. Woodrow Wilson, a historian before he was president, wrote, "The battle of Trenton was not more significant than the battle of Manila. The nation that was one hundred and twenty-five years in the making has now stepped forth into the open arena of the world."

But the battle weighs less in our national annals than does the subsequent decision to annex and colonize the Philippines. This was precisely the kind of entanglement against which Adams—and George Washington before him—had warned. Throughout the nineteenth century we had been content to serve merely as an example to others. Our infant republic offered, as Jefferson had said, "a standing monument and example" to the world. But with the conquest of the Philippines, as Hans Morgenthau observed, "an activist conception of America's mission in the world was added to this passive one." We would become not merely "missionaries," but "crusaders." The annexation of the Philippines was a blunt assertion of power by a state bursting with political and moral self-confidence, but from the distinctive tension between raw power and high purpose emerged the world's first self-conscious exercise in democracy promotion, and in democratic nation-building.

The United States did not premeditate its colonial experience in the Philippines. President William McKinley had not sought a war with Spain, and did what he could to forestall it. The issue became inescapable when Spain's long campaign to suppress an insurgency in Cuba turned especially brutal in the mid-1890s. This was the era of the "yellow press," and the popular dailies competed in depictions of atrocities. Soon the entire nation was inflamed with outrage at Spanish cruelty. War might nevertheless have been averted, for a moderate regime that gained power in Spain in late 1897 went to great lengths to mollify the Americans, and President McKinley pronounced himself satisfied with their efforts. Then, in February 1898, the *Maine* went down with 266 hands in Havana Harbor. Despite the lack of evidence pointing to Spanish involvement—an accident on board seems to have set off the great stores of gunpowder—the American public now demanded satisfaction. Two months later, Congress passed a resolution of war without being asked for one by the president, insisting that Spain withdraw from Cuba within three days—an obvious impossibility—or face "the entire land and naval forces of the United States."

The war combined elements of unbridled jingoism with what we would now call "humanitarian intervention"—the penny broadsheet version of a "CNN war." It wasn't a strategic war; it wasn't a necessary war. But it was an eminently winnable war, and a noble enterprise to boot—or so Americans quickly came to feel. Spain put up little resistance, making the war yet jollier. The war, at least in its Pacific theater, was over almost before it began. The speed of events forced the McKinley administration to figure out what to do with this remote sprawl of Pacific islands long before it was ready to do so. McKinley ordered the army to secure the chief island, though at the time he had no intention of staying. He told Secretary of State John Hay that he would be quite content with "a port and necessary appurtenances."

But once again, McKinley could not, or would not, face down public fervor, which demanded that we gain the prize for which we had fought, if ever so briefly. McKinley was deeply torn; he later told a delegation of clergymen that he had paced the halls of the White House night after night, and then had fallen to his knees with a prayer for insight. "It came to me," he explained, that it would be "cowardly and dishonorable" to return the islands to Spain; "bad business and discreditable" to hand them over to other European imperial powers; and irresponsible to "leave them to themselves," and thus to anarchy. There was thus "nothing left to do" but to "take them all" and "do the very best we could by them."

The anti-imperialist faction argued that a nation dedicated to the principle of liberty, having broken the shackles of colonial rule, was obligated to restore the country to its own people. But men such as McKinley viewed such a course as profoundly irresponsible. We were enjoined to make the Filipino people capable of self-government before handing them the reins of government. As Woodrow Wilson wrote in 1902, "It were easy enough to give [the Philippines] independence, if by independence you mean only disconnection from any government outside the islands, the independence of a rudderless boat adrift. But self-government? How is that 'given'? Can it be given? Is it not gained, earned, graduated into from the hard school of life . . . ?" And so, having taken the islands, it was our duty to "impart to [the Filipino people], if it be possible by contact and sympathy, and example, the drill and habit of law and obedience which we long ago got out of the strenuous processes of English history." As England did for us, so we would do for the Philippines.

But there was a problem with this great project of regeneration. The Filipinos, who had come to despise the Spanish friars who owned the best land and ruled in the name of a distant power, had fought their own war against a colonizer; they did not want to be adopted by another, allegedly more benevolent, master. And they naïvely assumed that the Americans had arrived to shatter the yoke of colonialism. Once the Spanish left, Emilio Aguinaldo, the leader of the Filipino rebels, returned from Hong Kong, whence the Spanish had exiled him, intending to become president of a new nation. For six months, the Filipino people ruled themselves. But all of President McKinley's sources assured him that self-rule would be a recipe for chaos and anarchy—which it quite possibly would have been. In December of 1898, he instructed his negotiators in Paris to insist that Spain surrender the islands (in return for $20 million). The Senate approved the Treaty of Paris the following February. And Aguinaldo and thousands of his followers turned their weapons on the American soldiers.

Over the course of the next two years, American policy-makers discovered the wisdom of John Quincy Adams's admonition, for the U.S. Army fought a war no less savage than the Spanish had in Cuba. Seventy-five thousand troops—three quarters of the U.S. Army—were required to subdue the rebellion. More than 220,000 Filipinos are thought to have died in battle, as well as more than 4,000 American troops. Our textbooks tell us little about the Filipino-American War, perhaps because it bore so little resemblance to the "splendid little war" we fought against Spanish imperialists. It was, in many ways, the prototype of the many guerrilla wars that lay in our future. Each side routinely tortured the other. American soldiers practiced what they called the "water-cure" torture, placing unforthcoming Filipinos under the tap of an iron tub, forcing water into their mouths, and then stomping on their stomachs to make them vomit. If that didn't produce the desired information, a medic would use a syringe to squirt salt water up the man's nostrils.

But even as they were harshly suppressing the Filipino insurrection, American officials were also engaging in the kinds of nation-building activities designed to give local people a stake in the new order. The commander of the armed forces, Maj. Gen. Elwell Stephen Otis, though a zealous warrior, was a Harvard Law School graduate who took seriously the obligation to build institutions of governance. Otis established municipal and town governments led by Filipinos ultimately accountable to U.S. military advisers, replaced Spanish judges with Filipino ones, and began to reform the judicial system. He set his soldiers to teaching children, vaccinating villagers against smallpox, distributing food, and building sewers. This dizzying combination of warmaking and what we would now call peacekeeping led his predecessor, Gen. Lloyd Wheaton, to ridicule the practice of "going with a sword in one hand, a pacifist pamphlet in the other hand, and trailing the model of a schoolhouse after." But President McKinley and the civil authorities he had appointed believed that they could subdue the insurrection through benevolence as much as gunfire.

Political development and military pacification proceeded simultaneously. In January 1900, President McKinley summoned William Howard Taft, the former solicitor general and now a federal circuit judge in Cincinnati, to meet with him at the White House. Taft was a stout and peaceable soul who had steadily climbed the ladder of Republican politics in Ohio. His consuming ambition in life was to join the Supreme Court (which he would eventually do in 1913, after serving one term as president).

He was hoping that McKinley intended to propose just that. When instead the president asked Taft to head up the Philippine Commission, which would administer the newly acquired territories, "He might as well have told me that he wanted me to take a flying machine," as Taft later recalled. Taft had opposed the invasion, opposed the Monroe Doctrine, and in general had trouble fathoming why people tried to tear one another to bits when they could be doing business with one another instead.

Taft did not relish the prospect of transporting his great bulk to some godforsaken Pacific island. He suggested that the president find someone "more sympathetic with the situation." McKinley, who didn't much like the situation himself, replied, "I think I could trust the man who didn't want [the islands] better than I can the man who did." And his advisers were as one on Taft's merits, for he was, like the president himself, circumspect and shrewd, conservative in temperament but thoroughly pragmatic. When Taft continued to temporize, Secretary of War Elihu Root made an irresistible appeal to patriotism and manliness: "You have had an easy time of it holding office since you were twenty-one," Root said. "Now your country needs you . . . You may go on holding the job you have in a humdrum, mediocre way. But here is something that will test you; something in the way of effort and struggle, and the question is, will you take the harder or the easier task?" A man like Taft, imbued with an ideal of public service, could scarcely ignore such a call. Just to be on the safe side, however, McKinley added that he would put Taft on the Court if and when the occasion arose.

Root himself was the third member of the troika chiefly responsible for establishing America's nation-building experiment in the Philippines. The secretary of war was a New York corporate lawyer—formidable, straitlaced, and secretive, like Dickens's Tulkinghorn. He was a man who knew the world; though a staunch Republican, he counted among his clients Boss Tweed, the grand sachem of Tammany Hall, New York's Democratic machine. Root also had a mind that moved far beyond courthouse strategy. He had taken up his position in July 1899, and had had to solve the problem of Cuba before he got to that of the Philippines. The McKinley administration had accepted from the outset Cuba's right to self-government, but Root felt that America could not leave until it had devised a workable form of democracy there. He explained in a letter that the United States had to help the Cubans "avoid the conditions which have subjected Hayti, San Domingo and the Central American republics to continuous revolution and disorder." The great problem, he went on, is that the Cubans "have had no experience in anything save Spanish customs and Spanish methods which have grown up for centuries under a system opposed to general education and to self-government. To succeed in their experiment the Cubans must necessarily acquire some new ideas and some new methods. That is a very hard thing for a whole people to do, and it cannot be done by having outsiders preach at them. It is something that they have to do for themselves. The best that anybody else can do is to afford them opportunity of seeing and studying new methods."

Root recognized that self-government required not only formal institutions but the "methods" and "ideas" that lay behind them. A whole people could acquire these habits only slowly and laboriously, at least in the absence of general education. Outsiders could not implant such values, though they could model or perhaps teach them. Root was wary of popular democracy; he felt that democracy had to be arrived at by degrees. In another letter, he explained that in devising a system of suffrage for the Cubans, he had concluded we could not simply adopt the system used by Spain, which "controlled every pretend election with force and fraud," but neither could we offer the American principle of universal suffrage, which relies upon "the traditions of self-government and respect for constitutional methods and principles continuing through centuries and permeating the most ignorant social strata." Strong institutions depended on strong methods and ideas. In their absence, popular democracy could produce "revolution and disorder." Root and his chief advisers decided to limit the vote to property owners, the literate, and former Cuban soldiers, thus making the ballot a "reward" for thrift, "self-respect and ambition," and "patriotism and love of liberty." And when the United States granted independence to Cuba in 1902, the franchise was limited to these categories. (Universal suffrage was extremely rare at the time; women did not win the right to vote in the United States until the Nineteenth Amendment passed in 1920.)

Root believed, as did McKinley, Taft, and others, that the Philippines, unlike Cuba, was a poor candidate for self-government on any terms. "There is no Philippine people," he wrote, reflecting common wisdom. "The hundreds of islands . . . are inhabited by more than eighty different tribes, speaking more than sixty different languages." Self-government would be a formula for civil war. Root was well aware that colonial rule violated the principle of consent, which Americans held to be universal; the thought did not faze him. "Nothing can be more misleading than a principle misapplied," he wrote. "It is true wherever a people exist capable and willing to maintain just government, and to make free, intelligent and efficacious decisions as to who shall govern. But Jefferson did not apply it to Louisiana. He wrote to Gallatin that the people of Louisiana were as incapable of self-government as children, and he governed them without their consent." Raising up a people to self-government was a vastly more difficult undertaking than merely granting them sovereignty; but this was the burden that had fallen to us by virtue of our conquest.

Since the War Department was to retain jurisdiction over the Philippines so long as the insurrection lasted, it fell to Root, in the first months of 1900, to devise principles for the operation of the Philippine Commission. Though Root did not question America's right to exercise authority over a people "incapable of self-government," he puzzled over the question of how far American law, and the American body of rights, should be extended to cover noncitizens. Can a right that Americans considered universal nevertheless not apply to our colonial charges? The Constitution was silent on the colonial question. Root wrote to a friend that he had compiled "a list of a great number of books which covered in detail both the practice and the principle of colonial government under the English law." But after much study, he decided that an American system of colonial government had to arise from American principles. And Root concluded that those principles, embodied in the Constitution, must indeed be universally applicable. Even if the right of self-government was not absolute, there are nevertheless, he wrote, "certain things the United States government couldn't do because the people of the United States had declared that no government could do them." Root added ruefully, "We haven't always stuck to it."

Root formally issued his instructions in early April. This remarkable memorandum offered a kind of blueprint for the development of self-government. And when Root, Taft, and others spoke of self-government, they did not mean mere sovereignty; they meant rule by the people. We should pause to recognize how very strange and new this task was. However much they sought to develop their overseas possessions, colonial powers did not seek to cultivate self-rule; in fact, even the most liberal-minded among them went to great lengths to ensure their continued control. Moreover, non-Western peoples were not thought capable of democracy. While Asia had a number of sovereign states, none was remotely democratic; they were ruled, in the phrase of the day, by "Oriental despots." Root and the others did not put great store by the Filipino capacity for self-rule, but they could see no justification for their dominion save the development of this capacity.

Root enjoined the Philippine Commission first to establish a system of local government, then to move on to the provincial level, and finally to develop a national legislative apparatus that would take over from the military structure that had operated since annexation. At that point the commission would, in effect, constitute a new Filipino state, issuing orders for the raising and spending of revenue and for the creation of an educational system, a civil service, courts, and all the other functions of civil government. In an explicitly American touch, Root ordered that in the distribution of powers among local, state, and federal entities, "the presumption is always to be in favor of the smaller subdivision." And he added that local government was to be entrusted to the Filipinos, and that at higher levels natives were to be preferred to Americans "if they can be found competent and willing to perform the duties."

In the most extraordinary passage, Root reminded the commissioner that the government that they would be creating "is designed not for our satisfaction, or for the expression of our theoretical views, but for the happiness, peace and prosperity of the Philippine Islands," and thus that whatever measures they undertake "should conform to their customs, their habits and even their prejudices" as far as possible. Even their prejudices! Root would not have found this sentiment in his library of English colonial regulations. But neither would he have found his ensuing, and contrary, thought, which is that "certain great principles of government," and "certain practical rules," must apply in the Philippines even if they conflict with local custom. And Root then offered a roll call of the fundamental rights enumerated in the U.S. Constitution, starting with the Fourteenth Amendment—"no person shall be deprived of life, liberty or property without due process of law"—and then progressing through the rights of criminal defendants; the prohibition against slavery; freedom of speech, press, and assembly; and the separation of church and state.

The commission arrived in the Philippines in June 1900. The members, in addition to Taft, included an attorney, a judge, and a historian, among others. All were Americans; only Dean Worcester, a zoologist, had any prior familiarity with the islands. Few of them spoke Spanish, the language of the elite. Taft knew next to nothing of the nation he had been asked to rule. Taft's father, Alphonso, also a lawyer, had served as attorney general and then a diplomat for Republican administrations in the 1870s and '80s. Taft himself was a jovial enthusiast, a congenital optimist, a steady climber who rubbed no one the wrong way. Asked many years later by the journalist William Allen White how he had so deftly deployed his influence to rise up the ranks, he said, "I got my political pull, first, through my father's prominence; then there was the fact that I was hail-fellow-well-met with all of the political people of the city convention-going type." Another editor described the young Taft as possessing the "sunny disposition of an innocent child."

Taft, all 325 pounds of him, stepped off the boat from Hong Kong into a blast of heat and humidity that would not subside for months. The setting must have been every bit as miserable as he had imagined, but he was not only as big but also as industrious as an elephant, and he got straight to work meeting the people whose destiny he was to direct. Taft was a warmhearted man, and he quickly made friends among the Manila elite. But he knew and judged the world more or less as any other Anglo-American clubman of his time would. Both the country and its people were a shock to his system. "The population of the islands," he reported in a letter to Root a few months after his arrival, "is made up of a vast mass of ignorant, superstitious people, well-intentioned, light-hearted, temperate, somewhat cruel, domestic and fond of their families, and deeply wedded to the Catholic church." They were not only lighthearted but "light-fingered," and the "greatest liars in the world." Even the members of the elite "are generally lacking in moral character."

Whatever his doubts, Taft fully accepted the obligation to raise the natives from their abject state. As Root had proposed, the commission focused right away on local government. Here, after all, was the foundation of American democracy. In an early meeting of the commission, Taft cited Tocqueville on the "town conditions of New England," and observed that the "town spirit" he had found in the Philippines affords the "greatest hope of success" in evolving toward self-government. The commission held extensive hearings on the question, and ultimately devised a system in which local citizens would elect a municipal council and its chief officers; the council would be entrusted with tax collection and the enforcement of local ordinances, but any of its decisions could be contravened by the provincial government, in turn controlled by colonial authorities. What's more, as in Cuba, a strict control over the franchise was to curb the excesses of popular democracy. Only males twenty-three or older who had either served in the Spanish local government, paid taxes, or could demonstrate literacy in English or Spanish would be allowed to vote. This constituted less than 3 percent of the population.

The Americans were providing self-government with training wheels. Taft estimated that it could be fifty to a hundred years before the people had fully grasped the principles of "Anglo-Saxon liberty." This was not, as it would be today, a euphemism for "It's impossible" but rather a call for patient and steady commitment. Taft explained to a Senate committee that "it is the duty of the United States to establish there a government suited to the present possibilities of the people, which shall gradually change, conferring more and more right upon the people to govern themselves, thus educating them in self-government," until they were ready for statehood, protectorate status, or even independence.

At the same time, Taft recognized that the commission could not govern the islands by itself; it needed to work with and through the indigenous elite, and to give its members a vested interest in the project's success. Taft called this the "policy of attraction." In late 1900, the Americans officially recognized a native political party, the Federalistas, drawn almost entirely from the country's educated, pro-American class, known as the *ilustrados*. This Europeanized class identified more with the American rulers than with the peasantry; their platform called for American statehood. Taft gave the Federalists a monopoly over jobs reserved for Filipinos, thus turning the party into a patronage bank. He also refused to permit the forming of any other party, especially an anti-imperial one. In September 1901, the commission invited three Federalist leaders to join. Taft reassured Root that the new officers would prove "as orthodox in matters of importance as we are." He was so confident of their loyalty, or perhaps so eager to demonstrate America's willingness to share power with the locals, that he had pushed hard to induct two more Filipinos to the governing body, and to include among them Emilio Aguinaldo, the former rebel leader, who had been captured only six months before.

In the first months of 1902, Taft lobbied Congress to include a provision for a popular assembly in the "organic law" on the Philippines it was then debating. This, too, Taft argued, would operate as a form of political education. He ultimately carried the day, and the legislation signed by President Roosevelt in July (McKinley had been assassinated the previous September) provided for an assembly to be elected two years after the completion of a national census. The Popular Assembly convened for the first time in October 1907. It was a gathering of the national elite. Of the eighty delegates, sixty-five had university or other postsecondary education; fifty-six had legal training. One historian estimates that the average educational level was approximately equal to that of the U.S. Congress. The Assembly was yet another, grander form of self-government with training wheels, since the commission, now operating as the nation's upper house, could veto whatever legislation it didn't like. The Americans themselves often introduced legislation into the Assembly. And yet this system of tutelage, which lasted until the Filipinos gained full power over legislation in 1913, really did constitute a form of political education.

By the time the Assembly first convened, the United States had been administering the islands for eight years, and popular opinion, or at least elite opinion, had shifted considerably. The Federalists, having found to their chagrin that the United States had no intention of granting the Philippines U.S. statehood—Root had explained that it was hard enough dealing with the "Negro problem" without adding a Filipino one—now called vaguely for "ultimate independence." But incrementalism itself had fallen out of fashion. The Nationalist Party, many of whose members had served in the insurrection, called for immediate independence. Taft had earlier refused to let the party operate, but in the first meeting of the Assembly, it controlled almost three quarters of the seats. The Nationalists provided the Philippines with a new generation of political leaders, including Manuel Luis Quezon and Sergio Osmeña, enormously deft figures who would dominate national politics for the next quarter century. In short, the political system Taft devised took on a life of its own, greatly accelerating the schedule of independence Taft and others had in mind.

Training in governance was an instrument for the Philippines' ruling class. But the American colonizers believed that the only way to fit ordinary Filipinos for democracy was through education. Root had stipulated that the commission "should regard as of first importance the extension of a system of primary education which shall be free to all." He and his colleagues shared Jefferson's devout belief in the democratizing effect of public education. As one scholar of the colonial period writes, "The faith of the American officials in education as an engine of social, political, economic and moral reform was apparently infinite. It was expected to reduce the power of the *caciques*"—the local strongmen—"to furnish economic motivation, and to regenerate morally not only the student generation but also their parents."

Even before sailing for the Philippines, Taft had hired Fred Atkinson, the thirty-five-year-old principal of a high school in Springfield, Massachusetts, as the first general superintendent of public instruction. Atkinson knew nothing of the Philippines, but he had a Ph.D. from the University of Leipzig and the mixture of rugged determination and idealism that marked so many of the first generation of administrators in the Philippines. Atkinson spent his first several months in studying the meager, church-based system the Spanish had left behind. He concluded that instruction could not be offered in Spanish, a language known only to the upper classes, or in the native languages, for which neither texts nor teachers would be available. The medium of instruction would have to be English. This was itself highly unusual: elsewhere, the colonial powers restricted literacy in Western languages to the compliant elite.

Atkinson also wanted the schools to be nonsectarian, but he was overruled by the commissioners, who were politically more astute than he. As Taft observed, "It was of the highest importance that the Filipino people should understand that the Commission did not come here to change the religion of anybody." The *mission civilatrice* was, after all, a secular one, and the Filipinos had already fought to throw off the yoke of the Spanish friars. The commission decided on a compromise that sounds extremely contemporary: teachers or priests could conduct religious education after school three days a week. Atkinson failed in another, and more fundamental, goal. Both he and the *ilustrados* of the Federal Party wanted schooling to be compulsory to age twelve, with fines exacted on parents who failed to send their children to school. The commission refused, for the simple reason that it did not have the money to provide universal primary school education. Indeed, local communities would be expected to build and repair schools and pay the salaries of teachers—an obvious impossibility in much of the country. The U.S. Congress, with none of the zeal of the colonial administration, had no intention of appropriating the kind of funds that would be required to educate the whole country.

Atkinson advertised for a thousand American teachers. And in August 1901, the *Thomas*, a converted cattle ship, arrived in Manila with five hundred eager young Americans, "the men wearing straw boaters and blazers," writes the journalist and historian Stanley Karnow, "the women in long skirts and large flowery hats. Like vacationers, they carried baseball bats, tennis rackets, musical instruments, cameras and binoculars." The Thomasites, as they and all other American teachers quickly came to be known, saw themselves as missionaries and as ambassadors of goodwill. They were naïve, but they were not quite neophytes. Almost all had at least attended college; four fifths had prior teaching experience. Many were overwhelmed by the challenge of teaching enormous classes of deeply impoverished children in remote towns. But collectively, along with the growing cadre of local teachers, they established the Philippines' first national school system, offering literacy to the masses and the opportunity for higher education to a much smaller number. Beyond that, the Thomasites both incarnated and preached egalitarianism and the Protestant work ethic; they were, in short, doing their best to form Americans. To the Filipinos, they represented, for the most part, a truly benevolent face of colonialism and an endearing introduction to America—a precursor to the Peace Corps.

David Barrows, who took over from Atkinson in 1903, believed that the goal of the schools, and of the civil administration itself, should be to shatter the social system that kept farmers bound in perpetual debt and servitude to the land-owning *caciques*. He hoped, in his own version of the Jeffersonian vision, to use the schools to forge a new class of "peasant proprietors," in whom economic self-reliance would ultimately breed political and social independence. He reduced the primary course of schooling from four years to three, in order to reach more children, and he focused on academic rather than vocational training. He introduced new readers with characters and situations familiar to rural children. The texts, according to one account, gave teachers the following instructions after a set of math problems involving tenant-landlord relations: "Explain to the pupils carefully the right which the Filipinos have to take up land, and urge them to carry the information to their parents." Barrows wrote in 1904 that two years of such instruction would suffice, a generation hence, to "destroy that repellent peonage or bonded indebtedness that prevails throughout this country."

Perhaps, with enough time and breadth, the schools could have had the liberating effect Barrows dreamed of, though there is something almost touching about the extremely American faith in the idea that knowledge alone, in the absence of social change, can destroy an ancient system of indenture. But the commission never appropriated enough funds to educate more than half of Filipino children; and rural areas often could not afford to sustain the schools themselves. In 1907 only 7 percent of Filipinos were enrolled in school, though this still exceeds the fraction educated in other colonies at the time. What's more, many of the Filipino teachers were barely literate in their own languages, much less in English, and most had to deal with huge classes and high levels of absenteeism. Graduation rates were thus extremely low. Dean Worcester notes that in 1912, only 11,200 children (in a country of 8 million souls) graduated from primary school, and 221 from high school. And Barrow's faith in the miracle-working effects of education did not survive for long. His replacement shifted the schools' focus to vocational training, while the administrators reduced the education budget in order to spend more on roads, reasoning that the consequent increase in revenue could then be spent on the schools.

Schools were the most powerful and pervasive instrument of psychic transformation, but scarcely the only one. Although sober figures such as Root understood that they could not promote democracy in native peoples by preaching at them, preachment was at the very heart of the American presence in the Philippines. The Americans established YMCAs around the country to introduce physical fitness, and the Christian ideals then associated with it, to Filipino men and boys. They taught the Filipinos baseball, a game that they were quite sure embodied all the highest values of sportsmanship and manhood. Girls sent away from home lived in dormitories, and these "dormitory girls" became famous for their American-style fearlessness and ambition. A much smaller number of promising students were sent off every year to study in the United States, thus establishing a future cadre of sympathetic leaders for the Philippines. Everything the administration introduced, very much including the institutions of governance, was designed to turn Filipinos as much as possible into Americans.

But would even fifty or a hundred years suffice for this alchemical process? After all, America itself had not been shaped by a conscious external force; it had evolved, incrementally and organically, like fruit given its distinctive flavor by the local soil and climate. And the Philippines did not resemble the United States at any point in its development; you could not succeed by speeding up the effect of the native conditions. The idea of inalienable individual rights had come naturally to the yeoman farmer and the tradesman of colonial America, who stood on their own two feet. But in the Philippines, almost everyone depended on the favor of powerful clans. The habits of deference were deeply ingrained. Filipinos considered the relationship of patron and client every bit as rooted in the nature of things as

Americans did the bonds of equality among citizens. Politics depended far more on kinship ties and on personal friendship than it did on abstract principle or belief. Politicians gained office with the support of their actual and metaphorical kin, and then offered recompense with jobs, contracts, and the like. The Americans called this corruption, but for the Filipinos it was simply an extension of the family system. José Avelino, a well-known Filipino politician, once said, "When Jesus Christ died on the cross, he made a distinction between good crooks and bad crooks. We can be good crooks."

Some leading members of the elite absorbed the ethos of self-reliance and equality; others learned how to parrot it back to their gullible masters. "We pushed them," one perceptive commission official later observed. "They appeared to yield with that Old World courtesy . . . but they interfered as little as possible with things as they were—with municipal officials incompetent and venal; with municipal police, tattered and inefficient . . . and with all the chaotic conditions which changes of government and greater changes of ideals of government had brought about."

The American administrators understood very well that this body of ideas, habits, prejudices, and values rested on a deeply entrenched social system. And they understood that democracy could not flourish in a world of patrons and clients rather than of self-reliant citizens. But they chose to take on the ideas rather than the social order that had produced them. They could have tried, for example, to break the stranglehold of local landlords by taking away some of their land and distributing it to tenants, who would then have formed the class of "peasant proprietors" upon whom much of the Western democratic tradition had been founded. Land reform, at least done well, would later prove to be a critical means of empowering the rural poor and also of defusing their frustration and resentment. But this lay in the future; and in any case, the free-market Republicans at the helm of the Philippine Commission were not about to forcibly redistribute assets. What's more, Taft's "policy of attraction" depended on the goodwill of the *ilustrados*, who would have been disadvantaged by such a step.

The commission did, in fact, institute an American-style homesteading program in order to distribute to rural folk much of the land they had seized from the Spanish friars; but most of it wound up in the hands of the landed class. They tried as well to spur economic growth by encouraging American investment. The commission proposed raising the ceiling on the foreign purchase of Philippine land from 2,500 to 25,000 acres, with the hopes of spurring the development of a plantation economy, as was happening in Hawaii. But here they were blocked by the U.S. Congress, which rejected the plan. The anti-imperial bloc in Congress would not permit the Philippines to become a playground for American capital. At the same time, acting out of protectionism rather than misplaced idealism, Congress also refused, until 1909, to remove tariffs that made Filipino goods prohibitively expensive in the United States. This precluded the kind of rapid economic growth that might have produced a new middle class, and the sort of productive clash of interests from which competing political parties often rise. The net effect was that the colonial administration prevented Americans from exploiting the Filipinos, but in no way disturbed the system whereby Filipinos had immemorially exploited one another.

Taft had said that he would confer more autonomy on the natives as they proved themselves worthy of it. He and his successor, William Cameron Forbes, who became governor of the Philippines when Taft returned home in February 1904, cautiously and gradually expanded the ambit of self-rule, as if dealing with a valetudinary whose system needed to be prepared for solid food. The civil service became increasingly Filipinized, but chiefly in its lower and middle ranks; as late as 1913, twenty-one of the twenty-four heads of bureaus, and twenty-nine of the thirty-five assistants, were Americans. An increasingly emboldened Assembly passed bills expanding the reach of its authority, only to see them vetoed by the Philippine Commission. The system continued to work because the *ilustrados* at the very top, men such as Osmeña and Quezon, were almost as skeptical about their fellow citizens' capacity for self-government as the colonizers were, and in addition they worried about any upheaval that might jeopardize their own position. But they, too, eventually became restless with their long tutelage. In 1910, Osmeña publicly complained that his people would never learn self-government so long as they remained under the colonial thumb. This was, in effect, turning the American argument on its head.

What's more, colonialism was a Republican project. William Jennings Bryan promised in the 1900 presidential campaign to give up the Philippines. The Republicans, however, held on to the White House until Woodrow Wilson won in 1912. Wilson had no higher opinion of the Filipinos' capacity for self-rule than Taft had; five years earlier he had tartly observed that self-government "is a form of character rather than constitution. Only a long apprenticeship of obedience can secure them the precious possession." As president, he opposed those in his party who wanted to immediately yield the islands back to their people, but he vowed to speed the path to independence. In the Philippines, Wilson's victory was greeted as an act of historic deliverance.

The Philippines' first Democratic governor, Francis Burton Harrison, arrived in Manila in October 1913, and before a tremendous, cheering throng delivered a message from the president: "Every step we take will be taken with a view to the ultimate independence of the islands." The Assembly then passed a euphoric resolution, stating that "colonial exploitation has passed into history." That wasn't quite Wilson's view, but Harrison, who knew no more about the reality of the Philippines than Wilson did, was fired by a progressive faith in self-determination that

Wilson himself was to adopt only in the aftermath of World War I. Harrison told Osmeña that he was prepared to replace every single American bureau chief with a native. The Assembly speaker, aghast, responded, "We want not only a Filipino government, we want a good government." He advised Harrison to "go more slowly." And Quezon, now in Washington, worked with pro-autonomy legislators to craft a bill that would not abruptly cast the Philippines adrift. Quezon was prepared to put off independence until a distant era when Filipinos were literate in English and prosperity was widespread, but he was afraid to tell Harrison his plan. He helped shape the Jones Bill, which passed in 1916. The law replaced the Philippine Commission with an upper house, thus vesting all legislative power in Filipino hands; expanded the franchise to include all adult males; and put off independence until the establishment of a "stable government," whenever that should be.

Harrison also tried to stimulate the kind of economic growth that his predecessors had ignored. He established the Philippine National Bank and appointed as its head a dodgy Filipino who ran up $30 million in losses by extending loans to cronies and peddlers of dubious ventures, and who eventually was jailed for fraud. The relaxation of tariffs, and then the huge demand created by World War I, provided a temporary boom market for Filipino exports. But the economy itself remained primitive, with a small manufacturing class and a yet more modest sector of middle-class professionals. Few jobs were available for those who completed secondary school. Almost all the benefits of economic growth went to the elite, while much of the country remained locked in poverty. A survey in the 1930s found that almost a quarter of the population consisted of landless rural laborers. Isolated peasant uprisings, generally directed against the landed rich, sprang up throughout the decade; none led to lasting change.

By this time the two sides seemed to be clinging listlessly to each other. In 1930, Quezon foresaw independence in another decade or two. In 1933, the U.S. Congress voted to give the Philippines commonwealth status for ten years, and then independence. President Herbert Hoover, who still believed in the colonial enterprise, bravely vetoed the measure, claiming that it violated "the idealism with which this task in human liberation was undertaken." The veto was easily overridden. Quezon, now president of the commonwealth, moved into the royal palace and threw magnificent parties on the presidential yacht. The new constitution gave the president autocratic powers, which Quezon proved quite willing to exercise.

In retrospect, America's aspirations for the Philippines were more remarkable than its achievements there. We acquired the country by force, just as the European powers had obtained their own overseas empires; and yet once we had the islands, we could find no rationale for keeping them, save to establish there the republican principles that we took to be the noblest of human achievements. "Kings can have subjects," as the diplomat and historian George Kennan grandly observed; "it is a question whether a republican can." Kennan, who shared John Quincy Adams's aversion to self-righteous adventurism, deplored the annexation of the Philippines, viewing it as a kind of national loss of grace. It's true that successive American administrations found reason to hold on to our Asian prize, just as did the colonial powers we affected to despise. And yet we sought to gain very little from it. Surely it's no coincidence that after the first few years and until the 1930s, we faced few if any domestic uprisings there. Even well after many Filipinos had tired of our presence, American rule, unlike that of the Spanish, never felt onerous enough to spark rebellion.

American rule came with all the blind spots of the American character of the day. The secular *mission civilatrice* coexisted with the doctrine, or rather the axiom, of racial superiority. We would instill in the Philippines the principles of Anglo-Saxon liberty, but these benighted souls might take a century to grasp them. Yet we shouldn't make too much of the widespread racism of the day. How different, at least in effect, is our own belief that democracy takes root only in nations with the tradition of social equality, inalienable individual rights, and the like—places, that is, much like the United States of America? Men such as Taft spoke of race as an impediment to self-rule, while we more enlightened souls speak of history and culture. Both modes of thinking lead to the same conclusion: That the work of promoting democracy in historically undemocratic nations is generational, and has as much to do with the slow transformation of ingrained habits and values and social relations as it does with governing institutions and legislatures and elections.

"Race" was a more intransigent factor for Taft's generation than culture is for us. Yet thanks to their deep skepticism of Filipino capacity, along with their recognition that self-rule depended on the slow fashioning of self-reliant citizens, the democracy promoters of 1900 undertook their task with a far more serious and steady sense of purpose than those of, say, 2003. In *America's Mission*, a history of democracy promotion, Tony Smith describes American efforts in the Philippines as "a textbook example of good government," noting that "the gradual expansion of democratic practices from the grassroots level to the center, on the one hand, and the gradual devolution of powers retained by the American authorities to Filipinos, on the other, correspond well to the findings of academic literature." Smith also concludes that the democracy campaign was "without obvious parallel" in the colonial experience of the time.

Of course, many educated Filipinos chafed at their nonage, and at the premise that they were incapable of producing democratic governance on their own. And yet even here, it can be said, first, that much of the Filipino political elite shared the doubts of the Americans about native capacity, and second, that the colonial administrators were sometimes more willing to take risks than were their interlocutors, who had a vested interest in the status quo. The Americans, in general, recognized that the greatest obstacle to self-rule lay with the islands' social structure, which they tried, unsuccessfully, to undermine through education and acculturation. What's more, for all that they were unwilling to surrender sovereignty, when it came to devolving power, the colonizers generally erred on the side of trust.

The United States ruled the Philippines for almost half a century; the nation that emerged was broadly Americanized in its talk and its tastes, but much less so in its politics and civic culture. By the 1950s, the Philippines was plainly a democracy, but a brittle, corrupt, and ineffective one. The failure to deliver prosperity or social justice led to increasing instability, including peasant rebellions, breakaway movements, and a growing communist presence. The combination of official corruption and social turbulence, in turn, provided President Ferdinand Marcos with the rationale to declare martial law in 1972. The Philippines is a democracy once again, yet it is still dominated by family dynasties. There are now said to be approximately 250 such families, who operate through the civil service, electoral politics, and the business and professional classes.

In the most recent ratings by Freedom House, an organization that monitors and reports on political behavior, the Philippines was characterized as "partly free"—a little better than Sri Lanka or Venezuela, a little worse than Senegal or Serbia. And in the most recent edition of the UN Development Programme's Human Development Report, the Philippines ranked 84th out of 177 on a wide array of social and economic indicators—just ahead of Tunisia and Turkey, just behind Peru and Lebanon. By the standards of the developing world, the Philippines is, in short, a middling country. And owing in part to continuing impoverishment and lack of opportunity, and also to inveterate neglect of the predominantly Muslim parts of the country, the Philippines now faces a very real problem of Islamic fundamentalism, including terrorist bombings.

What, then, should or could the American colonial apparatus have done to leave the Philippines on a surer footing? An all-knowing version of William Howard Taft could have taken direct aim at the country's social structure, but that was never in the cards. A more meaningful proposition is that the United States could have done more of the same. It could, for example, have built more schools and trained more teachers and educated more children—and more engineers and accountants and doctors. Or perhaps the crucial variable was time, rather than money: we could have devolved power more slowly, and thus extended the period of political education, as figures such as Dean Worcester and perhaps also Woodrow Wilson would have wished. Either course was possible, but a recalcitrant U.S. Congress precluded the first, and Filipino nationalism, the second. Maybe we did about as well as could be expected.

We established something new in the Philippines—the global projection not just of American power but of American ideals. Henceforward, we would, perhaps all too often, go abroad in search of monsters to destroy. But while the military part of that grand project would often prove attainable, the missionary one would turn out to be far harder. Our universalism, our sense of chosenness, impelled us to seek to reproduce abroad the price-less blessings we enjoyed at home. We would learn, through painful experience, that the world was a recalcitrant place. But it wouldn't stop us from trying.

2

From Woodrow Wilson's Noble Dream
to George Kennan's Sober Realism

The enduring faith that democracy had been established in America not only as a precious boon to its own people but as a model for men everywhere reached its full flower in the presidency of Woodrow Wilson. Taft's successor was a historian by training, and his study of the history of the American republic had left him with a sacramental, and indeed providential, view of America's role in the world. Wilson knew next to nothing about foreign affairs when he became president, but his deepest instinct told him that just as America must safeguard democracy at home through a program of progressive reform, so it must propagate it abroad through such means as presented themselves. Indeed, within a week of taking office in January 1913, he issued what we would nowadays call a new national security policy, aimed specifically at Latin America. "We hold," he declared, "that just government rests always upon the consent of the governed, and that there can be no freedom without order based upon law and upon the public conscience and approval . . . We shall lend our influence of every kind to the realization of these principles in fact and practice, knowing that disorder, personal intrigue and defiance of constitutional rights weaken and discredit government."

Wilson immediately found the opportunity to put this new doctrine into action, for just ten days before he took office, a Mexican general, Victoriana Huerta, had murdered that country's reformist president. Wilson broke with the European powers by refusing to recognize the Huerta regime. He armed Huerta's opponent, persuaded the British to withhold aid, and occupied the key port of Veracruz. The Huerta government fell in August 1914. Wilson's role may not have been decisive, but he felt that his deepest principles had been vindicated. "They say the Mexican people are not fitted for self-government," he told *The Saturday Evening Post*, "and to this I reply that, when properly directed, there is no people not fitted for self-government."

This was, however, not a conviction born of experience but an a priori faith, as almost everything was with Wilson. The experience with the Philippines was not bearing out his credo nearly so well as was Mexico. And his own most ambitious venture in democratic nation-building, in the Dominican Republic, proved to be a fiasco. Wilson had sent the Marines to occupy the capital city of Santo Domingo in late 1916, after a duly elected government had fallen; he filled the vacuum of authority with an American military government. As in the Philippines, the Americans tried to promote rural reform and development; as in the Philippines, the ultimate effect of their efforts was to strengthen the hand of the wealthy landed class. The military government established a national constabulary to replace the bosses' hired guns. Conflict resumed almost as soon as the United States withdrew in 1924, and it was the commander of the new National Guard, Rafael Trujillo, who assumed power and initiated a dictatorship that would last until the 1990s. "Wilson's dreams of a constitutional order," as historian Tony Smith writes, "had become a nightmare."

It was World War I, of course, that offered the greatest scope to Wilson's moral aspirations. Though we entered the war for a variety of reasons, the president explained his decision to send American soldiers to fight and die in the trenches of Europe in terms very similar to those he had adduced in Latin America. The United States, he said in his speech seeking congressional ap-

proval for a declaration of war, would fight not for national interest or even self-defense but, rather, for "the right of those who
submit to authority to have a voice in their own governments, for
the rights and liberties of small nations, for a universal dominion
of right by such a concert of free people as shall bring peace and
safety to all nations and make the world itself free at last."

The United States did, indeed, play a decisive role in winning
World War I, but Wilson's vision of a war fought to "make the
world safe for democracy" proved every bit as evanescent as his
hopes of transplanting American-style government to Latin
America. He failed to persuade the Senate to approve the treaty
establishing the League of Nations, that "concert of free people"
of which he had spoken. American accession might not have
made much of a difference, for the League was an unwieldy body,
requiring a consensus of all its members to act, and possessing no
real means to enforce its decisions. Even more ruinously, Wilson
found that none of his partners in establishing a postwar peace
shared his faith in either the benefits of democracy or the rights
of people everywhere to self-determination. The French, British,
and Italians used the postwar negotiations to expand their own
colonial empires, while in the Treaty of Versailles they imposed
ruinous and humiliating terms upon the Germans. Wilson had issued a noble call for "a peace without victory"; here, in response,
was the cold slap of reality. Over the next several decades, under
the sway of Republican presidents, who took a dim view of Wilson's romantic pieties, the United States largely withdrew from a
diplomatic world so little to its liking.

The United States was in a vastly better position to impose its
own terms at the end of World War II than it had been at the
end of World War I. The United Nations, designed largely inside
FDR's State Department, joined a visionary scheme to enforcement powers undreamed of in the League of Nations (though it,

too, would soon come to grief in the cold war). Only the two chief Axis powers were denied membership in the UN, but the administration of President Harry Truman decided that Germany and Japan would be incorporated into the postwar community through an act of democratic conversion—an astonishing contrast with the punitive terms imposed on the losers after World War I.

It is hard to appreciate today how audacious a plan this was. First, it was scarcely obvious that the treatment would work. In both countries, an intensely nationalist and chauvinist political culture had produced states united around the projection of military power. Germany had had brief experience with democracy during the interwar Weimar Republic, while in Japan a much more modest reform had been crushed by the military and industrial elite. Both countries had waged a battle to the death against the Allies; neither seemed an ideal candidate for democratic transformation. And there was no lack of alternatives. Henry Morgenthau, FDR's treasury secretary, had favored a plan to "pastoralize" Germany, lest it ever regain the capacity to wage war. Both George Kennan and Winston Churchill wanted to restore Germany and Japan's economic power in order to bolster the West in the emerging struggle against the Soviet Union, but they envisioned both as docile and dependent instruments of Western power rather than as fully autonomous democracies.

But there was a pragmatic case for democracy, just as there had been a pragmatic case for an improved version of the League of Nations. Democratization was arguably the most effective way to ensure that Germany and Japan would never again threaten the world's peace. These authoritarian states had gained their legitimacy through expansion and conquest; a state that relied instead on the consent of the governed would gain legitimacy through democratic performance. An effective democracy, it was believed, would marginalize extremist ideologies. In short, one could apply sober means in the service of Wilsonian ends.

American military authorities in both countries rebuilt political structures from the ground up. They released jailed dissidents and excluded from public life both leaders and cadres of the former regimes. The Germans, who had a long constitutional tradition, were permitted to write a new constitution of their own. The military commander of Japan, Gen. Douglas MacArthur, who had grown impatient with Japanese efforts to do the same, imposed on the country a constitution that guaranteed previously unknown civil liberties, while reducing the emperor to a figurehead and effectively replacing his authority with that of the legislature, known as the Diet. In Germany, the American authorities decided to encourage incremental self-government, as colonial officials had in the Philippines—first at the county level, then the provincial, and then, finally, the federal. But the process was much quicker: Germany elected its first postwar chancellor, Konrad Adenauer, in 1949. In Japan, where MacArthur had ruled through the existing government, the Diet held new elections in 1946.

In both countries, the United States spent billions, first on humanitarian relief and then on reconstruction. Despite initial misgivings, both countries were encouraged to rapidly reindustrialize, for American planners were eager to shore up the West in the face of the communist threat. The Americans had less success in dismantling economic cartels in both countries than they had with political structures. In Japan, however, MacArthur enfranchised millions of landless farmers through land reform and shifted the balance of power between industrialists and workers by establishing trade unions—precisely the kind of deep-seated reforms the United States had failed even to attempt in the Philippines. Both of these steps solidified Japan's nascent democracy by creating a more equal distribution of wealth.

The American governors also understood that democratic institutions would not hold absent democratic habits and attitudes. They therefore consciously set out to uproot authoritarian modes of thinking and replace them with democratic ones. In doing so, the occupying forces had the enormous advantage in both countries of dealing with a shattered, defeated people. As General MacArthur put it, the collapse of faith in nation and emperor "left a complete vacuum, morally, mentally, and physically. And into that vacuum flowed the democratic way of life." MacArthur and his staff, and his counterparts in Germany, sought to promote that democratic way of life through the schools, the media, and the rhetoric and behavior of the occupying forces, including the war crimes tribunals held in both countries.

The consequence of the billions in aid, the immense program of political reform, and the root-and-branch campaign of reeducation, was that two of the world's most powerful nations left behind a monstrous past and joined the camp of the democracies within a few short years. By 1955, German democracy was so solidly founded that the country joined NATO and commenced to rearm. In Japan, MacArthur said that he was prepared to fold his tents by 1947, though in fact the American occupation would last much longer. The democratization of Japan and Germany was one of the greatest achievements in the history of American diplomacy.

Why did this effort succeed, and so swiftly, when the democratic *mission civilatrice* in the Philippines had achieved so much less after thirty years (and the one in the Dominican Republic less still)? Above all, because of the difference in the countries. Germany and Japan had been modern, industrialized powers for several generations. Their people were generally well educated and prosperous—as the Filipinos, of course, were not. And then there was the difference in circumstances: the Axis powers had been destroyed by war, and were desperate to return to normalcy, while the Filipinos had only sought liberation from Spanish rule, if anything. Finally, the occupying forces in Japan and Germany insisted on uprooting at least some elements of an unjust and malevolent social order, while their counterparts in Manila trod with greater care. These lessons would, over time, slip from the memory of American statecraft.

The world that emerged from World War II was not divided between "democrats" and "communists" but rather between two camps led by, respectively, a democratic nation and a communist one. Many of the countries in the democratic camp were, in fact, thoroughly undemocratic. This meant that while American rhetoric during the cold war celebrated the virtues of democracy, and American policy sometimes actively sought to forge democracies, as it did in Japan and Germany, the imperative of fortifying "our side" against "their side" frequently meant lending support to authoritarian anticommunist regimes. Woodrow Wilson had never had to face such a choice, for Germany posed no threat to the security ensured by two oceans. He could, in effect, conduct his crusade with impunity; President Truman had no such luxury.

Thus in 1947, with the Balkans threatened by communist insurgency, Truman proclaimed to Congress that the United States must "support free peoples who are resisting attempted subjugation by armed minorities or by outside pressures." The people of Greece and Turkey were in fact ruled by corrupt, autocratic regimes, but we would defend right-wing tyrannies against the threat of communism. Truman asked for $400 million in foreign aid, which Congress duly granted. The Truman Doctrine, as it came to be called, served as a precursor to the Marshall Plan, which Secretary of State George C. Marshall would announce three months later. The countries of Western Europe, like those of the Balkans, suffered from war exhaustion. Staggering under poverty and unemployment, they offered a tempting target for Moscow, which had already begun funding local Communist parties. Over the next four years, Congress would appropriate $17 billion for the sixteen nation recipients. The aid proved to be such a tonic that the program was halted with $4 billion left in the till. The Marshall Plan is rightly thought of today as the greatest success in the history of foreign aid. But it succeeded for the same reason the rebuilding of Japan and Germany had succeeded: we were coming to the aid of some of the most advanced industrialized nations in the world.

Of course, the cold war dynamic that produced the Marshall Plan produced as well a policy of supporting reactionary regimes and reactionary elements inside democratic regimes. Indeed, the imperative of blunting the communist advance led the United States for the first time to a policy of intentionally, if not openly, siding with antidemocratic elements. American operatives helped mastermind the overthrow of democratically elected leaders in Iran in 1953, and in Guatemala in 1954. The CIA covertly funded legitimate publications in Europe and the United States that helped make the intellectual case for democracy and liberalism; it also supported "psychological warfare" and disinformation campaigns aimed at opposition movements in the third world deemed dangerously left-wing. New media outlets such as Radio Free Europe offered a source of real hope to people living behind the iron curtain while at the same time serving as an outlet for raw propaganda. Throughout the 1950s, Washington promoted democracy largely as a fortuitous, and very occasional, consequence of the war with communism.

And with the advent of the cold war came the rise of an explicitly anti-Wilsonian theory of international relations. The "realists," chief among them George Kennan, Reinhold Niebuhr, and Hans Morgenthau, argued that both Wilsonian moralism and the faith in international law upon which the United Nations had been founded were bound to come to grief in a world that respected neither. The only professional historian to become president had insisted that the central force in American history was the perfection of our democratic system, and had then sought to project this historic dynamic onto our relations with the world. Morgenthau, too, believed that "the essence of international politics is identical with its domestic counterpart." But he turned Wilson on his head, for he held almost the opposite view of political man. "Both domestic and international politics," Morgenthau wrote, "are a struggle for power, modified only by the different conditions under which this struggle takes place in the domestic and in the international spheres."

Realism, for Morgenthau, meant being realistic about human nature. He viewed the ideologies under which leaders supposedly conducted affairs of state—whether missionary or imperialist or even "status quo"—as masks designed to "render involvement in that contest for power psychologically and morally acceptable to the actors and their audiences." The heirs of the nineteenth century liberal tradition, in which Morgenthau included Wilson and his fellow idealists, had been swift to condemn "power politics" as a form of archaic barbarism, and had sought to immunize mankind from its effects through institutions like the UN. But it was all vain, for society is fashioned by man's "elemental biopsychological drives"—to wit, "to live, to propagate, to dominate." In trying to understand statecraft, therefore, we do not look to the fine words of leaders or to their motives, lofty or otherwise, but rather to their country's objective interest—what Morgenthau called "interest defined as power." Statesmen under the influence of liberal ideas may at times act according to principle—as Morgenthau said, Neville Chamberlain did in forestalling war with Hitler through his policy of appeasement—but they will live to regret it, for others will not reciprocate.

To the realists, the argument for rapprochement with Russia was appeasement in a new key, and leftists such as Vice President Henry Wallace were the new camp of Chamberlain. But the realists were every bit as concerned about conservatives eager to "roll back" Soviet advances, through military means if need be. In his famous "Long Telegram" of 1947, and then in the article in *Foreign Affairs* based upon the cable, George Kennan tried to explain to American policy-makers what the world looked like to the men who led Russia. Yes, their ideology dictated that socialism would eventually crush capitalism, but centuries of turbulent history had taught them the virtues of "caution, circumspection, flexibility and deception." As they were not prepared to fight a holy war, we need not seek one of our own but rather apply a policy of "long-term, patient but firm and vigilant containment of Soviet expansive tendencies."

Kennan favored the use of economic aid to support our allies, and he was fascinated by the potential of covert psychological and propaganda efforts to weaken the grip of communist ideology. But he shared Morgenthau's view that the crusade to replicate democracy across the globe was laced with a typically American combination of naïveté and hubris. "Political realism," as Morgenthau had written in his typically dry and withering manner, "refuses to identify the moral aspirations of a particular nation with the moral laws that govern the universe." Kennan concluded a series of six lectures he delivered in 1951 with the hope that "we will have the modesty to admit that our own national interest is all that we are really capable of knowing and understanding—and the courage to recognize that if our own purposes and undertakings here at home are decent ones, unsullied by arrogance or hostility toward other people or delusions of superiority, then the pursuit of our national interest can never fail to be conducive to a better world." After conceding that such a policy of restraint was bound to strike some listeners as cynical and reactionary, he added, "I cannot share these doubts. Whatever is realistic in concept, and founded on an endeavor to see both ourselves and others as we really are, cannot be illiberal."

Realism recommended a policy of prudence—the cardinal political virtue, according to Morgenthau—and of modesty and restraint. It suggested, in general, doing less rather than more. Long before neoconservatives spoke of "the law of unintended consequences," figures such as Niebuhr spoke eloquently of the inevitably flawed designs of men. Realism was not necessarily a policy of the left or the right; rather, it posed itself against the crusades of the day. The same thinkers who had argued against "roll-back" in the 1950s later opposed the war in Vietnam as a classic act of American folly and overreaching. And nothing excited Morgenthau's ever-ready scorn quite so much as the extravagant claims made on behalf of foreign aid. In *A New Foreign Policy for the United States*, written in 1968, Morgenthau argued that foreign aid was perfectly acceptable as a species of bribery in which rich countries give money in exchange for political support. As "economic development," however, it was doomed to fail, since the backwardness of the recipient nations was due not to a scarcity of resources or injustices perpetrated against them, but to their own political culture or human deficiencies. "As there are bums and beggars," Morgenthau tartly noted, "so there are bum and beggar nations."

As a general rule, and with important exceptions, postwar Republican administrations found realism a more congenial guide to policy than Democrats did. Eisenhower's caution, patience, and professionalism made him in many ways the ideal realist president. The restless, crusading John Kennedy, on the other hand, undermined that policy of restraint both from the right and the left. Kennedy famously vowed in his inaugural address that "we shall pay any price, bear any burden, meet any hardship, support any friend, oppose any foe, in order to assure the survival and the success of liberty." And one may interpret the two great fiascoes of his time—the Bay of Pigs invasion and the beginning of the war in Vietnam—as making good on that pledge. But Kennedy also shared Wilson's belief in the irresistible force of the wish for self-determination, and Truman's faith in the value of foreign aid. Indeed, in that same speech, he also said, "To those peoples in the huts and villages across the globe struggling to break the bonds of mass misery, we pledge our best efforts to help them help themselves, for whatever period is required—not because the Communists may be doing it, not because we seek their votes, but because it is right." Kennedy redeemed that pledge as well, in the form of the Alliance for Progress, a kind of scaled-down Marshall Plan for Latin America.

The return of Republican rule in 1968 meant the return of the status quo (though President Nixon's high-wire diplomacy with China scarcely constituted status quo statecraft). Henry Kissinger, President Nixon's national security adviser and secretary of state, and himself a student of the history of diplomacy, was the high architect of political realism. In 1969 he summarized the administration's view of statecraft by saying: "We will judge other countries, including communist countries, on the basis of their actions, not on the basis of their domestic ideologies." Kissinger was entirely at home with America's right-wing allies, including the Shah of Iran, a profoundly unpopular autocrat to whom Washington sold $16 billion worth of weaponry from 1972 to 1977; and he appears to have assisted Gen. Augusto Pinochet in the 1973 coup that led to the ouster and murder of Chile's Marxist president, Salvador Allende. At a time when an increasing number of Americans viewed these dictators as a greater moral evil than an increasingly arthritic Soviet empire, Kissinger did more than any other figure to confirm the public suspicion that *realism* was a euphemistic term for an amoral policy. The communist threat had called forth the realist response; the doctrine would not survive Russia's rigor mortis.

The democratic world order that men like Wilson hoped to conjure from the ashes of the Great War had proved to be a chimera. Fascism had swallowed Germany, one of the most advanced of the European states, while liberal forces in Russia had proved no match for the revolutionary allure of communism. Many of the states in the European perimeter, whether in the Balkans to one side or the Iberian peninsula to the other, lived under authoritarian regimes. And in the "emerging nations" of the third world, whose numbers were growing rapidly, the few parliamentary systems left behind by colonial empires had in most cases disintegrated, or had been liquidated by despots. And all this raised a series of fundamental questions. Why did some states become, and remain, democracies while others didn't? Why did brittle democratic institutions survive in some places and not in others? And what were the prospects for the development of democracy in authoritarian states? What, in short, was democracy's future? These questions preoccupied many of the leading political theorists of the postwar generation.

In *Political Man*, published in 1960, Seymour Martin Lipset made the first systematic effort to determine the attributes that were necessary and sufficient for democracy to arise. Lipset began with a view apparently ratified by common sense: nations became democratic as they became prosperous. The middle-class nations of the West were democratic, while the poor nations elsewhere, with very few exceptions, were not. Democratization had worked in Japan and Germany but not in the Philippines or the Dominican Republic. This was a theory with an ancient lineage, for Aristotle himself had observed that democracy develops where "citizens have a moderate and sufficient state property," while "where some possess much, and others nothing, there may arise an extreme democracy, or a pure oligarchy."

Lipset sorted a group of countries according to the strength and stability of their democratic institutions, and then ranked each group according to indices of wealth, industrialization, education, and urbanization. He found, not very surprisingly, that as you went higher up the democratic scale, per capita income increased, as did the incidence of doctors, cars, and telephones; and that citizens in more democratic countries were less likely to work in agriculture and more likely to be literate, enrolled in school, and living in cities. But Lipset then asked why this should be so. First, he suggested, prosperity mutes class strife: "A belief in secular reformist gradualism can be the ideology of only a relatively well-to-do lower class." Also, "the wealthier a country the less is status inferiority experienced as a major source of deprivation." Increased wealth increases the size of the middle class, which, *pace* Aristotle, "tempers conflict by rewarding moderate and democratic parties and penalizing extremist groups." National income also shapes "the political values and style of the upper class," for in a society with a more abased lower class, the rich are far likelier to treat the poor as "a lower caste beyond the pale of human society." (Think of the Philippines.) Income also shapes a society's "receptivity to democratic norms," for citizens will more easily be able to accept shifts in political power, and the accompanying redistributions that go with it.

But socioeconomic development was not itself a sufficient condition for democracy—otherwise Germany would not have embraced fascism. States needed to have "democratic legitimacy"; and this, in turn, depended on specific historical conditions. (In fact, Lipset accepted that even poor nations could make the transition to democracy given a sufficiently favorable political culture.) Thus democracies that come into being by toppling a monarchy will have trouble establishing their legitimacy with beneficiaries of the ancien régime; better to integrate preceding institutions. New groups seeking to become politically active must enjoy ready access to the new political institutions. Political parties with limited and explicitly political goals—i.e., securing votes in elections—tend to bolster democracy, while parties that seek to offer citizens a total identity, whether religious or nationalistic, tend to threaten it.

Political Man is an optimistic book: if democracy is largely a consequence of a process of "modernization," then it is open to any state that embarks on that path. But it was also implicitly prescriptive: if democracy is a consequence, not a cause, of modernization, then nations must first develop a middle class, as well as legitimate political institutions, before they can hope to become democracies. Lipset found few countries in Africa and Asia that had embarked on this path. Most, he expected, would either adopt a communist or military dictatorship or follow a familiar pattern involving "an educated minority using a mass movement and leftist slogans to exercise effective control, and holding elections as a gesture toward ultimate democratic objectives." Lipset held out greater hope that "many Latin American countries will follow in the European direction."

There were other ways of thinking through the model of political modernization. In *Civic Culture*, published in 1963, Sidney Verba and Gabriel Almond lined up countries on an axis of democratization, as Lipset had, but then looked not at socioeconomic data but rather at political attitudes. Each of the five nations in which they gathered data turned out to have a distinctive political culture. The Italian pattern was one of "relatively unrelieved political alienation and of social isolation and distrust," while in Germany, "though there is a high level of cognitive competence, the orientation to the political system is still relatively passive." This explained why neither country had a fully consolidated democracy. In the United States and the United Kingdom, however, the authors found what they called "the civic culture." Americans, they said, "report political discussion and involvement in political affairs, a sense of obligation to take an active part in the community, and a sense of competence to influence the government." Verba and Almond traced Anglo-American political culture to its origins in early Protestant Great Britain, where the disestablishment of the Church of Rome created a secular space in public life, while shifts in the economy produced a thriving merchant class and, most important, an aristocracy willing to immerse itself in the new world of trade and commerce. They thus reversed the terms of Lipset's argument: values determined social structures, rather than the other way around.

What all the early modernization theorists had in common, though, was the notion that states had to negotiate an arduous process of development before ultimately reaching the social and economic levels sufficient to support democracy. Verba and Almond acknowledged a rapid, even revolutionary, change in the political culture of the third world, which they christened a "participation explosion"—the demand for inclusion. But the West had had centuries to develop the habits and the structures required to accommodate this demand. Democratizing nations would need somehow to establish not only representative institutions, such as a parliament and political parties, but a democratic culture as well. These habits and attitudes, they wrote in a language Taft and Dean Worcester would have understood very well, "are subtler cultural components. They have the more diffuse properties of belief systems or of codes of personal relations, which the anthropologists tell us spread only with great difficulty, undergoing substantial change in the process." The authors speculated that the demand for inclusion in third world countries would find satisfaction in totalitarian rather than democratic systems.

Modernization theory fit quite comfortably with the orthodoxies of realism. If democracy was the precipitate of a vast and almost vegetable evolutionary process, and if the clamor for inclusion in countries unready for participatory systems was likely to lead to authoritarianism, we were well advised to support rulers who offered stability over their populist challengers. There was an economic correlate as well: autocratic rulers who could marshal the productive forces of a state were far better positioned to promote development and economic growth than was the ruler of a state with the diffused powers of a fragile democracy. This argument was made most extensively by Samuel Huntington in his 1968 *Political Order in Changing Societies*, in which he argued that the "single-party system," whether of the left or right, promotes the "concentration" of economic energies and the "assimilation" of disparate groups. Huntington, Lipset, and others took the view that the kind of strongman rule popular in East Asia and

South America offered the best route to economic growth and the development of stable institutions—the essential preconditions for democracy.

These scholars, writing in the first generation after World War II, shared a deep respect for Anglo-American democracy. Democracy, Lipset had asserted, "is not only or even primarily a means through which different groups can attain their ends or seek the good society; it is the good society itself in operation." But a rising generation of left-wing academics, shaped by the Vietnam War and the growing contempt for the American role in the world, came to see this liberal consensus as fraudulent. In *Social Origins of Dictatorship and Democracy*, published in 1966, Barrington Moore consigned liberalism to the wastebin of history. "Both Western liberalism and communism (especially the Russian variety) have begun to display many symptoms of historical obsolescence," Moore declared. For Moore, as for many scholars of the day, the model of incremental development toward a liberal democratic model was neither an accurate picture of recent history nor a particularly desirable outcome. "The costs of moderation," he claimed, "have been at least as atrocious as those of revolution, perhaps a good deal more." What Verba had scorned as populist totalitarianism should instead be viewed as an indigenous third world response to the search for just governance.

In his 1973 study, *Liberal America and the Third World*, Robert Packenham criticized what he took to be the underlying assumptions of the political development approach. Why do we imagine that states rise up an escalator of modernization from the ground floor of primitive authoritarianism to the uppermost story of liberal democracy—i.e., the United States and England? Why do we suppose that this latter model is universally desirable or applicable? Packenham suggested that this formulation tells us more about the blinders of the liberal tradition than it did about the development of states. The liberal fallacy Packenham called "All Good Things Go Together" prevented scholars from seeing, for example, that economic growth sometimes fueled social injustice; the liberal dictum that "Revolution and Radicalism Are Bad" similarly blinded them to the virtues of radical left-wing movements in the third world. While he himself considered liberal democracy a fine thing, Packenham wrote, perhaps it was a bad solution for poor countries. A preferable answer, he suggested, might be "greater national integration and identity, more governmental capacity and authority, and increased participation in national affairs (which sometimes may be 'mobilized' participation as well as democratic participation in the Western sense) . . ." Packenham looked not to Taiwan but to Cuba.

It is hard for us to recall today, in our era of hegemonic capitalism, and of universal professions of faith in the virtues of democracy, that democracy did, indeed, seem threatened with obsolescence in the 1960s and '70s. The decolonized nations of Asia and Africa preferred socialism to capitalism; the "nonaligned movement" called for a "new world economic order" in which global resources would be redistributed from rich nations to poor, and for a "new world information order" in which the collective good of states took precedence over the right of free expression. All this felt a great deal like a rationalization for maintaining authoritarian control, and in fact it generally was; but democracy still seemed to be in ideological retreat.

And democracy was rare. Even in Europe, it was a recent invention. According to a tally by political theorist Robert Dahl, only 8 of 48 sovereign nations in the first decade of the twentieth century qualified as "polyarchies," a term he used to denote states with the chief elements of democratic government. The figure rose over the next two decades, fell in the 1930s, and rose again with postwar decolonization. But over time many new nations shook off the parliamentary trappings they had inherited from their colonial master. By the 1960s, Dahl counted only 40 of 119 nations as polyarchies. Samuel Huntington offered a slightly different calculus: In 1962, he wrote, 13 governments were the products of coups d'etat; by 1975, the figure had reached 38. Huntington cited an estimate that a third of the 32 democracies in 1958 had become authoritarian by the mid-seventies. In the face of this reality, it was difficult to believe that the spread of democracy was either inevitable or altogether desirable.

3

Swept Along in the Democratic Revolution

Jimmy Carter ran for president in 1976 as the antidote to Richard Nixon—though Nixon had, of course, resigned in disgrace two years earlier. Carter didn't have much to say about foreign policy, a subject of which he knew very little. But during the campaign he found that his occasional pledge to restore a moral basis to our international affairs, as he vowed to do at home, resonated with voters. The idea of defending human rights became increasingly central to his candidacy. In his inaugural address, he promised that his administration's commitment to human rights abroad would be "absolute." By this he meant not that human rights alone would determine American foreign policy, though his listeners may have understood it that way, but rather that we would no longer practice the unofficial double standard of the cold war, by which we would exempt right-wing allies from the censure or pressure applied to left-leaning regimes.

Carter was without question our most "Wilsonian" president since Wilson himself. He was, like Wilson, deeply shaped by religious faith. He understood politics as, first and foremost, a moral activity, and he believed that the cold war realism of Nixon and Kissinger had not served our national interests. Nixon and Kissinger had opposed the movement to confront the Soviets on their treatment of dissidents and Jews; Senator Henry Jackson, the Democratic conservative, had had to fight the White House to win passage of his Jackson-Vanik bill linking favorable trade terms to increases in Jewish emigration from the Soviet Union. Jimmy Carter embraced this cause, championing individual dissidents such as Andrei Sakharov, as well as the cause of the Soviet Jews. And in the process he exacerbated tensions with Communist Party leader Leonid Brezhnev.

Carter also made common cause with Democrats in Congress who had been seeking to condition foreign aid on respect for human rights. The Carter administration reduced funding for dictatorial regimes across Latin America. And the president used his diplomatic powers to enforce his new policy goals. Starting in 1978, he tried to pressure Anastasio Somoza, the Nicaraguan strongman whom FDR had once allegedly labeled "our SOB," to leave office. He joined the international boycott of the white-run government of Rhodesia, while Vice President Walter Mondale sharply criticized South Africa's apartheid government. When Joaquín Balaguer, who had succeeded Rafael Trujillo as president of the Dominican Republic, delayed reporting results of an election he had lost, the United States weighed in strongly on behalf of the democratic opposition, which was then found to have won the ballot. Sixty years after Woodrow Wilson intervened there, the Dominican Republic finally honored the outcome of a democratic election.

In the end, though, Carter's human rights campaign, while inspiring to many, demonstrated the limits of an explicitly moral foreign policy, just as had Wilson's crusade for democracy. The president came to grief in two very different ways. On the one hand, human rights could not in fact be "absolute": Carter was often forced to swallow his own views and put his arm around authoritarian allies, just as all of his cold war predecessors in office, from Truman onward, had done. We would lean on Balaguer but not on the vastly more consequential Shah of Iran or on Ferdinand Marcos in the Philippines, both deemed bulwarks against communist advance. The question of the Philippines provoked a virtual civil war inside the State Department, with Patricia Derian, assistant secretary for human rights, eager to confront the martial-law government, and Richard Holbrooke, the assistant secretary for East Asia, charged with extending the leases on our massive naval and air bases in the islands, regularly assuring the regime of continued American support. In the end, President Carter came down firmly on Holbrooke's side. The administration also backed the Shah unconditionally in the face of revolutionary agitation. And when he fell, in January 1979, the Shah virtually took the Carter administration with him. After the United States agreed to admit the deposed leader for medical treatment, students in Tehran seized our embassy, and the endless hostage crisis began. Carter was condemned both for his hypocrisy and for his naïveté.

Carter also discovered what Reinhold Niebuhr or George Kennan would have been happy to tell him: the capacity even of the United States to shape events inside other countries is quite modest, and always secondary to the internal dynamic of those countries. After Somoza cut off negotiations with Nicaraguan moderates in early 1979, the Carter administration ended military support and called for him to step down. Carter believed that Somoza would be replaced by the social democrats whom the administration supported. In fact, the Sandinistas, who came to power in July 1979, turned out to be Marxist-Leninists, just as American conservatives had insisted all along that they were, and began to use Nicaragua as a beachhead for the advance of their revolutionary cause across Latin America.

What's more, Carter had urged Americans to get over their "inordinate fear of communism." But Russia's full-scale invasion of Afghanistan in the last days of 1979, while in fact a desperate gambit by a failing empire, made the president's reassurances look absurd. Carter had set himself against both hard-liners such as Henry Jackson and realists such as Kissinger; now he appeared to have been naïve. Humiliated and outraged, preoccupied and paralyzed by events in Iran, Carter began to mute his calls for change abroad. By the time he left office, he had become, like Wilson, a defeated figure.

In the late 1970s and early '80s, the Soviet Union enjoyed a last hurrah before the wheels fell off the juggernaut. Conservative Democrats as well as Republicans, alarmed by what they viewed as liberal appeasement of not only the Russians but also their proxies, joined forces to oppose the Carter position on arms-control talks with the Soviets and on relations with the third world. Cold war rhetoric became as superheated as it had been in the 1960s (the last time the Democrats had held office). In 1979, Jeane Kirkpatrick, one of the group's chief theoreticians and polemicists, published "Dictatorships and Double Standards," a diatribe against the Carter policy that appeared in *Commentary* magazine. Taking Iran and Nicaragua as examples, Kirkpatrick argued that "the American effort to impose liberalization and democratization" had not only failed but had helped empower a new regime under which "ordinary people enjoy fewer freedoms and less personal security" than they had before.

Kirkpatrick claimed that the Carter administration's left-wing sympathies had made officials see revolutionary movements in far too rosy a light, while they had equally failed to recognize the virtues of our undemocratic allies. She described Somoza and the Shah not as tyrants but rather as "traditional rulers of semi-traditional societies," and said that such states "are less repressive than revolutionary autocracies" and "more susceptible of liberalization." She poured scorn on the liberal faith that such countries could be transformed into democracies. Kirkpatrick had little use for impersonal and ineluctable forces such as "modernization." Only committed democrats could give birth to democracy. Such a state, she asserted, requires citizens who "think of themselves as participants in society's decision-making" and leaders who "eschew (at least in principle) violence, theft, and fraud" and who "accept defeat when necessary." And it rests on institutions such as political parties and professional associations in order to channel competing interests and opinions. "Decades, if not centuries," Kirkpatrick wrote, expressing a sentiment several of the Philippines' colonial administrators would have readily accepted, "are normally required for people to acquire the necessary disciplines and habits."

Kirkpatrick was arguing for a return to staunch and single-minded anticommunism; and Ronald Reagan was so impressed with her views that after he defeated Jimmy Carter to become president, he named her ambassador to the UN (though she would become a far more influential figure in the president's inner councils than UN ambassadors normally are). Reagan's other confidantes on foreign policy were strong conservatives such as William Casey, head of the CIA; National Security Adviser Richard Allen; Defense Secretary Caspar Weinberger; and Secretary of State Alexander Haig. All had chafed not only at Carter's blandishments to left-wing regimes but also at the mainstream Republican faith in containment; Henry Kissinger had only a few more friends in high places in this administration than he had had in the previous one.

Leading figures in the administration saw a tide of communism flowing toward America's southern borders. Haig described "a four-fold operation" mounted by the Soviets in Latin America: "First is the seizure of Nicaragua. Next is El Salvador, to be followed by Honduras and Guatemala." Reagan insisted that the communists were "aiming at the whole of Central and possibly later South America—and I'm sure, eventually, North America." Reagan was the first president to truly believe in the aggressive anticommunist policy of "rollback" rather than détente. For Reagan, the war against communism was, preeminently, a war of ideas and belief. He spoke rapturously of America's mission to "nourish and defend freedom and democracy." And of course he famously described the Soviet Union as "the Evil Empire."

Reagan and others around him believed that the Western

democracies had been far too modest about spreading their own gospel, too abashed by the fashion for socialism and collectivism in the developing world. In June 1982, the president gave a speech on democracy in a setting designed to sound the deepest chords of history. Speaking to the British Parliament in Westminster Abbey, he asserted, in the sunny tones for which he was famous, "optimism is in order, because day by day democracy is proving itself to be a not-at-all fragile flower." Totalitarianism, by contrast, was provoking "an uprising of the intellect and will," and retreating before a "democratic revolution." It was an audacious claim at a moment when the Soviets had subdued Afghanistan, and Cuban forces were making inroads in Africa. The United States, Reagan announced, would seize this historic opportunity with a new initiative to "foster the infrastructure of democracy— the system of a free press, unions, political parties, universities," through which men and women peacefully reconcile their differences. The Soviets, he said, had long given "covert political training" to allies; Europeans had begun to do the same thing openly. Now the United States would be joining them. Jeane Kirkpatrick's historically rooted skepticism vanished beneath the thunder of Reagan's millennial euphoria.

Later that year, Congress agreed to provide modest funding ($15 million at first) for a new National Endowment of Democracy, which would in turn distribute funds to organs connected to the parties, to labor, and to business. The NED would be a private organization funded by the government but accountable to its own board, while the National Democratic Institute and International Republican Institute, as they were called, would depend on the NED for funding but remain independent of it. The institutes were also made largely autonomous of the parties themselves, an arrangement designed to placate legislators who feared, quite reasonably, that they would otherwise become bottomless sources of foreign junketeering for their colleagues. The groups began to operate in earnest in 1985.

But what exactly did Reagan intend by his speech? For him, as for his predecessors, anticommunism certainly took precedence over democracy. Soon after taking office, Reagan had asked Congress to lift the ban on exports to the military dictatorship in Chile, and then to the equally brutal, and equally pro-American, regime in Argentina. In Reagan's first term alone, Washington directed $1.1 billion in civilian aid, and $496.0 million in military aid, to El Salvador, where a military government was conducting a savage war against an insurgency. And the White House clandestinely spent millions funding the right-wing force known as the Contras, who sought to overthrow Nicaragua's Sandinista regime. Like Kirkpatrick, Reagan did not acknowledge the existence of a legitimate opposition to autocratic rule, progressive but not communist, nationalistic but sympathetic to the West. Unlike Kirkpatrick, however, the president refused to concede that our anticommunist allies were, in fact, authoritarian leaders. He stoutly defended the democratic bona fides of El Salvador's military junta, and famously described the Contras, led by Somoza's former chief operatives, as "the moral equivalent of our Founding Fathers."

Reagan also put an end to our ambivalent relations with the Philippines' devoutly anticommunist, if grossly kleptocratic, regime. President Ferdinand Marcos had come to power in 1965 as a reformer. It was Marcos, ironically, who finally succeeded in pushing through a land-reform process designed to weaken the asphyxiating grip of the old elite. But he proceeded to replace one crony system with another, perhaps more corrupt one. Over the years, Marcos and his shopping-besotted wife, Imelda, were alleged to have stolen $5 to $10 billion from the national treasury. Marcos's open theft and his bid to centralize power provoked growing social turbulence; and this in turn provided him with the rationale to declare martial law in 1972.

If Marcos was an SOB, however, he was a very pro-American one; and in December 1980, just before taking office, Reagan arranged a private dinner with the ruling couple. In 1982, Reagan bestowed upon the Marcoses an honor they had long craved—an official reception at the White House. Reagan believed that he had to choose between the Marcoses and a communist insurgency. And yet long years of American colonialism had left behind a large class of educated Filipinos who took seriously all that they had heard about democracy, and who reviled Marcos and his predatory entourage. It was no coincidence that the threat to Marcos arose from the heart of the old elite; Benigno Aquino, the leader of the democratic opposition, was the scion of one of the baronial families, and had in turn married into another of the clans. Marcos had ordered Aquino's arrest when he imposed martial law; Aquino was released in 1980, probably owing to the regime's fear that he might die in jail. He returned to the Philippines on August 21, 1983; as he stepped out onto the tarmac at the airport, he was murdered with a gunshot to the head. The brazen killing, which was widely attributed to Marcos, provoked an explosion of popular outrage unheard of during the dictator's years in office.

The White House offered no sign of support to Aquino's widow, Corazon, who emerged as the figurehead of the opposition. In early 1985, under increasing pressure from Democrats in Congress, the administration began to press Marcos to initiate economic, political, and military reforms. Reagan even sent his close friend Paul Laxalt to deliver a personal warning. Marcos, confident that Reagan would support him come what may, refused. Later that year, however, the increasingly beleaguered dictator called snap elections. What's more, he promised to permit anyone, including Cory Aquino, to run, and, even more recklessly, to permit observers to monitor the election. Marcos had miscalculated the depth of public outrage, the capacity of the country's long-dormant democratic institutions, and the role of the Americans. A monitoring group, NAMFREL, deployed an astonishing fifty thousand volunteers to polling places around the country. The National Democratic Institute, which until that time had limited its activities to workshops, received $1 million to support NAMFREL's parallel count. An American delegation led by Senator Richard Lugar was also dispatched to Manila.

And now the dynamic of what Samuel Huntington christened "the stunning election" played itself out. Huntington observed that authoritarian leaders often sought to shore up their flagging legitimacy with an election, confident either that their popularity or their capacity to rig the outcome would carry the day. But of course they were loathed; and the mechanisms of fraud often failed. On Election Day, November 7, 1986, Marcos engaged in the rampant ballot stuffing that had become second nature to him. But this time NAMFREL's parallel count exposed his machinations; and the American delegation, after fierce internal debate, accused the president of cheating. Cardinal Jaime Sin, a deeply respected figure, denounced the vote in even more unvarnished terms.

In mid-February, leading military figures, though the beneficiaries of fortunes lavished on them by Marcos, staged a rebellion. And when Marcos moved to crush the coup attempt, thousands of Filipinos poured into the streets and blocked the tanks. Reagan, who had defended Marcos to the last, finally agreed to cut him loose. On February 25, Marcos and his family fled the country in four American helicopters, and Corazon Aquino became the Philippines' democratically elected president. Even then, Reagan was reluctant to endorse her rule. Secretary of State George Shultz, who had been remonstrating with Reagan for weeks to cut ties with Marcos, informed the president that any hesitation could "turn a triumph of democracy into a catastrophe." Reagan relented. It could be said that the White House had helped restore democracy to America's laboratory in democratic nation-building, but it would be more accurate to say that the Filipino people managed to reclaim democracy with the help of both national and international nongovernmental bodies and a push from Washington at the last, decisive moment.

Events increasingly exposed the speciousness of Kirkpatrick's supposed binary choice. In 1982, the Argentine junta fell and was replaced by a democratic one. In El Salvador, the Reagan administration had endorsed an electoral process to restore civilian rule; by the time of the presidential election in 1984, it had become plain that the only broadly acceptable candidate was José Napoleón Duarte, a moderate Christian Democrat. The administration supported him against Roberto D'Aubuisson, a ferocious anticommunist and death squad leader. Duarte won handily. At the same time, the Salvadoran military gained the upper hand in the fight against the rebels. The administration's anticommunist hard-liners felt sufficiently mollified to abandon El Salvador policy to the moderates in the State Department.

The administration's composition had also begun to change. Alexander Haig had given way to George Shultz, a more moderate figure. Both Shultz and his new assistant secretary for East Asia, Paul Wolfowitz, believed that the United States had to press autocrats as well as left-wing regimes to change; both men had played an important role in finally persuading Reagan to abandon Marcos. Elliot Abrams, a specialist in Latin America, became assistant secretary for human rights, and moved again in 1985 to become assistant secretary for inter-American affairs. Abrams had been deeply involved in funneling clandestine aid to the Contras, and later pled guilty to two misdemeanor counts of witholding information from Congress. (He was pardoned by the first President Bush.) Abrams was reviled by many in the human rights community for his single-minded defense of the Contras; he once baldly insisted on a television debate that the notorious death squad killings had "never happened." Like Wolfowitz, he was identified as one of the "neoconservatives," a group consisting largely of ex-Democrats, most of them Jewish, who in foreign affairs favored an aggressive anticommunist policy. But the neoconservatives also shared Reagan's evangelical fervor about democracy and, unlike Kirkpatrick, felt confident about America's ability to shape a better world.

Abrams began pushing for a shift in policy toward Chile, where Augusto Pinochet had been ruling with an iron fist since leading the military coup of 1973. Pinochet was not a crook, like Marcos; he had instituted a series of free-market reforms that had made Chile the most prosperous country in South America. He had, however, done far more grievous harm to the nation's democratic institutions and traditions than Marcos had. Chile had been electing its own rulers in an almost unbroken line since 1840. One index of democracy published in 1965 had ranked Chile ahead of the United States and France. The junta had systematically destroyed the country's democratic institutions and arrested or killed thousands of party leaders, union officials, and civil-society figures. Pinochet operated through a pervasive and terrifying secret-police apparatus. The Carter administration had made the country one of the chief targets of its human rights campaign. President Reagan, however, had moved swiftly to shore up the Pinochet regime, lifting bans on finance and opposing UN resolutions condemning human rights violations. Ambassador Kirkpatrick had met with General Pinochet and expressed the administration's "desire to fully normalize our relations with Chile."

But the collapse of the economy in 1983 weakened Pinochet's hold on businessmen and the middle class. A wide array of opposition parties agreed in 1985 to make common cause. President Reagan continued to speak of Pinochet as a friend and suggested bringing him to Washington; but in the end the administration distanced itself from Pinochet more quickly, and less grudgingly, than it had from Marcos. Washington supported, or abstained from, UN resolutions condemning Chile, though it had previously opposed almost identical measures. Elliot Abrams declared, with perhaps more clarity than was warranted, that "U.S. government policy toward Chile is straightforward and unequivocal: we support a transition to democracy." Abrams also prevailed on Democratic senator Tom Harkin to introduce legislation authorizing the expenditure of $1 million for democracy promotion in Chile. Much of this funding went to the NDI, thus marking one of the first attempts to strategically deploy the democracy institutions that the administration had brought into being.

The White House was still taking modest steps: rather than seek a change in government, it called on Pinochet to follow a constitutional process that he himself had established, which called for the holding of a plebiscite on his continued rule. At first the opposition parties demanded direct elections. But when the junta proved intransigent, opponents agreed to contest the plebiscite, which was scheduled for June 1988. Abrams and other officials publicly admonished the regime to permit an honest and transparent ballot. And the official organs of democracy promotion played a meaningful role for the first time. The NDI brought in experts to help the so-called No campaign organize itself and develop a message, sample public opinion, design ads, and register voters. The organization, which was supposed to be fortifying democracy rather than bolstering Pinochet's opponents, had to be careful to offer advice without actually shaping the campaign. It was a fine line. When in the final weeks the No campaign planned to devote a series of crucial fifteen-minute television ads to the regime's brutal violations of human rights, pollster Peter Hart reported that undecided voters in fact wanted to hear about jobs. The opposition reluctantly agreed to scrap its ads and replace them with a talk-show format illustrating the gauzy slogan "Happiness Is Coming." The regime countered with scare-mongering images of a headless horseman. "That," recalls Kenneth Wollack, an official with NDI (and now its president), "was the end."

The plebiscite turned out to be another "stunning election."

With no equivalent of NAMFREL, the NDI had funded a random sample of the voting rather than an actual parallel count. Early returns showed the No side winning. Opposition leaders quietly brought the results to some of Pinochet's less ardent supporters and then read out the results on radio. The regime, which had surrounded the No headquarters with tanks, vacillated. "At eight p.m.," recalls Wollack, "there was still no official response. Nine o'clock, nothing; ten, nothing; eleven; twelve. Finally, at one or two in the morning, a member of the junta walks into the presidential palace, the press sticks a microphone at him and says, 'Who won?' and he says, 'The No vote won.'" The sample vote count, he later admitted, had already become so widely accepted that the junta was trapped.

It was not, of course, the Reagan administration, or the NDI, that had carried the day but rather Chile's own democratic culture. Opposition parties with almost nothing in common had worked together for months, and would continue to work together to preserve a stable democratic government in the years ahead. Chileans themselves had remained calm, thus denying the regime a pretext to clamp down. The military had had no stomach for electoral fraud. "Even in the army," notes Arturo Valenzuela, a scholar and former official with the National Security Council, "institutional loyalties and respect for 'legality' were more important factors than allegiance to the ambitions of the commander in chief." Fifteen years of despotism had failed to crush a civic culture that had been a century and a half in the making. At the same time, the Reagan administration deserved credit for conditioning its support of the regime on the constitutional process and for warning Pinochet about the consequences of fraud. And the new instruments of democracy promotion had shown that at a decisive juncture they could tip the electoral process toward fairness and transparency. The Chilean plebiscite was one of the events that proved to scholars and policy-makers that the United States could help forge democratic outcomes if it acted firmly, consistently, and circumspectly.

Ronald Reagan was, in effect, our first conservative Wilsonian. In his evangelical faith in the power of freedom he was little different from Wilson himself; what made Reagan conservative was the dim regard in which he held government itself, and his accompanying belief in the liberating effect of the free market. Reagan spoke of "the vital nexus between economic and political freedom," fully equating "political restrictions on the rights of assembly, speech or publication" with "economic repression through high taxation and excessive bureaucracy." Capitalism was democracy in the economic sphere. And at a time when socialism, or at least social democracy, was fashionable among elites in the West and in the third world, Reagan advanced his old-fashioned liberalism with great vigor. The historian Tony Smith, generally no enthusiast of laissez-faire economics, writes, "It appears that one of the most powerful impetuses to democratization in the late 1980s was a form of economic argument that, while not unique to the United States, was articulated with special force by the Reagan administration."

At the same time, it is also true that Reagan clung to the last to some of the world's most pitiless dictators. And in almost every case he was forced by events to act. Thomas Carothers, an expert on democracy with the Carnegie Endowment for International Peace, notes that Reagan did nothing to disturb tyrants such as Joseph Mobutu of Zaire or Suharto of Indonesia, neither of whom was threatened by rebellion or popular discontent. "We didn't lead," Carothers concludes, "but rather, when our friends got in trouble, we didn't come to their aid."

Reagan was far too much a creature of the cold war to be counted an unalloyed champion of democracy. But even those who disdain Reagan as an archconservative must recognize that during his presidency the promotion of democracy became a conscious public form of diplomacy for the first time since the era of Harry Truman.

President Reagan had certainly been right about one thing: totalitarianism was, in fact, retreating before a "democratic revolution." Twenty years earlier, left-wing critics both in the West and in the third world could view liberal democracy as an archaism; no longer. The last authoritarian holdouts in traditional Western Europe, Spain and Portugal, had joyously cast off dictatorship in the mid-seventies; military governments in South America began to topple; a wave of reform swept the East Asian "tigers"; and of course the Soviet empire had begun to crumble. In his pathbreaking 1990 book, *The Third Wave*, Samuel Huntington, who in earlier work had touted the virtues of one-party rule, wrote that between 1974 and 1989, democratic regimes replaced authoritarian ones in thirty countries. A number of remaining authoritarian nations showed clear signs of liberalization; in still other countries, democratic forces gained in strength. "Although obviously there were resistance and setbacks, as in China in 1989," Huntington wrote, "the movement toward democracy seemed to take on the character of an almost irresistible global tide moving on from one triumph to the next."

Huntington argued that a "long wave" of democratization from 1828 to 1926 had been followed by a "reverse wave" from 1922 to 1942; then a "short wave" from 1943 to 1962 had been followed by another reverse wave from 1958 to 1975. The third wave had begun with the overthrow of Portugal's military dictator in 1974. No one factor accounted for these surges and relapses. Huntington traced the first wave of democratization to industrialization, the rise of the middle class, and the decrease in economic inequality; to the influence of Enlightenment philosophy; and to the victory of the Allies in World War I. He traced the second wave to the triumph of the democracies in World War II and to the subsequent decolonization. And then he turned to examine in detail the phenomenon of the Third Wave.

By this time it had become abundantly clear that many countries that did not satisfy Lipset's economic criteria could in fact become democracies, and that many countries that did satisfy them nevertheless would remain authoritarian. Events had forced a rethinking of the modernization paradigm. Lipset himself concluded that economic development was not a strict prerequisite for the development of democracy. Huntington wrote that while "an overall correlation" existed between the two, "no level or pattern of economic development is in itself either necessary or sufficient to bring about democratization." Huntington did, however, agree with Lipset on the important role played by an expanding middle class and increasing access to education. He also observed that involvement in the global economy opened society to new ideas, while increasing levels of economic complexity created a situation difficult for autocrats to control (which was one reason leaders of oil-rich states, where wealth did not lead to complexity, were able to resist democratization). But rapid growth had not led to chaos and authoritarianism, as Lipset and others had predicted. It had, rather, overwhelmed the mechanisms of control in one nation after another—first Greece, then Spain, then Brazil, then South Korea and Taiwan.

Huntington put great stress on noneconomic and nonstructural features. With the free world emerging victorious from World War II, "people in most countries came to accept—if not to implement—the rhetoric and ideas of democracy." That rhetoric proved to be a rallying point for reformers, and a biting source of contrast for dictators. Huntington also noted a structural feature of governance: regimes tend to lose legitimacy over time. In a democratic regime, one set of democratic leaders can replace another. In the case of one-man or one-party rule, public opprobrium over perceived failure attaches to the man or the party, and thus to the actual system of rule. Autocratic regimes thus have a problem of "performance legitimacy." The oil price hikes of the 1970s damaged the standing of democratic leaders of the West, many of whom were turned out of office; but they significantly weakened authoritarian regimes the world over.

All this was a way of saying that democracy could succeed, even under very adverse conditions, if people believed in it. A group of scholars who edited the Latin America edition of the series *Democracy in Developing Countries* concluded that virtually every factor that had promoted both the development and the consolidation of democracy in nations such as Brazil, Argentina, Chile, and Colombia had to do with legitimacy. "Stable democracy," they wrote, "requires that the broad mass of the public and all significant political actors (at the level of elites and organizations) believe that the democratic regime is the most right and appropriate for their society, better than any other realistic alternative they can imagine." Voters would even accept poor performance, at least in the short run, "so long as they perceive that democracy delivers on its political promise of freedom, transparency and accessibility to power." In the longer term, of course, democratic leaders had to grapple successfully with the profound economic and social problems that plagued Latin nations. Democracy, that is, had to produce results.

Huntington added to his list of causal categories one that an earlier generation of scholars would not have thought to contemplate: the role of external actors. By the late 1980s, Huntington observed, "the major sources of power and influence in the world—the Vatican, the European community, the United States, and the Soviet Union—were actively promoting liberalization and democratization." In other words, it was possible not only for authoritarian countries to go democratic far more rapidly than had once been imagined but also for outsiders to accelerate, or for that matter impede, that process. Huntington discussed the effect of the "Helsinki process" in strengthening advocates of liberalization in the Soviet orbit; the role of the Catholic church in fostering reform in Latin America and Poland; the contribution of President Jimmy Carter's human rights policy to the growth of democracy in nations such as Uruguay, Ecuador, and the Philippines; and the implicit pledge of successive American administrations—"a democratic version of the Brezhnev doctrine"—to prevent the overthrow of democracies within America's sphere of influence.

By the end of the Third Wave, the future of democracy looked very different than it had a quarter century earlier. Nations with low levels of economic development and education, with an immature political culture, with fledgling institutions, had become democratic—though for such brittle states, staying democratic was as serious a problem as getting there in the first place. No single model explained democratization. Economics seemed less important than politics and political ideas. Democracy flourished in unlikely places because people believed in it. As Huntington observed, "Democracies become consolidated when people learn that democracy is a solution to the problem of tyranny, but not necessarily to anything else."

What would the future hold? Huntington considered a "third reverse wave" unlikely, but neither did he expect a fourth. Very few of the ninety or so countries still nondemocratic in 1990 had prior experience with democracy, as many of the Third Wave countries had; few had experienced substantial Western influence, as many of the Third Wave countries did; neither Confucian nor Islamic culture seemed particularly sympathetic to democracy; and the economic obstacles to democratization seemed dauntingly high in sub-Saharan Africa, if not in South Asia or the Middle East. Robert Dahl, performing his own *tour d'horizon* in 1989, similarly concluded that conditions for democratization were ripe in only a very few countries, though he, too, thought backsliding at least as unlikely as progress.

Dahl concluded that in the short run the capacity of outsiders to transform nondemocratic states was very limited. Yet, he added, the United States and others could make a difference in the long run by supporting democratic reform and discouraging retrogression. Indeed, democracy studies seemed to have a built-in bias for optimism, even if it was optimism of a very tempered, very chastened sort. "Time is on the side of democracy," Huntington confidently concluded. "For a century and a half after Tocqueville observed the emergence of modern democracy in America, successive waves of democratization washed up on the shores of dictatorship. Buoyed by a rising tide of economic progress, each wave advanced further and ebbed less than its predecessor."

4

Second Thoughts

Was Democracy Just a Moment?

Ronald Reagan's successor, George H. W. Bush, was cut from a very different cloth—a cautious and pragmatic figure deeply versed in affairs of state. Bush and his chief foreign policy advisers, James Baker and Brent Scowcroft, were the spiritual descendants of Eisenhower and Kennan. They believed that history was on their side, and they practiced a statecraft of patience and of small steps. Bush and his team were quite clear about the distinction between national interest and moral principle, and willing where necessary to advance the former at the expense of the latter. Bush declined to publicly criticize Chinese leaders after the massacre at Tiananmen Square in the summer of 1989. He was equally reticent when faced with human rights violations in places of no strategic importance, as when military figures ousted Jean-Bertrand Aristide, Haiti's democratically elected leader. Most famously, he declined to get involved when Slobodan Milosevic, Serbia's populist rabble-rouser, turned on Croatia in the summer of 1991, and then on Bosnia the following year. Secretary of State James Baker famously explained, "We have no dog in that fight."

And yet this eminently managerial figure happened to become president at a moment when the status quo was disintegrating. The fall of the Berlin wall in November 1989 precipitated the collapse of the Soviet Empire, and with it an almost dizzying sense of possibility. Bush partook, at least rhetorically, of that sense of open horizons; he spoke of a "new world order" emerging from the rubble of the cold war, an order characterized by democracy and free markets. At his inaugural address, in fact, he delivered a fervent paean to democracy. "Great nations of the world are moving toward democracy through the door of freedom," he declared. "We know how to secure a more just and prosperous life for man on earth: through free markets, free speech, free elections, and the exercise of free will unhampered by the state."

This was majestic language for a man so famously averse to the "vision thing"; America's triumph in the cold war had, in effect, made everyone a Wilsonian. In his actions, however, Bush, unlike Reagan, was preoccupied with ensuring a soft landing for the old order rather than with accelerating the birth of the new. He forged a deep partnership with Mikhail Gorbachev, the Communist Party leader, whom he saw as the Soviet Union's greatest source of hope for a democratic future. And when he visited Ukraine in 1991, he cautioned giddy citizens to resist the "suicidal nationalism" of separating from the Soviet Union. This later became known as the "Chicken Kiev" speech.

In effect, George Bush oversaw one of the great historical transitions to democracy while keeping his feet planted firmly, perhaps even stubbornly, on terra firma. "We were driven by events that were occurring on the ground east of the Elbe," recalls Robert Blackwill, then the head of European and Soviet affairs in the National Security Council. "Once the vibrations began we had to manage it. Of course, we knew that 150 million people would be liberated if we could get this done, but that wasn't the language of our discussion. The language of our discussion was geopolitical. We were concerned with the withdrawal of the Red Army from the center of Europe." Blackwill says that his young Russia expert, Condoleezza Rice, shared his hardheaded view.

———

Bush was a transitional figure, delivering America safely into the post–cold war era. Until his tenure, the idea of democracy promotion had been inextricably bound up with the struggle between the "free world" and the communist one. The wish to spread democracy had often been subordinated to the imperative of supporting undemocratic allies. Now that calculus no longer applied; we no longer needed to distinguish between good "authoritarians" and bad "totalitarians." And in his campaign against George Bush, Bill Clinton insisted that "no national security issue is more urgent than securing democracy's triumph around the world," and proposed that America lead "a global alliance for democracy." The strategic rationale had changed: no longer a bulwark against a hostile ideology, democracy was now understood as a means of incorporation into an emerging world of global trade and prosperity.

In February 1995, the Clinton administration published "A National Security Strategy of Engagement and Enlargement." The chief goals of the new strategic doctrine, authored largely by National Security Adviser Anthony Lake, were to sustain military readiness, to ensure economic growth at home, and "to promote democracy abroad." The spread of democracy was a matter of national interest, the document explained, because "Democracies create free markets that offer economic opportunity, make for more reliable trading partners, and are far less likely to wage war on one another." The document regularly made use of the expression "democracy and markets," as if democracy were the sole political medium within which free-market economies grew. This was scarcely the case; what the new strategy really argued was that we needed to help nourish infant democracies with the benefits of the global marketplace. President Clinton proposed to encourage democracy and market reform in "states that affect our strategic interests," and especially those where citizens were "pushing for reform or have already secured it."

The new strategy of engagement and enlargement applied,

above all, to Russia and its former constituent parts, especially Ukraine. George Bush had been chiefly concerned with coaxing the Soviet Union to a peaceful end, and he had succeeded. For Clinton and his team, the democratization of Russia represented the unfinished business of the cold war, and an opportunity for a world-historical transformation. "Think of it," President Clinton said rapturously a few months after taking office, "land wars in Europe cost hundreds of thousands of American lives in the twentieth century. The rise of a democratic Russia, satisfied within its own boundaries, bordered by other peaceful democracies, could ensure that our nation never needs to pay that price again." The expression "satisfied within its own boundaries" was a kind of code for the doctrine that democracies "are far less likely to wage war on one another"—an idea first raised by Immanuel Kant (though he was talking about republics, not democracies).

What Clinton envisioned was not merely a democratic Russia but a free-market one, enmeshed in, and thus constrained by, the global economic system. Of course, Clinton went on, "the history of Russia must be charted by Russians." But, he added, "we must do what we can and we must act now." "Act now" was also shorthand for "spend real money." The Russian economy was in free fall, and Clinton believed that a swift infusion of emergency aid could help stabilize the government of Premier Boris Yeltsin. Clinton proposed, and Congress passed, a package of $1.6 billion in food aid and technical assistance; officials in the Treasury Department pushed the IMF to loan Russia billions of dollars without the usual demands for marketplace reform, which they considered Russia too brittle to meet. The IMF loaned Russia $1.5 billion in 1994, $6.8 billion the following year, and then $10.2 billion for the next three years. These were enormous sums, but in financial terms Russia would prove to be a bottomless pit.

The campaign to nurture democracy in Russia turned, to an astonishing degree, on Bill Clinton's feelings about Boris Yeltsin.

Strobe Talbott, deputy secretary of state and overseer of administration policy toward Russia, describes again and again in his memoir, *The Russia Hand*, how Clinton hitched his wagon to Yeltsin's very unsteady star. Clinton never wavered in his support, even when Yeltsin arrogated dictatorial powers to himself in his battle with a refractory legislature, or when he sent troops into Chechnya to brutally repress a bid for regional autonomy, or even when he slid into drunken buffoonery. "He's a genuine democrat—small *d*," Clinton said when taxed by the press, "and he is leading a country that is bravely trying to do two things: one, escape from communism into market economics, a world they never lived in before, and second, to preserve real democracy." Clinton believed that he could help sustain Yeltsin with his support and his advice—which in fact he did on numerous occasions. In the final days of Russia's nerve-racking presidential election of 1996, Clinton said, according to Talbott, "I want this guy to win so much it hurts." Clinton plainly identified with Russia's mercurial, intuitive, charming, and reckless leader. But he was also, as Talbott argues, right in believing that Yeltsin was vastly to be preferred to the apparatchiks, communists, or even fascists who vied with him for power. A single intransigent figure—a Marcos or a Pinochet—must often be removed in order to make democracy possible. Here was the rarer case where one crucial figure had to be sustained if democracy were to have a chance.

Two central themes ran through Clinton's policy of democracy promotion in Russia: prop up Yeltsin, and put the economy on its feet. This was the administration of "It's the economy, stupid," and the principle was taken to apply to Russia as much as to the home front. In his confirmation hearings, Deputy Treasury Secretary Lawrence Summers, whom Clinton entrusted with the financial side of the Russia file, said that "the task of rebuilding the Russian economy is the greatest economic restructuring job since the Marshall Plan." The billions from the IMF went to help stabilize the ruble, to finance a social safety net, to balance the budget. Russia, in turn, was to increase taxes and improve tax collection, reduce subsidies, lower inflation, privatize industry, and slowly turn itself into a "normal country," to use a favorite phrase of the time. The World Bank gave Russia $3 billion to help "restructure" its hopelessly inefficient agriculture, mining, and other sectors. American funds, funneled largely through USAID, went to emergency aid, technical assistance, and training on reform issues such as privatization.

For an administration famously focused on domestic policy, at least in the first term, the campaign to promote democratization in Russia was remarkably costly in money, effort, and thought. And yet the results were meager. "It is striking," write Michael McFaul and James Goldgeier in *Power and Purpose: U.S. Policy Toward Russia After the Cold War*, "how little power the United States exercised over domestic change in Russia." President Clinton could not stop his dear friend Boris from hiring and discarding economic advisers the way Henry VIII went through consorts; and when the all-important moment arrived to privatize public industries, he could not prevent Yeltsin from staging a thoroughly corrupt fire sale designed to win the favor of oligarchs in advance of the 1996 election. And it wasn't just Clinton: neither the World Bank nor the IMF made much headway with the reforms tied to their loans and grants. Yeltsin's chosen successor, Vladimir Putin, drove through some of the legal and regulatory changes Yeltsin had resisted, but proved to be an autocrat with little patience for a free press, a political opposition, or even independent mayors and governors.

Why did democracy promotion fail in Russia? First, the Clinton administration had many other priorities with Russia. Questions of democracy took a backseat to matters of national security, be they securing Russian support for the enlargement of NATO or defusing a confrontation over Kosovo. Second, the money never even approximated the levels of spending of the Marshall Plan; the $1.6 billion aid package of 1994 was quickly sliced to a tenth its size. Or perhaps the problem wasn't so much one of magnitude as of purpose: in the grip of modernization theory, Goldgeier and McFaul write, Clinton officials persuaded themselves that democratic reform would follow economic growth and stabilization. Goldgeier and McFaul note that only $130 million of the $5.45 billion the United States spent on Russia from 1992 to 1998 went to democratic reform. The obsession with global economic integration may have blinded Clinton officials to the centrality of politics: what Russia may have needed most of all were checks on the power of a tiny political and economic elite. Indeed, in recent years Russia offered powerful disproof of the theory that economic growth leads to political development: the boom Clinton tried so hard to spark has arrived, and brought with it aggressive nationalism and the ruthless centralization of power under a virtually omnipotent leader, Vladimir Putin.

Perhaps, then, a more conscientious attempt to seed change through civil-society groups, political parties, labor groups, and the like might have shifted the balance of power or popular opinion toward the forces of democracy. Or maybe we simply didn't have levers powerful enough to dislodge this immovable object. Russia was far more deeply corrupted by seventy years of communism than were its unwilling satellites in Eastern Europe, all of which progressed toward democracy. Talbott says that he found it almost impossible to find local groups in Russia legitimate and effective enough to receive American funding. Nor does he think it likely that Russia could have usefully absorbed a Marshall Plan. "The place was a sieve," says Talbott, "and the structures of the old Soviet Union, and the mentality of the people we were dealing with, and the place as a whole, were so messed up as a consequence of decades of Soviet misrule" that billions of dollars would have ultimately wound up in Switzerland—as so many in fact did—or in people's mattresses. Talbott still wonders if they could have prevented the privatization calamity, but he does not question the decision to stick with

Yeltsin, and neither, by and large, do Goldgeier and McFaul. The problem, in short, was less in the execution than in the task itself.

Russia turned out to be hopelessly recalcitrant, but those same tools could work in a more auspicious setting. The administration's greatest success in the founding of new democracies came in Serbia, whose bellicose nationalism had tormented its neighbors, and frustrated Europe, throughout the Clinton years. The outbreak of hostilities in Kosovo in 1999 persuaded both Washington and its chief allies that they had to get rid of Slobodan Milosevic, the Serbian dictator who had already wreaked terrible havoc in Bosnia. But Milosevic was a democratically elected figure, and the era in which the CIA dispatched troublesome leaders was long over. At the same time, the strongman's need for democratic legitimacy gave his opponents inside and outside the country critical leverage. Milosevic had permitted the IRI and the NDI to operate since 1997, perhaps viewing them as harmless. The White House started to increase the flow of funds in mid-1999, through USAID even more than through the democracy bodies; the spigots were turned on fully once Milosevic announced in July that he would hold elections in the fall.

The two-party bodies trained thousands of local election monitors and party activists. Working with the nonextremist parties, the IRI and NDI explained how to craft and disseminate a political message. The NDI brought in Clinton's chief polling firm to survey voters' attitudes. The IRI worked on a massive get-out-the-vote campaign with OTPOR ("Resistance"), the student movement, which had bravely stood up to Milosevic and was leading protests against his rule. Private groups such as George Soros's Open Society Institute, as well as European governments and the European Union, also poured in money, supporting Serbia's independent media, providing aid to opposition-controlled cities, and funding dozens of civic organizations, student groups, think tanks, and so on. Official U.S. aid was later pegged at $40 million, a very large sum in a poor country with ten million people.

Milosevic lost in the first round of the elections to Vojislav Kostunica, the candidate of the Democratic Opposition of Serbia. And then, in a classic unspooling of the logic of the "stunning election," Milosevic refused to accept the results, citizens took to the streets en masse, and this maestro of Balkan nationalism and xenophobia, who had plunged the region into a decade-long nightmare, was forced to step down, and ultimately to stand before a war crimes tribunal in The Hague. (Milosevic died, under mysterious circumstances, before a verdict could be reached.) In another election later that year, the democratic party took two thirds of the seats in Parliament.

Serbia turned toward democracy not because the United States and other external actors poured in more money per capita than they did elsewhere, or because they "got it right" after making a mess of things elsewhere. Serbia had a peaceful revolution, as a succession of other Eastern European states, including Ukraine and Georgia, were to do later, because the forces of civil society proved to be powerful enough, and were willing to act bravely enough, to overcome the determined efforts of a dictator and to defy threats of violence. The internal balance of power in Russia or in China was very different. And outside actors were able to tip that balance, as they had in Chile or in the Philippines, because the regime had lost legitimacy and because the demand for change was widespread and vocal. Serbia would engage in a fair amount of backsliding in the years to come: one president, Zoran Djindjic, would be assassinated; subsequent leaders would prove reluctant to track down and hand over indicted war criminals; and extremist nationalist parties would remain highly popular. Nevertheless, Serbia is now a more or less democratic state that aspires to join the European Union. And the Balkans, though scarcely at peace, are at least not at war. The experience of 2000 demonstrated that, under the right circumstances, patience, persistence, and money can help determined citizens achieve more just and democratic outcomes.

The end of the cold war offered the West the opportunity to adopt its neighbors, most of them of respectable birth, so to speak, even if badly neglected—the nations of Central Europe and the Baltic region and some of the former Russian provinces. But the collapse of the Soviet Union left behind a far more brutalized and helpless class of orphans in the form of the failed and failing nations of Africa, Central Asia, and elsewhere. And it was the Clinton administration's unsought destiny to deal with them. This obligation first presented itself in Haiti. For decades the United States had turned a blind eye to the brutality of the ruling Duvalier family. The Bush administration had supported the populist priest Jean-Bertrand Aristide, despite his left-wing rhetoric, when he became Haiti's first democratically elected president, in January 1991; but when Aristide was ousted in a coup eight months later, the White House adopted a studiously neutral position on the restoration of democracy. James Baker had remonstrated, but the administration was chiefly concerned with preserving the American assemblage industry on the island.

Clinton came to power vowing to reverse our Haiti policy. In July 1993, administration officials reached an agreement with the generals to permit Aristide's return, but when a troopship with a small American and Canadian force reached Port au Prince in October, the generals sent armed thugs to the harbor, setting off a planned melee, and in a humiliating denouement, the ship turned around and steamed home. After more fruitless discussions, the administration began simultaneously to assemble an invasion force and to seek UN approval for an assault. In July 1994, the Security Council passed a resolution authorizing the use of "all necessary force to facilitate the departure from Haiti of the military leadership"—the first time the UN had ever defined the restoration of democracy as a matter of international peace and security. The Haitian junta refused to comply, and in September, President Clinton delivered a televised prime-time address in which he threatened an imminent assault. Several days later, a multinational force of twenty-one thousand troops, commanded by and largely composed of Americans, landed in Haiti, where they met little resistance. The generals quietly departed, and Aristide was jubilantly welcomed home. Here was a new paradigm for a new era. "For the first time," writes Nancy Soderbergh, a former Clinton national security aide, "a U.S. President had considered force not to defeat direct threats to Americans, such as fascism or communism, but rather to defend American principles—respect for democracy and human rights—and interests—and stability in its own hemisphere."

Having restored Haiti's democratically elected leader to power, we had completed our military task, as we had defined it. With Congress demanding that Clinton withdraw American troops as rapidly as possible, the president ordered UN ambassador Madeleine Albright to get the UN to quickly take over the burden of peacekeeping. In March, six months after the invasion, the United States handed off control to a 6,000-man UN force (including 2,400 Americans), a number reduced to 1,200 the following year. The Haiti mission was counted a great success, since American troops had done the job they were sent for and had left without taking casualties—or, for that matter, barely suffering a scratch.

But keeping the peace was the least of the country's problems. Haiti was like the Philippines circa 1900—a crushingly poor country with virtually no effective or honest institutions. In some ways, it was worse off than the Philippines, since the local political elite had been feeding off the helpless citizens for generations. Here was a task of an entirely different order than the forging of democracy in Germany and Japan, or the managed exit of tyrants in Chile or South Korea. Those countries had already done the painstaking work of building political and economic institutions—or at least had the muscle memory that comes of having done so in the past. Haiti had long experience of self-government, but it was almost entirely predatory. Haiti was not only "unready" for democracy in the way that modernization theory understands political evolution; it was so enfeebled by generations of political and economic failure that it was unlikely to survive as a democracy, with or without Aristide. It did not simply need to have its democratic forces supported—though that was hard enough—but to have democratic institutions built. And doing so would be the work of a generation.

A new kind of effort was being born in Haiti and kindred states: democratic nation-building. New organizations, and new forms of expertise, were coming to the fore. As the troops withdrew from Haiti, international experts, the modern version of the colonial apparatus of generations past, set to work on Haiti's police, its judiciary, its schools and hospitals. The United States worked with the UN and other bilateral donors, especially France and Canada. Over the next few years the international community would pour $2 billion into the effort to make Haiti stand on its own two feet. And the effort would fail. Neither the Clinton administration nor its international partners took the full measure of Haiti's woes, or of the stupendous difficulty of creating the solid foundations of democracy in such a state. They lacked the patience of colonial regimes; and of course they could not wield the authority the colonial powers had, for Haiti was a sovereign nation with its own democratically elected president. And that president, alas, turned out to be as autocratic and corrupt as the men who had deposed him. More money might not have mattered, as it might not in Russia. "You could have put in three, four, five billion dollars, and you would have had the same result," said one of the country's leading economists. Aristide would have seen to that.

The experience in Haiti taught the Clinton administration several powerful lessons, some encouraging and some cautionary. It was possible to use force, or the threat of force, in order to restore or preserve democracy. We could not do it alone, if only because the American people would insist that the commitment be sharply limited in scope and duration. We needed to have international partners, and above all the UN. But you could not simply restore a democratic leader, hold an election, and walk away. Democracy rested on institutions, not elections, and the act of building those institutions in weak states was a vast and frustrating undertaking. Indeed, Haiti demonstrated a new kind of problem characteristic of the post–cold war era—not weak states but failed ones, which would suck their neighbors into a vortex of violence absent outside intervention. Somalia had been another such state, abandoned by both great powers after the cold war, and it had absorbed American and UN troops like a great lake of quicksand. Africa was dotted with failed or tottering states. Slobodan Milosevic left several of them in his wake after tearing the former Yugoslavia to shreds.

The questions of intervention and of state-building came to the fore in the decade between the end of the cold war and the terrorist attacks of 9/11. Humanitarian intervention offered one important answer to the question of what force should be used for after the demise of communism; nation-building, with its democratic end point, offered a lasting solution to the problem of the failed state. The Clinton administration would engage twice more after Haiti in intervention and nation-building—in Bosnia in 1995, and in Kosovo four years later. White House officials even created a template for the process, drawing up a "generic political-military plan" that ultimately ran to sixty pages. Ousting the aggressor was the easiest part, at least if you were willing to use or threaten real firepower. The hard part was building the institutions and the habits that would enable self-government. In Bosnia and Kosovo, and in East Timor, sovereignty rested with the international forces, as it had not in Haiti; but the effort to create an effective and trusted police force, an independent judiciary, a responsive civil service, and the like proved maddeningly difficult. East Timor, like Haiti, relapsed into violence when the occupying force went home. The arc of democratic development, it seemed, was vastly longer than the arc of international attention.

The clamps of the cold war had held much of the globe in place; with the screws suddenly loosened, nations throughout the third world spun off into their various, eccentric destinies. Many, like Somalia or the Democratic Republic of the Congo, experienced state collapse; in others, dictators fell, journalists exercised newfound freedom, and citizens euphorically thronged the polls. Democracy arrived in many of the deeply impoverished and tradition-bound states that an earlier generation of theorists had consigned to a long autocratic apprenticeship. *Democratic Experiments in Africa*, a book written in 1997, describes the almost miraculous tale of the arrival of democracy in Benin, where in 1989 president Mathieu Kérékou, installed by the military, reacted to widespread strikes and economic collapse by abandoning his party's monopoly on political power and its commitment to Marxist-Leninist doctrine. Still in retreat before unremitting popular outrage, Kérékou accepted a new constitution, which led to elections in which the leader of the democratic opposition won a smashing victory. Kérékou asked forgiveness for his abuse of power and withdrew from public life.

Michael Bratton and Nicolas van de Walle, the authors of *Democratic Experiments in Africa*, observe that from 1990 to 1994 the Beninois pattern was reproduced, if not quite so dramatically, across the continent. At least ten other nations experienced democratic changes of government. Of the forty-seven countries in the sub-Saharan region, thirty-eight held elections; the authors describe twenty-nine of them as "founding elections" that "paved a route away from the monopoly politics of authoritarian regimes." Overall, during this period, sixteen countries, including South Africa but also Malawi, Zambia, and Mozambique, experienced transitions to democracy. It was a time, the authors write, "when Africans experienced a broad and pronounced ferment of political change."

But *experiment* was a just, and telling, word. Few of these states had much prior experience with democratic rule, and in most, tribal loyalties ran much deeper than national ones. The lack of a private economy produced a never-ending scramble for state power, and thus endemic corruption, and the winning party brooked little real opposition. These fledgling democracies seemed at once flashy and feeble. They had changed—but only at the very top, so the change often proved transitory. Elected civilians were ousted in coups, or themselves put an end to democracy. Bratton and van de Walle describe the rise of "big-man democracy," in which "the formal trappings of democracy coexist with neopatrimonial political practice."

What was one to make of these new states? Were they bogus democracies, vindicating the view that economic development and political legitimacy had to precede elections and the rest of the formal panoply of the democratic state? If so, attempts to provoke a "fourth wave" were deeply misguided. Indeed, in 1993, Samuel Huntington published an article in *Foreign Affairs* titled "The Clash of Civilizations?" which sounded a far more discouraging note than he had only a few years earlier. Huntington now believed that "the efforts by the West to promote its values of democracy and liberalism to universal values" had provoked "countering responses from other civilizations." These values had "little resonance in Islamic, Confucian, Japanese, Hindu, Buddhist or Orthodox cultures," which had turned out to be far more durable than theorists of modernization had imagined. Countries such as China might well modernize without Westernizing. Some, in fact, would pose a grave threat to the West: Huntington foresaw a "Confucian-Islamic" axis trading in weapons of mass destruction. "The next world war, if there is one," Huntington melodramatically predicted, "will be a war between civilizations."

Others soon corroborated Huntington's dark vision. In "The Coming Anarchy," which appeared in *The Atlantic Monthly* in early 1996, journalist Robert Kaplan argued that much of the developing world was on the verge of political collapse and environmental catastrophe. "We are entering a bifurcated world," Kaplan wrote. "Part of the globe is inhabited by Hegel's and Fukuyama's Last Man, healthy, well fed, and pampered by technology. The other, larger, part is inhabited by Hobbes's First Man, condemned to a life that is 'poor, nasty, brutish, and short.'" The combination of the relentless Malthusian logic of resource scarcity and the ricketiness of the third world's jury-rigged states would lead not to Huntington's civilizational war, but to endless, and pitiless, tribal combat.

Kaplan returned to the issue a year later with an article titled, "Was Democracy Just a Moment?" History, Kaplan grandly declared, "has demonstrated that there is no final triumph of reason, whether it goes by the name of Christianity, the Enlightenment, or, now, democracy." Democracy was not destined to conquer the globe. It had emerged in the West "only as a capstone to other social and economic achievements." Because those preconditions existed in the former communist states of Eastern Europe, our efforts to nurture democracy there had borne fruit. "What is less reasonable," though, "is to put a gun to the head of the peoples of the developing world and say, in effect, 'Behave as if you had experienced the Western Enlightenment to the degree that Poland and the Czech Republic did.'"

Though democracy was not quite so flimsy and transitory a phenomenon as Kaplan insisted, it had also become clear that it was far more fragile than Ronald Reagan had thought. The grandiose hopes that the Clinton administration had held out for Boris Yeltsin's Russia had proved to be wildly overoptimistic. Central Asia was mired in strongman rule, while in Belarus, the old Soviet Union had been virtually preserved in amber. The number of democracies had stalled at 117 of the world's 191 nations, according to the annual tabulation made by Freedom House. For every nation added to the list, another fell out. And in many of the fledgling democracies, elections seemed to promise little more than an exchange of kleptocrats, or a formal confirmation of the incumbent one—big-man democracy.

These Potemkin polities, all façade and no substance, compelled, at the very least, a redefinition of "democracy." For Seymour Martin Lipset, it had been quite enough to characterize democracy as "a political system which supplies regular constitutional opportunities for changing the government officials, and a social mechanism which permits the largest possible part of the population to influence major decisions by choosing among contenders for political office." In short, regular elections plus wide franchise equals democracy. But this would no longer do. Larry Diamond, a political theorist at Stanford, suggested a distinction between "liberal democracies" and merely "electoral ones." In a liberal democracy, he wrote, "the military is subordinated, the executive is constrained, the constitution is supreme, due process is respected, civil society is autonomous and free, citizens are politically equal, women and minorities have access to power, and individuals have real freedom to speak and publish and organize and protest." An electoral democracy just had elections.

And electoral democracies, Diamond observed, were growing, while liberal ones were not. "In the former Soviet Union, Africa, parts of Asia, and the Middle East," Diamond noted, "elections themselves are increasingly hollow and uncompetitive, a thin disguise for the hegemony of despots and ruling parties." During the 1990s, Diamond wrote, sixteen regimes had staged multiparty elections "so flawed that they do not meet the minimal criteria for electoral democracies." Across the developing world, the multiparty election accompanied by a universal franchise, which to Lipset's generation had constituted the sine qua non of democracy, had been reduced to a sterile ritual. This combination of ubiquity and vacuity, Diamond commented, demonstrated "not only the

ideological hegemony of 'democracy' in the post–Cold War world
system but also the superficial nature of that hegemony."

The great barrier, it turned out, was not the one separating the
nondemocracies from the democracies, but the solidly founded
democracies from the flimsy ones. Thomas Carothers observed
that "of the nearly 100 countries that experienced political open-
ings in the 1980s or early 1990s and were counted by exultant
democracy promoters as part of democracy's 'Third Wave,' only a
small number have succeeded in consolidating democracy." And
Carothers noted that democracy had been deepened almost
exclusively in the relatively affluent countries in Central Europe,
Asia, and South America. For the others, the obstacles had
proved insurmountable.

By the 1990s, democracy promotion had become both an industry and an academic field, with an extremely porous membrane
separating the two. Seymour Martin Lipset and Robert Dahl had
been diagnosticians with no desire to perform experiments on a
live patient; but democracy promotion was an applied field of
study, and so many of the chief operatives moved back and forth
from theory to study and practice. Thomas Carothers was perhaps the leading example of this new generation of democracy
scholars. Carothers was a tall, thin, melancholy figure with the
drooping features of a basset hound—a man formed around the
idea of doubt. He had, in fact, been attracted to the field after
reading Robert Packenham's *Liberal America and the Third
World*, a book whose central theme is the vanity of American foreign policy, very much including the hopes of exporting democracy. His was arguably a curious career choice.

Carothers's first assignment, in 1985, was to help USAID
reform the judicial system of Haiti, from which "Baby Doc" Duvalier had just fled. He soon found, as he later wrote, that Haiti
did not have a flawed or immature system of courts, prisons, po-

lice, and so on. Rather, "the system was an integral part of a predatory state that had long lived off the Haitian people for its own benefit, without any notion that a state might actually seek to serve the interests of its people." You couldn't change it unless you could get to the underlying political culture. USAID, of course, went ahead and launched a program of reform, which ran aground and was relaunched several times over before coming to grief altogether after President Aristide was restored to power. And Carothers was left with the sense, which he never lost, that there was something preposterous about the confidence with which Americans went around the world injecting the potion of democracy into the sickliest of patients. Only by attending to the most external and superficial of symptoms could one imagine that the subject was showing signs of health. "Clearly," as he wrote apropos of Haiti, "law is not just the sum of courts, legislatures, police, prosecutors and other formal institutions with some direct connection to law. Law is also a normative system that resides in the minds of the citizens of a society." And those normative systems, as Hans Morgenthau or George Kennan or Jeane Kirkpatrick would have been quick to point out, take a long time to form.

Carothers soon left the government, for which he may have been unsuited by reason of skepticism, and ultimately became perhaps the world's leading authority on democracy promotion. He returned often to the theme of national blitheness, and to the incongruity between the depth of the political and structural problems of democratizing countries and the thinness and sketchiness of the remedies applied by American officials. While he believed that adroit diplomacy, consistent rhetoric, and carefully targeted aid could make a real difference in promoting democracy abroad, he was doubtful about the magnitude of the change outsiders could make in a country's internal political life. In general, he thought, American administrations received too much credit and too much blame: "Democracy on the rise—

kudos to the administration! Democracy losing ground—what are those idiots in Washington doing?" Even the most extensive campaign of assistance, as in Serbia, "is at most a facilitator of locally rooted forces for political change," he asserted, "not the creator of them."

Carothers was skeptical not only about the leverage of outsiders but also about democratization itself. By the mid-nineties, a whole class of countries had stalled somewhere along the path from authoritarianism. Were they, as was often said, in "transition," however slowly and uneasily, toward democracy? Carothers thought not. In an essay titled "The End of the Transition Paradigm," he insisted that countries moving away from authoritarianism were not necessarily moving toward democracy. Most of them had instead fallen into a "gray zone" in which they enjoyed a certain "dysfunctional equilibrium." The gray zone was not a "precarious middle ground" but rather "the most common political condition of countries in the developing world and the post-communist world."

Others, less gloomy, emphasized the growing popular clamor for representation. Larry Diamond suggested that democracies would survive even in the absence of economic growth if leaders delivered "transparent, accountable, responsive, orderly government." But the bottom line was that it was extraordinarily difficult to accomplish in a matter of years what had slowly accreted over generations in the West. It was exponentially harder in societies beset by poverty and racked by tribal or ethnic division. And the more deep-seated the problem, the harder it was for outsiders to play any role in dislodging it. Scarcely anyone, for example, questioned the centrality of the rule of law, a broad term that refers to legal institutions such as the courts and prisons, to the body of law itself, and to the attitude of citizens and rulers toward the law. It was the absence of the rule of law, whether in Haiti or Kosovo, that allowed corruption to flourish, and the powerful to remain beyond the reach of justice. Rule-of-law reform thus became one of the mantras of the democracy world; a great torrent of funds issued from the UN and the World Bank, European governments, foundations, universities, and of course American government agencies and NGOs.

But when a society was built on impunity, as Carothers had asked about Haiti, how could even the most determined outsiders reform its courts or its police or prisons? "Rule of law reform," Carothers wrote, "will succeed only when it gets at the fundamental problem of rulers who refuse to be ruled by the law." And this, of course, was not a technocratic issue with a technocratic solution. Carothers pointed out that Russia, the largest recipient of rule-of-law funds, was "not even clearly moving in the right direction." And the same, he said, was true of other major recipients of U.S. aid, including El Salvador and Guatemala.

The rise of the electoral democracy had deeply chastened democracy's proselytes, at least the more thoughtful among them. And it had increased the ranks of the outright skeptics. A significant and respectable body of opinion looked at the chaos and bloodshed of illiberal states and concluded that the very attempt to transplant our model abroad was a national delusion, and a dangerous one at that. Fareed Zakaria, then the editor of *Foreign Affairs*, powerfully captured this line of thinking in a highly influential 1997 piece, "The Rise of the Illiberal Democracy."

Zakaria used the expression "illiberal democracy" to describe the states Larry Diamond had categorized as "electoral democracies." But whereas Diamond understood these places as grossly immature versions of democracy, and urged that they be helped along the path of development, Zakaria described them as the inevitable consequence of putting the cart of democracy before the horse of liberalism. In the West, Zakaria argued, the whole body of individual rights enshrined in law—"constitutional liberalism," as he called it—had evolved slowly over centuries, long before the advent of democracy, which to Zakaria meant nothing more than the choice of leaders through free and regular elections. The tradition of limited government had acted as a counterweight to the blind majoritarianism of democracy. In the third world, by contrast, democracy had arisen prematurely, before liberal habits and institutions had been able to establish themselves. And while Kaplan had looked at these states and seen pitiful disguises for the anarchy lurking just below, Zakaria had seen majoritarian tyranny, in which the head of state and his cronies usurped whatever power was available. And now, he asserted, democracy was on the rise and liberalism in retreat.

Zakaria had reshaped the definition of *democracy* in a way that made it almost a pejorative term. With its liberal virtues sheared off, democracy sounded very much like mob rule. The two chief models of democratic governance, he argued, were the American one, where electoral majorities were blocked from carrying out their will by an active judiciary and various procedural obstacles, and the one presented by the French Revolution, in which "the people" wield unlimited power in the name of a just society. "Most non-Western countries," he claimed, "have embraced the French model." There was a real danger that illiberal democracies would discredit democracy itself. Zakaria proposed that "instead of searching for new lands to democratize and new places to hold elections," the United States and other Western nations seek "to consolidate democracy where it has taken root and to encourage the gradual development of constitutional liberalism across the globe."

Zakaria offered a more nuanced prescription than Kaplan, who had argued that Africa needed fewer democrats and more strongmen—Bismarcks—who would consolidate power and jumpstart the process of development. Zakaria pointed to "liberal autocracies" such as Singapore and Malaysia, which, he said, "have accorded their citizens a widening sphere of economic, civil, religious and limited political rights," even though decision-making power rested with "patriarchs or open-party systems." These states offered their citizens a far more prosperous and secure life than they could ever know under despotic majoritarianism. In fact, Zakaria wrote, "the experience of East Asia and Central Europe suggests that when regimes . . . protect individual rights, including those of property and contract, and create a framework of law and administration, capitalism and growth will follow." And democracy would follow after that.

One obvious question provoked by these attacks on third world democracies was: Where were these Bismarcks of the developing world? Everyone mentioned Singapore, but any kind of government was likely to prove more effective in a city-state than in a sprawling, multi-ethnic, geographically variegated nation, much less in a nightmare like Congo. Kaplan had suggested Peru's Alberto Fujimori and Ghana's Jerry Rawlings as models, but Zakaria classed both as illiberal democrats. Most benevolent dictators turned out to be benevolent only in their own minds. In a memo written several months after Kaplan's article appeared, Princeton Lyman, a former ambassador and then the deputy assistant secretary of state, wrote that Kaplan's argument had served as "the rationale for two generations of dictators throughout the Third World," most of whom in fact "ran their economies into the ground." And despite promising domestic harmony, most ruled in an arbitrary manner that exacerbated ethnic tensions, ultimately undermining their own rule.

It was plainly true, as Zakaria observed, that you could have liberalism without democracy, just as you could have democracy without liberalism. Suffrage had expanded over generations in the constitutional monarchies and the republics of Europe, as it had in the United States. But could you really hold off demands for representation until a people were "ready"? In fact, the seed of democracy was always sprouting within liberalism. One of Zakaria's critics, Marc F. Plattner, wrote that "the political doctrine at the source of liberalism" holds that "all legitimate political power is derived from the consent of individuals, who are by nature not only free but equal." Locke had described the state of nature as one of "perfect freedom" and also of equality, "there being nothing more evident than that Creatures of the same species and rank . . . should be equal one amongst another without Subordination and Subjection."

Could it be that citizens in deeply illiberal places had gotten it into their heads that they too were equal to their masters, and thus had an equal right over their destiny? Was it possible, that is, that meddlesome outsiders weren't holding a gun to the heads of third world democrats, as Kaplan thought, but, rather, trying to speed a process already in motion? It was true that it often made more sense to hold off on national elections until liberal habits had begun to form and the rule of law had taken hold. But, as Thomas Carothers asked, "what to do if the people of the society are pressing for democracy? Should the U.S. government tell them not to? *Can* it?" Carothers agreed that "deferred democratization" was an effective formula in nineteenth-century Europe. But, he said, "the global political culture has changed. For better or for worse (and I think much for the better), people all around the world have democratic aspirations."

And if democracy promotion was not simply a liberal peccadillo but rather a response to a global demand for rights and representation, however inchoate and even subject to cynical manipulation, then the central question to be asked was not whether it should be done, but how it could be done effectively. People like Carothers feared that whoever succeeded President Clinton would react to the failures by eliminating the policy itself. It did not occur to them to worry that democracy promotion would be discredited not by timidity but by recklessness.

5

"Realism Died on 9/11"

But What Was Born in Its Place?

In the 2000 election, George W. Bush was the candidate of the Republican foreign policy establishment. The neoconservative thinkers associated with a doctrine known as "greatness conservatism," which proposed that American power be boldly deployed to advance American values, found the maverick candidacy of Senator John McCain far more appealing. McCain was deeply acquainted with foreign affairs; Bush seemed almost entirely uninterested in the world beyond America's borders. Though he had been raised in the kind of elite settings where virtually everyone traveled abroad, he had not so much as left the country until 1975, when he went to China, where his father was serving as U.S. ambassador. He next ventured beyond our borders in 1990, when his father, then president of the United States, asked him to go to Gambia. Thereafter he went to Europe several times with the Young Presidents' Organization, and as governor of Texas he traveled regularly to Mexico.

Bush began learning about the world only when he decided to run for president, and he enlisted Condoleezza Rice, his father's former aide, as tutor. Rice, in turn, assembled a group of experts known informally as "the Vulcans" and drawn largely from the elder Bush's circle. The only bona fide neoconservative among them was Paul Wolfowitz, who as assistant secretary of state under Ronald Reagan had advocated applying pressure to Ferdinand Marcos. The others, including Dick Cheney, Steven Hadley, Robert Zoellick, and of course Rice herself, were drawn from the more conservative end of the Republican mainstream. Their collective critique was less ideological than managerial: Bill Clinton had overcommitted the American military in morally driven adventures in the Balkans and elsewhere; had rashly thrown in his lot with the drunken and unpredictable Boris Yeltsin in Russia; and had staked America's prestige on a doomed Middle East peace process. America needed to recover from what was, in effect, a binge of foreign policy romanticism.

The Bush team laid out its agenda in a pair of essays written by Rice and Zoellick for the January/February 2000 issue of *Foreign Affairs*. Zoellick's contribution offered five principles for a Republican foreign policy. "First," Zoellick wrote, such a policy "is premised on a respect for power, being neither ashamed to pursue America's national interests nor too quick to use the country's might." Second, it "emphasizes building and sustaining coalitions and alliances." Third, "Republicans judge international agreements and institutions as means to achieve ends, not as forms of political therapy." In short, a Republican foreign policy, unlike a Democratic one, would be clear-eyed, unsentimental, and professional.

The Rice essay is now remembered—as the Zoellick is not—because it drew such a bracing, if hyperbolic, contrast between Democratic softness and Republican toughness. "Many in the United States," she wrote, "are (and always have been) uncomfortable with the notions of power politics, great powers, and power balances." For these latter-day Wilsonians, she wrote, "The 'national interest' is replaced with 'humanitarian interests' or the interests of 'the international community.'" The Clinton administration had put far too much store by treaties, international law, and the United Nations. The most striking thing about Rice's essay was not so much the doctrine it advocated, which differed only in emphasis from Zoellick's call for realism and consistency, but the bellicosity of its tone. Here was a disciplined realist who could barely restrain her contempt for a woolly-brained administration whose "pursuit of, at best, illusory 'norms' of international behavior" had become "epidemic." At times Rice adopted a tone of Reaganesque patriotism, writing that "American values are universal" and are bound to triumph in the long run. Her point was not that statesmen should actively promote these values, but the opposite: though we should seek an international balance of power favorable to our principles, "in the meantime, it is simply not possible to ignore and isolate other powerful states that do not share those values."

George Bush the candidate automatically fell back on Rice's brand of hardheaded realism in the rare moments when he was called on to discuss foreign policy. Asked in the second presidential debate about his "guiding principles" for the exercise of American power, Bush said, "The first question is what's in the best interests of the United States." His opponent, Vice President Al Gore, staked out what was, in effect, the opposite position. "I see it as a question of values," said Gore. The dichotomy was, of course, a facile one, for any rational policy must combine values with interests; but the difference was not merely rhetorical. Vice President Gore "believes in nation-building," Bush said accurately. "I believe the role of the military is to fight and win war." The Republican candidate had also absorbed his adviser's scorn for the sort of moral grandiosity that had led Madeleine Albright to call America "the indispensable nation." "If we're an arrogant nation, they'll resent us," he said. "If we're a humble nation but strong, they'll welcome us." He expanded on this theme of self-restraint in an unscripted response to Gore, saying, "I'm not so sure the role of the United States is to go around the world and say, 'This is the way it's gotta be.'" The United States could "help people help themselves" rather than flaunt the American way.

In January of 2001, I wrote a cover story about Bush and his team for *The New York Times Magazine*; the title was, "Downsizing Foreign Policy." In this new era of "worldly pragmatism," I wrote, George Bush the elder's euphoric "new world order" was "as distant a memory as the evil empire." Reagan's Wilsonianism of the right would prove as unfashionable as Clinton's "assertive multilateralism." I got one thing right: "What one feels, in talking to the people who are likely to determine foreign policy in the Bush administration, is . . . a preoccupation with threat, a suspicion about negotiations, a willingness to go it alone." I got everything almost absurdly wrong, though I did leave myself what turned out to be a very convenient escape hatch: "Perhaps the most hopeful thing one can say is that administrations rarely stick to the abstract principles they lay out during the campaign." Of course, I had a very different escape route in mind from the one the Bush administration would actually take.

The new Bush administration at first looked very much like the old one minus the faith in multilateral institutions and international law. Robert Blackwill, a member of the Vulcans who had been Rice's boss under Bush 41, says, "I think it would be fair to say that our transition preparations and the application of those ideas which had been approved by the president were routinely realist in character. We were on the way to be a conventional Republican administration." Reaganite neoconservatives occupied key second-tier positions in the Pentagon, the vice president's office, and the National Security Council; but all the top jobs went to cold war pragmatists, including Donald Rumsfeld, the secretary of defense; Colin Powell, the secretary of state; National Security Adviser Condoleezza Rice; and, of course, Vice President Dick Cheney. The focus of the early months was national missile defense; trade; the charting of new relationships with Russia, India, and Mexico. Lorne Craner, assistant secretary of state for democracy, human rights, and labor in an administration that had only a modest interest in spreading democracy and human rights abroad, spent much of the year preparing for the World Conference Against Racism in Durban, South Africa, where his goal was largely to prevent an auto-da-fé of Israel. When it ended, on September 10, 2001, Craner assumed that he had just seen the high point of his year.

And then, from the maelstrom of 9/11, a new world emerged. A president with no clear sense of purpose discovered his calling: to pursue and crush a monstrous adversary, "the heirs of all the murderous ideologies of the twentieth century," as he put it in his address to a joint session of Congress on September 20. That meant, above all, a direct assault on the forces of Al Qaeda and their state sponsors and protectors in Afghanistan. In the months after 9/11, the administration was consumed by the planning and execution of the war, and by the vast criminal justice effort to track down a supposed Islamic fifth column at home.

But the attacks also forced a rethinking of the nature, or the boundaries, of foreign policy itself. The Condoleezza Rice of early 2000 viewed diplomacy much as Clemenceau, or even Metternich, had—as the correct management of the behavior of states. Given the rise of such "transnational" issues as drug trafficking, infectious disease, and terrorism, her views were already archaic; the domestic policy and the internal conditions of other nations affected us every bit as much as did the statecraft of foreign leaders. But the terrorist assault made this conclusion self-evident. As Barry Lowenkron, a Rice aide first at the NSC and then at the State Department, says, "Realism died on September 11, 2001." Until 9/11, Lowenkron says, "what happens inside states is a humanitarian imperative"—precisely the kind of concern that the Rice of 2000 had ridiculed. Of course, President Clinton's doctrine of "enlargement" dictated that what happened inside states had very practical significance for the global economy. But there is all the difference in the world between a policy that promises to boost our GNP and one that aims to keep terrorists at bay. What happened inside states was now a matter of national security.

And Americans quickly came to understand that hunting down the terrorists would not be enough. They were a tiny band; but millions of ordinary citizens across the Arab and Islamic world despised the United States and the West, and rallied to the side of the killers. Some on the left, such as the writer Susan Sontag, argued that the problem lay in American policies toward the Middle East. But whatever truth this claim may have had, Americans were in no mood to hear it. A more popular, and maybe more plausible, suggestion was that the problem lay inside Arab states. V. S. Naipaul, the Nobel Prize–winning author, said that the angry young men of the Arab street really wanted an American green card; furious at the reactionary and paralytic states in which they lived, they lashed out at the world of prosperity and freedom that they desperately envied but could not enjoy. Conservatives agreed, of course; but this was no mere ideological hobbyhorse. In a cover story in the October 15, 2001, issue of *Newsweek* bluntly titled "Why Do They Hate Us?" Fareed Zakaria located the answer in "the sense of humiliation, decline and despair that sweeps the Arab world." Zakaria specifically attributed the rise of Islamic fundamentalism to "the total failure of political institutions" in Arab society. Of course the United States had to wage remorseless war against Al Qaeda and kindred forces, Zakaria wrote, but it must also "help Islam enter the modern world."

This was an idea profoundly congenial to President Bush, for whom the war on terror had already taken on the proportions of an antinomian struggle between "freedom and fear, justice and cruelty." In the months after 9/11, Bush began raising the idea of promoting reform in the Middle East. The president, says Douglas Feith, the former undersecretary of defense for planning and a key architect of policy on the Middle East and Iraq, "thought at the grand level. He is a strategic thinker—high-level, conceptual, long-term and global. And the idea that a substantial part of the answer to the ideological problem in the war on terror is democracy is his idea." A senior White House official agrees that the whole idea of democracy promotion "was driven by the president. He felt that we couldn't get to the bottom of this as long as we ignored the nature of these societies—that they were closed societies, they were unjust societies. There were plenty of discussions with the president about individual countries—Egypt, the former Soviet states and so on."

Less than a year earlier, of course, Bush had been warning against the arrogance of imposing the American way on others. But Bush's sudden conversion to the cause of liberty did not have the feel of mere expedience or of hypocrisy. If anything, the realism and restraint he had preached in the campaign seemed like a poor fit for his sunny and deeply moralistic nature; he had absorbed from Condoleezza Rice a doctrine that offered a satisfying critique of his opponent without necessarily fitting his own intuitive worldview. The president believed in transformation; he had, after all, abruptly reversed his own life trajectory. What's more, his politics were infused with an evangelical faith in America and the American way, a deep belief that people everywhere aspired to the American condition of freedom. The terrorist attacks may have reordered an incoherent world into a reassuringly clear alignment. Like Reagan before him, though far more dramatically, Bush experienced a Wilsonian conversion. Indeed, this most plainspoken and tongue-tied of presidents availed himself, apparently un-self-consciously, of the high diction and cadence of the Founding Fathers: "America, in this young century, proclaims liberty throughout the world, and to all the inhabitants thereof."

Rice's own conversion experience is harder to explain. As an academic and a policy-maker, she had a long-established reputation as a steely realist who scorned the idea that changes in a nation's internal political life would alter its diplomatic behavior. She was allergic to Reaganesque moralizing. "Like most Americans," she told an interviewer, "I listened with some skepticism to claims that America was 'a beacon of democracy.' When American presidents said that, I chalked it up to bad speechwriting and

hyperbole." As the Russia expert for Brent Scowcroft, national security adviser to the elder George Bush, she had distinguished
herself by being yet more hard-boiled than her colleagues. One
State Department official who worked with her closely recalls,
"She tended to be more dismissive of non-state-centered things
like the environment. I suspect that some of it was, as an African
American woman in the security field she needed to demonstrate
that she was hard and tough and understood power politics."

There was something almost atavistic about Rice's worldview;
she seemed to be a throwback to the realpolitik of Henry Kissinger. And yet, as a liberal Stanford colleague observes, Rice "always had a belief in American power as a force for good." She was
acutely conscious of her own life journey as a black girl who had
grown up in racist Birmingham, Alabama; who had absorbed
from her parents the lesson that "the only limits to our aspirations
came from within"; and who had reached heights that few blacks,
or few women, had attained. In congressional testimony she gave
in the course of being confirmed as secretary of state in 2005, she
spoke of her own life as "a story of the triumph of universal values over adversity"—a moral that the far earthier Colin Powell,
for example, would never have thought to draw. Those values, she
went on, offer "a source of hope to men and women across the
globe who cherish freedom and work to advance freedom's cause."
Rice, like Bush, was a deeply religious figure; and this evangelical mode of speaking appears to have come as naturally to her
as did her bleak dismissal of humanitarianism. It may be, of
course, that only someone who had not fully explored her own
thoughts could be equally comfortable in both of those modes.

Nor was it only personal experience that led Rice to see American power as a force for good. During the two years she had
spent in the George H. W. Bush National Security Council, she
had watched the cold war come to a close in a far more benign
and peaceful fashion than anyone could have imagined. She had
seen the unambiguous triumph of America, and of American val-

ues. She had played a role in the reunification of Germany. And according to the memory of Daniel Fried, the State Department desk officer for Poland, she had been receptive, as others had not, to the momentous sense that "history is open."

By September 2001, Rice "was juggling a number of ideas that weren't even consistent with one another," says Philip Zelikow, a colleague from the first Bush administration, a fellow academic, and a friend to whom she would frequently turn in the years to come. "She came in with a legacy view of a classic international system that was already coexisting uneasily with a lot of ideas about how the system has changed." Rice herself says that from the time she took office she had been thinking about ways to "rebuild a consensus about foreign policy." In July 2001, at the summit of the world's eight industrialized nations in Genoa, she met with Bono, the lead singer of U2, who had just created a new organization to lobby for increased aid to Africa. Bono suggested a plan his aides had been designing to direct funds to a small number of highly impoverished but well-governed countries. The program might well have fallen to the bottom of the pile; but the terrorist attacks had created an urgent demand for new tools of statecraft. And with a major UN conference on financing development in the third world scheduled for January, President Bush needed a "deliverable." Working frantically, Rice's staff and Bono's policy aides hammered together the Millennium Challenge Account, the first major innovation on foreign aid since Kennedy's Alliance for Progress.

The MCA was a startling departure from GOP orthodoxy. Generations of Republicans had denounced foreign aid as a preposterous waste of money. The critical insight behind the MCA was that while the corrupt and despotic regimes to which we had often given aid in the past did, in fact, squander the funds, that money could be used far more effectively in better-governed countries. More than that, aid could encourage good governance. Recipients would become eligible for MCA grants based on their performance on a range of indicators, including civil liberties, political rights, rule of law, and control of corruption; expenditures on health and education; fiscal and trade policy; and natural resource management. No less important, it would be the recipient countries themselves who identified projects to be funded and then carried out the programs, with consultation and oversight from Washington.

President Bush (along with Bono) was able to announce the MCA prior to the conference in Monterrey, Mexico. He vowed that the Millennium Challenge Corporation, as the organization was to be called, would be disbursing $5 billion by its third year—the largest single increase in American development assistance in years. But once the announcement was made, the entire project disappeared into dark bureaucratic byways. Only after two years was the MCC even chartered. It took more time before the organization was prepared to actually award grants. The delay, in turn, gave Congress all the rationale it needed to authorize less money than the White House requested; in no year did the sum appropriated reach $2 billion, much less the advertised $5 billion.

The Bush administration was scarcely alone in thinking about the connection between the failures of development and the kind of political failures that lead to terrorism. In mid-2002, the UN Development Programme produced a document that dramatized those failures as never before. The Arab Human Development Report, part of a regular series of studies on regional development produced by UNDP, astonished readers with its blunt and unforgiving analysis; the fact that it was produced by leading Arab academics made it impossible to impeach on grounds of Western bias or neocolonialism. Arab states, the authors argued, suffered from a "freedom deficit," a "women's empowerment deficit," and a "human capabilities/knowledge deficit." The Arab world scored dismally on indexes measuring all three of these attributes. The authors observed that the "wave of democracy" that had swept over much of the developing world in the 1980s and

'90s had "barely reached the Arab States." And they insisted, crucially, that education, political freedom, and economic development were linked in a tight nexus: "Human development, by
enhancing human capabilities, creates the ability to exercise freedom, and human rights, by providing the necessary framework,
create the opportunities to exercise it. Freedom is the guarantor
and the goal of both human development and human rights."

Colin Powell, who was in any case no theoretician, would
never have said that realism died on 9/11, but he did believe that
the Arab world needed "reform," and the Arab Human Development Report made that proposition inescapable. Under Powell's
direction, the State Department developed a new aid program
to address the deficits the UNDP report had identified. The Middle East Partnership Initiative, unveiled in December 2002, was
designed to provide short-term grants to encourage political,
economic, and educational reform and women's empowerment.
Some portion of the funds, including those for explicitly political
activities such as party-building, would go directly to the Arab
world's nascent civil-society groups. This was itself a serious departure, since traditional development assistance went straight
into the coffers of the state and was designed to strengthen the
state's capacity. The Arab Human Development Report had criticized Arab governments for stifling all forms of citizen initiative,
concluding that most treated relations with NGOs as "a zero-sum
game." MEPI was something genuinely new; but it was also
something modest. At a time when the U.S. Agency for International Development was spending more than $600 million a year
in Egypt alone, MEPI never disbursed more than $100 million
throughout the Middle East.

The terrorist attacks had forced administration policy-makers
to think about how they could reach the insides of states. But
they had also forced the president and his team to think about
how they could shape the way people thought about the United
States—above all, people in the part of the world where anger at

the United States translated into acts of violence. For President Bush, who had never traveled when young, who had maintained a scrupulous ignorance of the world beyond our borders, the very fact that the United States was hated was well-nigh incomprehensible. In a prime-time press conference held one month after 9/11, he said, "I'm amazed that there is such misunderstanding of what our country is about, that people would hate us . . . Like most Americans, I just can't believe it. Because I know how good we are, and we've got to do a better job of making our case." And so if one answer to "Why do they hate us?" pointed to the "democracy deficit" of the Arab world, another pointed to a marketing deficit on our part: too many people didn't know the truth of America.

The art of shaping the way people abroad think about you is known as public diplomacy. During the cold war, the United States spent billions promoting our image and ideals, in both open and clandestine ways, on both sides of the iron curtain. But when the cold war ended, so, it seemed, did the need to shape public opinion. In the 1980s and '90s, according to the 2003 Djerejian Report, named after its chairman, Edward Djerejian, a veteran Middle East diplomat, staffing for public diplomacy programs in the Arab and Muslim world fell by a third, and funding by a quarter. Only fifty-four officials in the entire State Department spoke fluent Arabic. Programs to bring future leaders to the United States had been all but eliminated, as had the widely appreciated American Studies centers. Actual spending on diplomatic outreach in the Arab world—as opposed to exchange programs or administrative overhead—came to a grand total of $25 million. This "process of unilateral disarmament in the weapons of advocacy over the last decade," the authors concluded, "has contributed to widespread hostility toward Americans and left us vulnerable to lethal threats to our interests and our safety."

Actually, it was impossible to prove that the hostility was a consequence of the unilateral disarmament. If Arabs hated us be-

cause they were enraged at their own repressive regimes, and because those regimes were all too happy to redirect that public
frustration at the United States (and Israel), then no amount of
advocacy would avail. And if it was our policies Arabs hated, then
we would have to change those policies to alleviate the hostility.
Indeed, the authors of the report pointedly observed that "surveys
show much of the resentment toward America stems from our
policies." But policy lay beyond the report's mandate.

For President Bush, rethinking American policy in the Middle
East in order to cool the rage of the Arab street would have
amounted to appeasement. Public diplomacy post-9/11 thus
meant selling America. Scant weeks after the attacks, the administration created the new post of undersecretary of state for public diplomacy and public affairs, and hired as its first occupant
Charlotte Beers, a celebrated advertising executive who had
successfully marketed such brands as Uncle Ben's Rice and
Head & Shoulders shampoo. For Beers, who had no prior experience in the Middle East, America was a uniquely powerful brand
that was poorly understood in its target markets. In testimony before Congress a week after taking over, she explained that "the
burden is now on us to act as though no one has ever understood
the identity of the United States, and redefine it for audiences
who are at best cynical." She was making sure that our embassies
received copies of articles showing America's compassionate
treatment of its Muslim population; she was striving to infuse official communiqués with the kind of emotional resonance that
advertisers use to reach potential customers.

By mid-2002, Beers had come to understand that the American brand faced far more formidable resistance than her favorite
shampoo had. In a speech in May, she described meeting a
teacher in an Arab capital—"she's a composite, but she's real"—
who had said that her students flatly refused to believe that Islamic fundamentalists had flown planes into the World Trade
Center, though they had seen a videotaped statement made by

one of the bombers before he died. "They refused to hear," Beers concluded. "It's a painful reality that we have to come to grips with every day. It's not what you say, it's what you hear—what they can hear, what they can take in, what's allowable." Beers was noticeably more rueful than she had been before. She was, she said, uncomfortable with the expression "winning hearts and minds." "I know it's intended to sound positive," she said, "but we need a more modest and substantive goal, which would be just to create a dialogue, to engage in a productive debate that allows anger and frustration and disagreements, but not hate—hate that's used to justify the killing of innocents."

But Beers felt that she had found a solution to the problem of willful deafness. The most powerful weapon in her quiver, she said, were exchange programs that let people see America for themselves. But how to reach the millions who would never leave home? That, Beers explained, was a "modern marketing question that we know something about." The trick was to listen to the audience, to empathize with it, to speak from its point of view. Muslims abroad believed that America was a corrupt and impious land. Beers had, in response, begun working on a set of TV spots called "Muslim Life in America," in which American Muslims would discuss the tolerance and respect for faith of their adopted home.

The Shared Values campaign, as it was known, debuted in late 2002 during the monthlong holiday of Ramadan, when television viewing is typically heavy. The brief segments featured Muslims who worked as paramedics or scientists or teachers talking about their lives and extolling America's religious tolerance and diversity. Beers said that 288 million people saw these messages two to three times during the month. Follow-up research in Indonesia had found excellent recall and "message retention." Perhaps that was so; but the elite response, and the state response, drowned out the popular one. Governments in

Egypt, Lebanon, and Jordan, where television was largely state-run, refused to air the programs at all. And Arab commentators generally condemned the exercise as crude and condescending counterpropaganda. The spots were pulled.

By early 2003, when the war in Iraq was drawing near, Beers had been thoroughly defeated. In late February, she told the Senate Foreign Relations Committee that in the Islamic world, "millions of ordinary people . . . have gravely distorted but carefully cultivated images of us—images so negative, so weird, so hostile that I can assure you a young generation of terrorists is being created." The following week, the sixty-eight-year-old ad maestro resigned for "health reasons." An anonymous administration official was quoted as saying that they had waited for the negative fallout from Shared Values to subside so that Beers could be afforded "an honorable exit." It's tempting to say that Beers had failed because she mistook public diplomacy for advertising. But public diplomacy *is* a species of advertising. Beers failed because, as she herself seemed to recognize, the problem she had been asked to solve lay beyond the reach of public diplomacy. The issue, in many ways, was the pathology of the Arab world, which expressed itself in unreasoning contempt for the United States, and which was, in turn, compounded by American behavior and policies.

Charlotte Beers stepped down on March 4, 2003. The war in Iraq began two weeks later. The job of explaining the ways of America to the Islamic world, and of encouraging the spread of democracy there, was about to become vastly more difficult.

President Bush began using new language in the months after 9/11, but the word *democracy* was not a major part of his lexicon. In his 2002 State of the Union address—the one in which he described a new "axis of evil"—Bush pledged his nation to support "the non-negotiable demands of human dignity: the rule of law, limits on the power of the state, respect for women, private property, free speech, equal justice, and religious tolerance." This came pretty close to a description of democracy, but it could also be understood (at least if you left aside "free speech") as accepting the distinction made by Zakaria and others between liberalism and democracy. That, says Philip Zelikow, was no coincidence. "The consensus," he says, "was in favor of limited government that respected human dignity." Rice had tasked Zelikow with writing the administration's new national security strategy, and the document (which appeared only in September 2002) echoes the language of the State of the Union speech. It includes the sentiment that the nonnegotiable demands "can be met in many ways," depending on local traditions of governance.

This cautious agnosticism about political forms appears to have lasted until the middle of 2002, when President Bush formulated a long-awaited policy toward Middle East peace. The Bush administration collectively viewed President Clinton's melodramatic efforts to forge agreement between Israel and Palestine as the perfect example of grandstanding and presidential overreaching. Bush was not about to push Israeli prime minister Ariel Sharon to make concessions. Along with Cheney and Rumsfeld, he had come to view Yasir Arafat, the Palestinian chieftain, as a "terrorist leader" who should not be courted or even engaged. But after returning from a swing through the Middle East in April 2002, Colin Powell concluded that the administration had to restart the peace process, if only to bolster its standing in the Middle East; he urged the president to call for a regional peace conference. Over the next several months, the administration was convulsed by internal debate. James Mann reports in *The Rise of the Vulcans* that the text for the speech Bush was to deliver on June 24 went through "at least twenty-eight drafts."

But the debate had three sides, not two. Rice, who viewed Middle East peace negotiations as quicksand that the president must at all costs avoid, had come to see Palestine as a test case of the new doctrine of internal reform. Philip Zelikow points out that Rice, the convert from hardheaded realism, did not share his own cautionary preference for limited government, but embraced "a positive vision of democracy as appropriate." Along with the administration's leading neoconservatives, Rice pushed for a new grand strategy offering the possibility of statehood for Palestine in exchange for democratic reform. The idea was in the air. A few weeks before the president was to give the speech, Natan Sharansky, the Israeli leader and former Soviet dissident, had proposed a new Palestinian administration, "which would be chosen by a coordinating body headed by the United States," to rule over the territories for "at least three years" while democratic institutions were taking form. Then, when they were deemed ready, the Palestinians would be permitted to hold elections and choose a government that would negotiate peace with Israel. Sharansky had laid out this vision at a retreat held by the conservative American Enterprise Institute in Beaver Creek, Colorado; the next day, he writes, he spoke for more than ninety minutes with Vice President Cheney, who was also attending the event. Soon afterward, he explained the idea to Rice, whom he found receptive.

Here was a bold, affirmative policy rather than the merely negative one of refusing to act until the Palestinians got rid of Arafat. Rumsfeld and Cheney, quite comfortable with the negative policy, opposed the statehood-for-democracy transaction. But the president, always attracted to the dramatic gesture, came down on Rice's side. In his speech, Bush said nothing about a peace conference; instead, he spoke directly to the Palestinian people. "If Palestinians embrace democracy, confront corruption and firmly reject terror," he declared, "they can count on American support for the creation of a provisional state of Palestine." Bush cast this prospect in epochal terms: "If liberty can blossom in the rocky soil of the West Bank and Gaza, it will inspire millions of men and women around the globe who are equally weary of poverty and oppression, and equally entitled to the benefits of democratic government." Bush never mentioned the word *Iraq*, but the administration had already begun its planning for a war to overthrow Saddam Hussein, and the dream of churning up a tidal wave of freedom in the Middle East would soon become a fixed element of his rhetoric. Perhaps the wave would begin in Ramallah and Gaza.

The offer, however, fell on deaf ears—as Powell and others must have imagined it would. The problem was not that the Palestinian people didn't hunger for an honest and democratic state—they did. But they were not a captive people looking to the West for rescue, like Poland or Czechoslovakia in the 1980s. Whatever they felt about their own leadership, the Palestinians believed deeply in the rightness of their struggle against Israel, loathed the government of Ariel Sharon, and profoundly distrusted the Americans. Why would they renounce that struggle when nothing remotely reciprocal was being asked of Israel? Here was an early-warning sign about the blithe hopes of making freedom bloom in the rocky soil of the Middle East—and about the president's own cast of mind. Bush had not reached his new set of convictions about democracy after fighting his way clear of old convictions or the lessons of old experience. He had switched from one view to something like its opposite without passing through any of the intermediate stages. The president had little sense of the rough terrain that lay beneath his splendid words, and thus of what it would mean for the United States not only to proclaim liberty but to somehow help it come to pass.

The United States did not go to war in Iraq in order to democratize the Middle East. Virtually all accounts agree that George Bush and his closest aides considered Saddam Hussein an intolerable threat to the region, and ultimately to the West. Conservatives had been making this case since the middle of the 1990s;

in 1997, *The Weekly Standard* had declared, "Saddam Must Go." The Clinton administration's national security team had entertained little doubt that Saddam had weapons of mass destruction, and that he had been rebuilding his weapons program under the nose of UN inspectors. "Regime change" was the official policy of both the Clinton and Blair administrations. And 9/11 only made those concerns more urgent—though the Bush administration insisted on fortifying the case by connecting nonexistent dots between Saddam Hussein and Osama bin Laden. Finally, the administration's volley of threats in late 2002 and early 2003, and Saddam's intransigent responses, established a logic of its own. According to Bob Woodward in *Plan of Attack*, an account of the months after 9/11, both Bush and Rice focused on the danger of letting Saddam flout the will of the international community. Rice is quoted as telling the president in late 2002, "To let this threat in this part of the world play volleyball with the international community this way will come back to haunt us someday. That is the reason to do it."

Maybe that was the reason to do it—that, and the wish to reassert America's potency, to fight a new kind of war with a new kind of army, to ensure a steady supply of oil, to defend Israel, to banish the ghosts of a father who had failed to "finish the job." But a democratic transformation of the Middle East, if not the war's underlying motive, was certainly understood to be its great consequence. The administration's chief intellectual supporters, including Fouad Ajami, William Kristol, and Charles Krauthammer, made this case. The neoconservatives inside the administration, such as Paul Wolfowitz and Elliot Abrams, made this case. And, most important, the president himself embraced the transformative vision.

Three weeks before the invasion of Baghdad, President Bush delineated his new philosophy of democracy promotion in the Middle East in a speech before the conservative American Enterprise Institute. "There was a time," Bush asserted, "when many said that the cultures of Germany and Japan were incapable of sustaining democratic values. Well, they were wrong. Some say the same of Iraq today. They are mistaken. The nation of Iraq— with its proud heritage, abundant resources and skilled and educated people—is fully capable of moving toward democracy and living in freedom." Bush went on to repeat one of Bill Clinton's favorite nostrums: "The world has a clear interest in the spread of democratic values, because stable and free nations do not breed the ideologies of murder." Therefore, he declared, "A new regime in Iraq would serve as a dramatic and inspiring example of freedom for other nations in the region." Bush seemed to have concluded that the chain reaction of freedom which he had hoped to set off in the West Bank would begin instead in Baghdad.

It was a powerful vision; but what was the reality it was based on? Even some democracy experts inside the administration viewed Iraq as a very stony field for the seeding of democracy. Iraq lay at the heart of a region that had no experience of democracy and almost none of liberal rule. These countries, as the Arab Human Development Report had made all too clear, lacked a civil society, a rule-of-law tradition, elementary political freedoms, an active middle class, and many of the other features correlated with democracy. And of all the Arab nations, Iraq had the most brutal history of repression. Moreover, its "proud heritage" was an authoritarian one, its resources had been exhausted by years of warfare and sanctions, and its skilled and educated workforce had been idle for years. The president had grandly declared: "It is presumptuous and insulting to suggest that a whole region of the world—or the one-fifth of humanity that is Muslim—is somehow untouched by the most basic aspirations of life." But even critics of the "clash of civilizations" theory agreed that democracy was likelier to grow in some places than others.

In October 2002, soon after Bush had begun talking about war in Iraq, four scholars at the Carnegie Endowment— including Thomas Carothers—published a paper speculating that" while overthrowing Saddam might prove easy enough, "democracy will not soon be forthcoming." First, they observed, prior experience in nations such as Haiti, Panama, and Afghanistan was scarcely encouraging. "Like Afghanistan," they went on, "Iraq is a country torn by profound ideological, religious and ethnic conflicts." The United States would have to reconcile Sunni, Shia, and Kurd, and then hold the state together until legitimate indigenous leadership arose. "In short," they concluded, "the United States would have to engage in nation-building on a scale that would dwarf any other such effort since the reconstruction of Germany and Japan after World War II." They also poured cold water on hopes for a democratic "tsunami" originating in Iraq. "For example," they wrote, "an invasion would very likely intensify the anti-Americanism already surging around the region, strengthening the hand of hard-line forces." What's more, "many Arabs, rather than looking to Iraq as a model, would focus on the fact that Iraq was 'liberated' through Western intervention, not by a popular Iraqi movement." If the Bush administration really wanted to democratize the Middle East, they concluded, "the goals must be initially modest, and the commitment to change long-term."

The problem was not only that Bush, Rice, and others believed that they could use the invasion of Iraq to spread democracy across the region, but rather that they undertook this stupendous adventure so blithely. The year before, they had prepared to overthrow the Taliban government in Afghanistan while virtually leaving the country's postwar status to the whim of fortune. According to *Bush at War*, three days before hostilities began, Rice and Paul Wolfowitz, Rumsfeld's top aide, had suggested seeking contributions from other nations to reconstruct Afghanistan after the war. When the president asked, "Who will run the country?" his national security adviser had no idea: Rice, Woodward writes, had thought, "We should have addressed that." At a press conference the following week, Bush had suggested that "it would be a useful function for the United Nations to take over the so-called 'nation-building' . . . after our mission is complete." The president apparently could not even bring himself to use the term without calling it into question.

In Iraq, unlike in Afghanistan, the administration had the time to prepare for the postwar effort. And this time, also unlike in Afghanistan, the United States would step in as sovereign until the Iraqis were ready to take over. But what form would that rule take? Planners in the State Department spent months assembling a vast body of material in what came to be known as the Future of Iraq Project. Yet after the kind of bruising interagency battle that had become routine in the Bush administration, the Pentagon, rather than State, won the job of running postwar Iraq. No one in the administration was more hostile to peacekeeping and nation-building, or more indifferent to the promotion of democracy, than Donald Rumsfeld. The defense secretary had tried to eliminate the Pentagon's Office of Peacekeeping and Humanitarian Affairs, established under Bill Clinton. In May 2002, with the postwar effort in Afghanistan just getting under way, Rumsfeld had ordered the Army War College to shut down its Peacekeeping Institute, another unwanted reminder of the Clinton years.

Rumsfeld had viewed postwar Afghanistan as a boondoggle from which the United States should extricate itself as rapidly as possible. And in late 2002 and early 2003, as he thought (or chose not to think) about the question of postwar Iraq, Rumsfeld looked upon Afghanistan, then being touted as a smashing success, as a counter-paradigm to the Clintonian principles of peacekeeping and nation-building. In mid-February, barely a month before the invasion of Iraq, Rumsfeld gave a speech in New York in which he extolled the "light footprint" in Afghanistan, and criticized the nation-building exercises in Kosovo and East Timor for distorting local economies and creating a culture of dependency. The defense secretary vowed that the lessons of Afghanistan would be applied to "post-Saddam Iraq." And he proceeded to dispose of the Future of Iraq Project, and to ignore the studies by experts in postwar reconstruction drawn up by virtually every national security–related think tank in Washington.

Defenders of Bush and Rice have come to view Donald Rumsfeld as a kind of rogue element in the administration. Philip Zelikow insists that "the president accepted the nation-building requirement for Iraq; that's the policy that the president believed he approved." But there is little if any evidence that either Bush or Rice tried to ensure that any such policy was carried out, or even that either had come to terms with the burden they were about to shoulder. As one former Rice aide puts it, "For eight years"—the Clinton era—"we heard, 'Nation-building—awful.'" President Bush's own views about postwar Iraq seemed to be based on an a priori faith in human nature, and on an analogy— to the democratization of Germany and Japan—that would be difficult for a person familiar with history to seriously entertain. But Rice herself made the same analogy, and also spoke of the democratic transformation of Eastern Europe that she had witnessed in the first Bush administration.

And so Donald Rumsfeld had his way. Jay Garner, the retired general chosen to head up the Office of Reconstruction and Humanitarian Affairs, a name chosen to indicate the narrowness of his ambit, was given seven weeks to prepare for postwar Iraq, though essentially the entire United States military had spent the previous six months preparing for the war itself. In *The Assassin's Gate*, George Packer describes Rumsfeld's spokesman, Larry DiRita, in Kuwait, addressing Garner's team as they prepared to head into Iraq behind advancing troops. DiRita vowed that the Pentagon would not make the hash that the State Department had in Bosnia and Kosovo. "We're going to stand up an interim Iraqi government," DiRita announced, "hand power over to them, and get out of there in three to four months."

Garner explained to people that he would rebuild Iraq's infrastructure, appoint an interim government, oversee a new constitution and elections, and then go home by August—all this in a country where even the tiniest breath of political life had been snuffed out by Saddam. That, in any case, is the brief he had been handed. At a meeting in late April between Garner and 350 Iraqi leaders, according to Packer, a sheik asked, "Who's in charge of our politics?" And Garner said, "You're in charge"—a response that provoked "an audible gasp." State-building would be the responsibility of the indigenous people. Good luck.

Though the war in Iraq was not fought to replace a fascist leader with a democratic one, it would forever after define, and discredit, the Bush administration's Freedom Agenda. The war would stand as irrefutable proof that the president and his team of neocons believed that democracy was something that could be imposed at gunpoint, and thus that any other nation to which they proposed to bring this great benefit, especially one in the Middle East, could expect an equally terrifying treatment. That wasn't true, of course; but there was no way of establishing the truth in the face of this overwhelming, catastrophic reality.

6

Bringing Democracy into Disrepute

Two days after winning his bruising reelection battle, President Bush, relaxing at his ranch in Crawford, Texas, looked through the galleys of a new book that a friend had recommended. The title was *The Case for Democracy: The Power of Freedom to Overcome Tyranny and Terror,* and the author was Natan Sharansky, a friend of the administration who had favored regime change in Iraq and democracy promotion in the Middle East. Sharansky shared the president's habit of thinking in grand terms. Unlike Jeane Kirkpatrick, who distinguished between "totalitarian" and "authoritarian" societies—and thus invited a certain moral nonchalance toward autocratic allies—Sharansky divided the world cleanly into two parts, with "fear societies" on one side and free ones on the other. It was, Sharansky argued, a terrible mistake to try to accommodate authoritarian states in the name of stability, as the realists had done with the Soviet Union—not only because such regimes responded to pressure rather than to blandishments, but because the stability so purchased was bound to be ephemeral. Autocrats manufacture external enemies to justify repression: "in order to avoid collapsing from within, fear societies must maintain a perpetual source of conflict." Classic realism was thus not only morally reprehensible but strategically self-defeating.

The United States, Sharansky wrote, had once understood

that repressive regimes had to be confronted head-on. Ronald
Reagan, casting aside the conventional wisdom of détente, had
"insisted that America use the advantage of a free society and a
free market to win the Cold War." Had Reagan and others listened to the realists "who called them dangerous warmongers,"
Sharansky wrote, "hundreds of millions of people would still be
living under totalitarian rule." Although most scholars and diplomats give Mikhail Gorbachev credit for recognizing that the Soviet Union was collapsing, and for ushering it to a more or less
peaceful demise, Sharansky insisted that it was the combination
of internal dissent and external pressure from outsiders, above all
Reagan, that had brought the Soviet Union to its knees. He drew
a sharp distinction between the heroic Reagan and the first President Bush, the latter determined to work with Gorbachev to preserve the Soviet Union and thus consign the Russian people to
perpetual servitude.

And now, Sharansky asserted, "the free world continues to un-
derestimate the universal appeal of its own ideas." "Freedom's
skeptics" waved off the prospect of a democratic Middle East
that President George W. Bush had conjured up in his speeches,
and had sought to bring into being through the invasion of Iraq.
In fact, Sharansky asserted, the desire to live free from fear was
universal. The tyrannical regimes of the Middle East had tried to
distract their citizens by blaming everything on the machinations
of Israel and the West, but it wouldn't wash. And of course
democracy was exportable: Look at what the United States had
accomplished in Germany and Japan, and look at what Reagan
and other resolute statesmen had accomplished by conditioning
relations with the Soviet Union on internal reform. The moral
was clear: "The nations of the free world can promote democracy
by linking their foreign policies toward non-democratic regimes
to how those regimes treat their subjects." The Soviet Union had
bent under pressure; so would Arab regimes. And just as Soviet
dissidents had taken heart from the knowledge that, if they were

punished or imprisoned, "the free world would stand by our side," so would Arab democrats. Sharansky was calling on the West to do for democracy what Jimmy Carter had done for human rights—but to do so with much greater singleness of purpose.

In *The Case for Democracy*, history and culture melt away before the universal hunger for freedom. Sharansky seemed to take it for granted that Arab citizens despised their governments, valued political liberties, and looked to the West for intervention to the same degree and in the same way as Russians or Poles did. Perhaps that explains why he had also believed that the Palestinians would accept a three-year tutelage from American governors, and then accept an American- and Israeli-imposed solution that offered no recognition of their claims to Israeli territory or to the right of return.

Bush was so impressed with what he read that a week later he met with Sharansky in the Oval Office. "Mr. President," his visitor said, "you are a real dissident." As this was a term Bush had probably not heard applied to him before, Sharansky explained what he meant: "You really believe that Arabs can live in freedom. People criticize you for this. They call you naïve. But you stick to the idea of bringing democracy to the Middle East even when it is unpopular . . . That is the mark of a dissident." One can only imagine the power of such a blessing, conferred by a man like Natan Sharansky upon a man like George W. Bush. The president had an a priori belief in freedom, but Sharansky was a martyr to the cause. Bush relished confounding the policy elites, and Sharansky had recast the debate over democracy promotion as a tale of St. George and the dragon. Bush was forever trying on the mighty cloak of Ronald Reagan, seeking to fill its dimensions. And the opportunity to break cleanly with the habitual caution of his father—well, one can only speculate. Several weeks later, Bush told his chief speechwriter, Michael J. Gerson, that he wanted to make democracy promotion the centerpiece of his second inaugural address.

Sharansky was scarcely the only influence on Bush's thinking. Bush and Condi Rice, who was to replace Colin Powell as secretary of state, had been talking about the need for bold new policy in the Middle East. And events themselves were confirming Bush's faith that the arc of history moved toward freedom. In late January, the Iraqi people were to hold the first democratic ballot in their history, which the president saw as the supreme affirmation of his decision to overthrow Saddam. A few months earlier, Rafik Hariri, the popular prime minister of Lebanon, had sparked protest by resigning rather than submitting to Syrian dominion. And in early December, hundreds of thousands of Ukrainian citizens had taken to the streets rather than accept the transparently fraudulent results of the presidential election. On January 10, two weeks before the inaugural, Bush's speechwriters and communications aides met with a group of conservative foreign policy thinkers to work out the speech's larger themes. The Yale historian John Lewis Gaddis, author of the recent pro–Iraq war volume *Surprise, Security and the American Experience*, proposed that Bush "throw an anchor into the future" by vowing to end tyranny by some specific date in the future. Michael J. Gerson later recalled that he was intrigued by such a "bold, but limited" goal—as opposed, for example, to "the universal triumph of democracy."

In his first inaugural address, Bush had delivered a rather windy sermon on the virtues of civility, compassion, courage, and personal responsibility. The terrorist attacks had given the president a clear and commanding sense of his role; and now, in the rolling cadences supplied by Gerson, he laid out the Freedom Agenda. "For as long as whole regions of the world simmer in resentment and tyranny," the president said, "violence will gather, and multiply in destructive power, and cross the most defended borders, and raise a mortal threat. There is only one force of history that can break the reign of hatred and resentment, and expose the pretensions of tyrants, and reward the hopes of the decent and tolerant, and that is the force of human freedom. We are led, by events and common sense, to one conclusion: The survival of liberty in our land increasingly depends on the success of liberty in other lands."

Even presidents as skeptical of grand formulations as Bush's own father had used the inaugural address to speak of America's democratizing mission. But in most cases, it had just been rhetoric. Not here. Bush 43 proceeded to lay out a policy of transformation breathtaking in its scope. "It is," he declared, "the policy of the United States to seek and support the growth of democratic movements and institutions in every nation and culture, with the ultimate goal of ending tyranny in our world." The president was, in effect, endorsing the Sharansky Doctrine. "We will persistently clarify the choice before every ruler and every nation," he went on. "We will encourage reform in other governments by making clear that success in our relations will require the decent treatment of their own people." The president concluded, as was very much his wont, with an evocation of transcendent forces: "History has an ebb and flow of justice, but history also has a visible direction, set by liberty and the Author of Liberty."

Whatever restraint had once tethered the president to the modest goal of "limited government" was long gone. Some of the less zealous officials in the administration were boggled by the sheer ambition of the speech. Michael Gerson writes, perhaps a bit defensively, that while "in some ways, the President's second inaugural was radical," he was saying nothing more or less than President Kennedy had when he asserted that "the 'magic power' on our side is the desire of every person to be free," or than Ronald Reagan had in his address to Westminster, or than FDR or Truman had before them. This president, like those, Gerson writes, believed that the United States benefits in the long run from "the growth of a liberal international order." There is, of course, a world of difference between positing that democracy or a liberal international order will triumph in the long run and vowing to produce such an outcome in real time. And as Stephen Krasner, then the State Department head of policy planning, observes, no matter how often Rice or Bush noted that democratization was the work of generations, "the body language was always, we can go in and do this in a relatively easy way."

Democrats and liberals criticized the speech as the reckless vision of a president increasingly unmoored from reality. But so, strikingly, did many traditional conservatives. It was in many ways a watershed moment for a class of Republicans who equated conservatism with caution, and who shared Edmund Burke's sense that the noblest human designs tended to go awry, thanks to the limits of human wisdom and virtue. How could a conservative, especially one who not long before had promised to stop telling countries how to behave, proclaim a "policy" of "ending tyranny in the world"? Did he understand the difference between the desirable and the possible? Peggy Noonan, speechwriter for Bush 41, wrote in *The Wall Street Journal* that the president might as well have "announced we were going to colonize Mars." To others, Bush's sweeping universalism sounded like liberal piffle. George Will observed, "Everyone everywhere does not share 'our attachment to freedom,'" and tartly suggested that advocates of building democracy in the Middle East "remember an elementary principle of moral reasoning: there can be no duty to do that which cannot be done."

The spring of 2005 was a giddy time for democracy enthusiasts in Washington and elsewhere: The "color revolutions" were sweeping across Eastern Europe, while in the Middle East "the Arab spring" was blossoming. Only days after the president's speech the people of Iraq would ignore death threats to vote for a national leader; the purple-dyed index finger was to become, if briefly, the icon of a Middle East liberated from tyranny. The

White House was working closely with France, with which it had been at daggers drawn after the U.S. invasion of Iraq, to defend a fragile democracy in Lebanon against Syrian encroachment. President Bush and his team believed that the war in Iraq had truly provoked the long-awaited wave of democratization.

The bull's-eye in the White House's target of Arab reform was Egypt—the most populous and politically important country in the region, the historic heart of Arab culture and politics. We had friendly relations with the regime of President Hosni Mubarak, and the $2 billion we had been giving the country annually since the Camp David agreements in 1979 meant that we had substantial leverage there as well. Cairo did little without calculating the likely reaction from the White House. And while Mubarak was an authoritarian leader, Egypt, unlike Saudi Arabia, our other major Arab ally, was no theocracy. There were an obstreperous press, free-thinking intellectuals, a large class of secularized professionals, opposition parties, and a profoundly cherished history of constitutionalism. Real reform in Egypt thus didn't seem nearly as far-fetched a prospect as it did in Saudi Arabia, Syria, or Iran.

Efforts to push reform in Egypt had begun years before. State Department officials had established modest benchmarks of reform that the Mubarak administration had to hit in order to have its aid released. Mubarak had removed a number of old party figures from economic ministries and replaced them with young, more forward-looking technocrats. But he and the old guard retained total control on political matters. In early 2004, Bush invited the Egyptian leader to the ranch in Crawford, Texas—itself a signal honor. Bush hoped that he could nudge Mubarak to make real political concessions. At the press conference after their talks, Bush lavished praise on the Egyptian supremo for his love of peace, his staunch opposition to terrorism, and so forth, and then added, "Just as Egypt has shown the way toward peace in the Middle East, it will set the standard in the region for democracy by strengthening democratic institutions and political participation." In private, Bush urged Mubarak to loosen the iron grip he kept on political debate and assembly.

Mubarak began ever so delicately opening the pressure valves that governed political expression. In March 2004, the regime permitted a group of intellectuals, diplomats, and businessmen to gather at the Alexandria Library and issue a declaration calling for increased freedom—though local observers were quick to note that the government had carefully vetted the group to exclude members of the opposition. And Egypt's feared and ubiquitous security apparatus, the Mukhabarat, relaxed its vigilance sufficiently to permit the kind of demonstrations heretofore almost unknown. In December 2004, the courts permitted a new political party, Al Ghad ("Tomorrow"), to register, normally a virtual impossibility under Egyptian law. The Arab Spring seemed to be dawning in Cairo. "It was getting toward the end of Mubarak's tenure," says Scott Carpenter, then an official in the State Department's Office of Near Eastern Affairs, "and we were hoping that he would be thinking about his legacy."

The Bush administration was determined to push hard on this half-open door. Several weeks after the inaugural speech, Bush called Mubarak to urge him to open up the political playing field, and to permit independent figures to monitor the election. The Egyptian press was astonished. One of the cheekier newspapers ran pictures of both men on the front page. Bush was quoted as saying, in Arabic, "Mr. President, we will not allow you to use the police to attack peaceful demonstrators." And Mubarak meekly answered, in English, "Yes, Mr. President." Soon afterward, Mubarak announced that he would call for an amendment to Article 76 of the Constitution, which limited presidential elections to a "yes" or "no" referendum on the incumbent. The decision was almost universally ascribed to White House pressure, though Mubarak clearly felt that he had to deal with rising demands for political participation. It was not a good omen, Scott Carpenter thought, that Mubarak had kept the parliament in the dark, apparently to demonstrate the irrelevance of his own legislature.

The Mubarak regime was plainly nervous about the forces it had unleashed. In early March, the security forces arrested Al Ghad's charismatic young leader, Ayman Nour, and charged him with forging signatures on petitions. The allegation may have had some substance, but it was plainly meant to eliminate a potentially popular opponent. Condoleezza Rice responded by canceling an upcoming trip to Cairo, in which she was to discuss a free trade agreement that Egypt had been eagerly seeking. The regime was stunned; Washington had never before exacted any price for acts of domestic repression. But Mubarak had, in effect, tested the Bush administration's bona fides; as one State Department official says, "You cannot have that inaugural address on January twentieth and six weeks later the Secretary of State shows up in Egypt as if nothing had happened."

State Department officials applied pressure on other issues. Elizabeth Cheney, a senior official in the State Department's Near East Bureau and the vice president's daughter, pushed the regime to allow the National Democratic Institute and the International Republican Institute, the two chief democracy-promotion NGOs, to work in Egypt, chiefly to train election monitors and offer technical assistance to political parties. The Congress was also getting involved. Egypt had always insisted on control over the expenditure of the vast American aid package, a privilege granted to no other major recipient of development assistance. But in December 2004, Congress passed an amendment to the foreign aid bill stipulating that all funds spent on democracy promotion would be disbursed directly by the U.S. Agency for International Development. This was quite possibly a bitterer pill to swallow than the actual presence of the NGOs, and there were protracted negotiations over the oversight of the $25 million the

United States planned to spend. But Egyptian officials felt that they could not reject either demand; in May, the NDI and the IRI set up shop in Cairo.

Rice rescheduled her canceled trip to Egypt for mid-June. By this time the security situation had begun to darken. Private goons retained by the government had beaten up peaceful demonstrators, even tearing the clothes from some women—a shocking violation of Egyptian norms. The secretary of state arranged to meet with President Mubarak in the resort town of Sharm el-Sheik but insisted on adding a speech at the American University of Cairo. The speech had been crafted with enormous care by her counselor, Philip Zelikow, among others. Rice would later tell friends that this was the most important speech she had ever given. Mindful of Egyptian pride and sensitivity, she began by flattering her hosts' sense of historical greatness, citing the reformist nineteenth-century ruler Mohammad Ali, the liberal interval between the world wars, and the bravery of Anwar Sadat. Then she went on to speak of her own government with a candor few Egyptians were accustomed to hearing—about the United States or about their own country. "For sixty years," she said, "my country, the United States, pursued stability at the expense of democracy in this region here in the Middle East—and we achieved neither. Now we are taking a different course. We are supporting the democratic aspirations of all people."

Rice offered what had by now become the standard White House tableau of freedom on the march in the Middle East—in Iraq, in Lebanon, in Palestine, and so forth. And then she turned back to her hosts. "We are all concerned," she said, "when peaceful supporters of democracy—men and women—are not free from violence. The day must come when the rule of law replaces emergency decrees—and when the independent judiciary replaces arbitrary justice . . . Egypt's elections, including the parliamentary elections, must meet the objective standards that define every free election." This was genuinely startling language. No high-ranking American official had ever admonished the regime so publicly. Bush had said that "success in our relations will require the decent treatment of their own people." Rice had just put Cairo on notice.

After the speech, Rice met with Ayman Nour, who had been released from jail pending trial, and one of Nour's chief lieutenants, Hisham Kassem, the founder and publisher of a respected new daily, *Egypt Today*. This, too, was a pointed statement to the regime. Rice spoke enthusiastically of reaching the Egyptian people with the message that America stood with their aspirations. "Not on your watch," Kassem recalls saying. "It's a lost cause trying to shift public opinion." Public opinion was, in fact, sharply split over Rice's democratic call to arms; leftists and nationalists denounced the speech as a new front in the Bush administration's campaign for regional domination. But others, including Kassem, were far more receptive. Strange though it seemed, the Bush administration could be simultaneously despised for its policies and welcomed for its democratic advocacy.

The three-week presidential election, terminating in early September, produced the expected landslide victory for Mubarak, at least given the state's near-total control over the media and its vastly superior funding. But in the first round of the parliamentary elections, held two months later, the candidates of the banned Muslim Brotherhood, running as independents, did far better than the regime had ever imagined; in the next two rounds, the state security apparatus and its shadowy crew of hired thugs beat up and terrorized Brotherhood voters, shut down polling places, and instigated riots in which a dozen or so Brotherhood supporters died. The ballot was denounced by Egyptian election monitors and foreign groups. Immediately after the results were announced, the White House was silent, while the State Department issued a statement noting that it had found "no indication that the Egyptian government isn't interested in having peaceful, free and fair elections." This bland expression of see-no-evil provoked such uproar that it had to be amended: the spokesman now declared that officials had "serious concerns about the path of political reform in Egypt."

Rice had put Mubarak on notice; and then Mubarak had called her bluff. One American diplomat in the region insists that there was little choice in the matter: "We can stand up on a soapbox any day of the week and complain about the way things are going in Egypt. But when we do, we play into the hands of the state, which would incite its own people against an outside power which otherwise would be seen as a friend and benefactor." But if that's so, then why had Rice issued her bold proclamation? "It trapped us," said Stephen Krasner. "We pushed for something we couldn't get." Perhaps Rice, and the White House, had gotten caught up in the euphoria of the moment, or had been hypnotized by their own rhetoric. "Did anyone think about the consequences?" asks Scott Carpenter. "What were you prepared to do if? If this, that? No. We believed in our own backbone."

American ambassador Frank Ricciardone, an Arabist and a professional diplomat, declined to issue a statement criticizing the elections, nor to privately read the riot act to Mubarak and his team. But White House officials were also afraid to threaten Mubarak with restrictions on the aid package, or with a future renegotiation of the terms. They worried that Mubarak would walk away, that he would incite his people against us, that we would damage our very substantial interests in the Middle East. Mubarak was, in this regard, little different from the cold war dictators whom we had once felt we had no choice but to support—even though Rice had announced that sixty years of such policies had proved self-defeating.

The Arab Spring had proved to be very brief—and perhaps illusory. By the end of 2005, the euphoria of the purple index finger in Iraq had faded to a dim memory. The sovereign Iraqi government barely functioned. Rather than stemming Iraq's terrifying violence, the election had, if anything, deepened sectarian rivalry by installing the Shias in power. Iraq was not progressing toward democracy by any recognizable standard. Between the fear that Iraqi violence could spill into the region, and the growing truculence of Iran over attempts to curb its nuclear program, the Middle East looked more and more like a zone of danger, and less like one of hope and possibility. Fearing a Shia tide rolling in from Tehran, from the Iraqi government in Baghdad, and from the forces of Hezbollah in Lebanon, the Bush administration came to rely increasingly on moderate Sunni states—moderate, that is, in their regional policy—such as Egypt, Jordan, and Saudi Arabia. We needed them; and this meant, as Mubarak and others understood very clearly, that we would be prepared once again to trade democracy for stability.

Meanwhile, the Bush administration's bid to forge a democratic Palestine moved toward a denouement. After Yasir Arafat died at the end of 2004, Bush threw his support behind Arafat's successor, the moderate Mahmoud Abbas. Rice began pressing Abbas to consolidate and legitimize the authority of his Fatah party by holding elections. Both Abbas and leading Israeli officials had warned that Fatah had lost so much of its support that it might lose to Hamas, the militant Islamic group; but the administration insisted on forging ahead.

Hamas defeated Fatah by a sizable margin. Philip Zelikow, who played a key advisory role in Middle East policy, insists that he and his colleagues were well aware of the dangers. "We thought about it and argued about it, and concluded that they needed to go ahead with the elections," he recalls. "If you postpone the elections you don't solve the problem, and you completely delegitimize Fatah." But outsiders like Dennis Ross, President Clinton's chief Middle East negotiator, were struck by the blitheness of White House and State Department officials. And Rice later admitted to an interviewer that she was so shocked by the news that she climbed off her elliptical trainer to call her aides. Told that Hamas had in fact outpolled Fatah, she said to herself, "Oh my goodness, Hamas won?" This was scarcely what she had imagined in 2002 when she took on both Colin Powell and Dick Cheney to argue for democracy promotion in the Palestinian Territories.

The Hamas victory, a State Department official says, "clarified many, many areas." First, it showed that Rice and Bush had been naïve to imagine that free and fair elections in the Middle East would bring democratic figures to the fore, as they had in the Balkans and Eastern Europe. The analogy was wrong—as more knowledgeable and dispassionate figures had been saying all along. Rice seemed not to have come to grips with the fact that elections could have bad outcomes. As Dennis Ross says, "She does have kind of a view that elections are a built-in self-correcting mechanism. You may bring in people you don't like, but account-ability will bring changes over time." That certainly wasn't true here: the White House was not about to do business with an or-ganization that openly avowed terrorism. The Bush administra-tion, along with its European allies, took the position that it would not recognize the new government unless Hamas re-nounced the use of violence—which of course it would not do.

The Palestinian election also cast a harsh retrospective light on the Egyptian one. Hamas was the Palestinian branch of the Muslim Brotherhood. In both cases, an election had bolstered Is-lamists at the expense of secular parties. The Brotherhood con-fined itself to democratic methods, though it stoutly supported Hamas policies in the occupied territories. In her Cairo speech, Rice had specifically ruled out support for the Islamists, formally a banned organization. But there had been, according to Stephen Krasner, little if any discussion about how to deal with the conse-quences of electoral gains by the Brotherhood. The administra-tion seems to have been taken by surprise in this case as well.

The realists, and the State Department Arabists, had been vin-dicated. We had demanded a democratic opening—and wound up emboldening our enemies. And the outcome had been a gift to

dictators like Mubarak, who offered themselves as the only bulwark against radical Islam. The message of the events was, stick
by your friends. Michael Gerson, one of the chief apostles of
democracy promotion in the White House, writes that he
protested the decision to go easy on Mubarak, but "with little
effect." Gerson bitterly complains that career diplomats in the
State Department—figures like Ambassador Ricciardone, no
doubt—ensnared efforts to raise human rights and democracy
concerns all over the globe "in a thousand sticky strands of objec-
tions and cautions."

In Washington, democracy promotion began to look like another species of neoconservative delusion. "After the Hamas
election," says Scott Carpenter, "I felt that the chill was on. Rice
and Bush were still committed to the idea. But for those who
were implementing the policy, it became much more difficult."

A nation that does not hold itself to democratic standards can no
more serve as a force for the propagation of democracy than a
parent with an unacknowledged drinking problem can lecture his
children on the evils of alcohol. Yet the Bush administration increasingly found itself in this position after the publication in late
April 2004 of photographs of horrific abuse in the Abu Ghraib
prison in Iraq. President Bush blamed the problem on a small
group of rogue soldiers. But it quickly became clear that prisoners in American custody elsewhere were being systematically
abused, humiliated, and even tortured, and that the mistreatment was a direct consequence of decisions made at the highest
levels of the White House—very much including the president
himself, who had signed an executive order exempting enemy
combatants captured on the battlefield from the terms of the
Geneva Conventions.

We now know, of course, that the same White House that had
vowed that "success in our relations" with other governments

"will require the decent treatment of their own people" had secretly formulated and approved a series of legal opinions giving the president unprecedented powers over the conduct of the war; authorizing the CIA to engage in interrogation tactics not permitted by the U.S. Army manual; and establishing the practice known as "rendition," in which individuals suspected of terrorist ties could be apprehended abroad—kidnapped, in some cases—and then secretly sent to a third country, often one where torture was routine. The administration had also established a prison on Guantánamo Bay, technically outside of American territory and thus arguably beyond the reach of American law, and there incarcerated hundreds of suspects without access to counsel, with no meaningful ability to challenge their status as enemy combatants, and with no access to civilian courts—even though few of them had any useful intelligence to offer and many had simply been swept up in raids on the battlefields of Afghanistan.

We also now know that principled men and women inside the Justice Department, the State Department, the Pentagon, and elsewhere tried to prevent the worst abuses—and, in almost every case, failed. The chief figures in the debate—Rumsfeld, Cheney, and Alberto Gonzales, first White House counsel and later attorney general—all favored the most single-minded possible prosecution of the war on terror, and at critical moments threw their support behind their own hard-line aides. None of these figures had any particular interest in the promotion of democracy, and in any case would have viewed a concern for how America looked in the world as pusillanimous and even threatening to our national security.

What about Condoleezza Rice, seen inside the Bush administration as the bearer of the democracy gospel? One of her close aides describes a policy process in which the hard-liners inside the White House Office of Legal Counsel systematically excluded Rice's own legal staff from the formulation of policy, whether the development of the judicial system at Guantánamo, the question of detainee treatment, or the establishment of a terrorist surveillance program at the National Security Agency. At the interagency meetings run by Rice's chief legal figures, he says, Rumsfeld's and Cheney's aides behaved with studied indifference. But Rice herself eventually took over these interagency meetings. She was familiar with the secret rulings as well as the growing evidence of mistreatment, yet she appears never to have used her privileged position with the president to demand a change in policy. Indeed, according to Seymour Hersh in *Chain of Command*, Kenneth Roth, the executive director of Human Rights Watch, met in June 2003 with Rice and her legal deputy, John Bellinger, and asked that the president promise to abide by the terms of the Convention Against Torture. Rice refused. In a second meeting a year later, soon after the revelation of Abu Ghraib, Rice insisted that the problem lay not with White House policy but with "implementation," and said only that "there's a need to clarify whether there's a need for better training."

Rice made a renewed push when she became secretary of state. In June 2005, just as Rice was preparing to go to Cairo to talk to the Egyptians about democracy, her counselor, Philip Zelikow, and the deputy secretary of defense, Gordon England, circulated a nine-page memo that proposed that the administration apply to prisoners the terms of the Geneva Conventions, including the treaty's ban on the use of "humiliating and degrading treatment." It also called for the administration to bring to trial prisoners held by the CIA overseas, and move toward closing the Guantánamo facility. Rice approved the memo and sent it on to the NSC. But Rumsfeld was so outraged, according to a report in *The New York Times*, that he and aides gathered up and shredded copies of the document. In subsequent discussions, David Addington, Cheney's counsel, opposed accepting the Geneva language or offering more legal safeguards to detainees at Guantánamo. Cheney's and Rumsfeld's aides continued to block the proposed reforms for months. Only when the Supreme Court struck down key elements of the Guantánamo legal system in late June 2006 did the White House move to adopt many of the memo's suggestions—though even then Cheney succeeded in significantly watering down the crucial language. And the vice president continued to argue publicly that interrogators should be permitted to use techniques like "waterboarding" if such techniques produced crucial information.

This, then, was the debate the world was overhearing as President Bush was rolling out the Freedom Agenda. Did anyone at the White House or in the State Department worry about the appearance of gross hypocrisy—not to mention the fact of hypocrisy? When I posed this question—in more delicate form—to one of the administration's most prominent advocates of democracy promotion, he said, "The argument that anger at America feeds an inability to promote democracy is a dictator's argument."

"What about torture?" I asked.

"I think that's very hard to measure. It *is* a logical point. Why would it not hinder our ability? I have to tell you that I don't find it to be true. It's an argument used by human rights violators. I have never heard a political prisoner say, 'Ah, a visit from the Americans. I don't want it because I'm mad about Abu Ghraib.'"

Another senior administration official insisted, "If you're looking at what affects negatively America's ability to operate in the Arab world, the perception that we're somehow falling victim to some of the debates in Congress"—over support for the Israeli incursion into Lebanon, for example—"that's what hurts our ability to operate. People say, 'If somebody like Bashir Assad'"—the president of Syria and backer of Hezbollah—"'can cause you this kind of damage to your image and he's paid no price, does that mean he's going to scare you out of the region? Is Iraq going to scare you out of the region?'" The Arab street, as well as the elite, respond to strength and fear, not justice and hope—a remarkable view for an advocate of democracy promotion in the Middle East.

Again, I asked about torture.

"I want an American president who will do everything possible to keep us safe," this official went on, "and that is much more important than whether it has made people in any other country think less of us as a nation. It would be ludicrous to have a president who said, 'These things'"—Guantánamo or "special interrogation techniques"—"'are going to keep us safe, but it's going to make some people in France, or some people in Morocco, angry.'"

This was the view among the conservative ideologues who were the figures in the Bush administration most inclined to bear aloft the flag of democracy promotion. Others, however, were appalled. One of Condoleezza Rice's key aides, both at the NSC and the State Department, said, "We've got a lot of people thinking that we don't believe in the rule of law or share the same values they do. And it's done us deep and lasting damage."

That, certainly, was what democracy activists and journalists in the Middle East were finding. Mikaela A. McDermott and Brian Katulis, democracy activists with long experience in the Middle East, wrote in *The Christian Science Monitor* in 2004, "On a recent trip to Syria, Bahrain, and Jordan, reformers told us, with great distress, that they can no longer even use the words 'democracy' and 'human rights' in their communities, let alone work publicly on US-funded democracy promotion projects. Sadly, these terms have become synonymous with military occupation, civilian casualties and abuse of prisoners in Iraq and around the globe." A reporter for *The Washington Post* quoted a prominent writer in Syria as saying, "The Americans came to Iraq to make it an example to the other countries to ask for change. But what happened was the opposite. Now everyone is saying we do not want to be like Iraq." The reporter noted that the bloodshed in Iraq "has accomplished what human rights activists, analysts and others say Syrian president Bashir al-Assad had been unable to do by himself: silence public demands for democratic reforms here."

Indeed, the association of democracy promotion with regime change was a tremendous boon to autocrats, who could enlist and exploit nationalist feeling in order to discredit international efforts to bring reform. A backlash against democracy promotion had been building ever since the "color revolutions" in Serbia, Georgia, Ukraine, and elsewhere had demonstrated the role that outside groups could play when elections hung in the balance. In Egypt, as well as in Bahrain and a number of other Middle Eastern countries, the NDI and the IRI were either prohibited from working or simply instructed to pack up and leave. The backlash was even stronger in Eastern Europe, where autocrats could plainly see the effectiveness of democracy strategies. Russia's president, Vladimir Putin, accused Russian NGOs that took money from Western groups to advance democracy and human rights of engaging in subversive, anti-Russian activity. In January 2006, Putin pushed through laws clamping tight controls on the activities of both international and domestic groups. Over time, Putin became a sort of sentinel of autocracy, issuing dark warnings about the perils of Western NGOs to his autocratic neighbors and to the Chinese. Belarus president Aleksandr Lukashenko banned all foreign funding of political or even educational activity. President Nursultan Nazarbayev of Kazakhstan enacted similar laws.

In a 2006 article in *Foreign Affairs*, Thomas Carothers ascribed the backlash to a combination of opportunism by powerful countries such as Russia and China, which would seize upon any useful pretext to crack down on sources of dissent, and a genuine fear among their weaker brethren of being overthrown in the next color revolution. But Carothers also observed that, thanks to the Bush administration's aggressive rhetoric and behavior, democracy promotion had come to be seen in much of the world as a synonym for regime change. And the Bush administration's own conduct in the war on terror had, Carothers added, "made it all too easy for foreign autocrats to resist U.S. democracy promotion by providing them with an easy riposte: How can a country that tortures people abroad and abuses rights at home tell other countries how to behave?"

The Bush administration was not prepared to change its approach to terrorism in order to present a different and more sympathetic face to the world; it was, however, eager to show the world, and especially Arab publics, that they had a mistaken view of American intentions and policies. Margaret Tutwiler, a longtime aide of the president's father, had replaced Charlotte Beers, but she lasted less than a year. In September 2005, as the hopes of an Arab spring were fading and Iraq was taking a turn for the worse, President Bush announced that he was appointing Karen Hughes as the new undersecretary of state for public diplomacy. Hughes had no more knowledge of the Middle East than either of her predecessors. But what qualified her for the job was that she had spent the previous decade crafting George Bush's message as both governor of Texas and president. She had largely written some of his most important speeches, including several on the Middle East. And she was one of the president's very closest friends and advisers. "She understands what we stand for," as Bush said in introducing her. "Karen will deliver the message of freedom and humility and compassion and determination." Hughes's appointment was intended to be a sign that the White House was taking public diplomacy seriously.

Hughes explained her role to her new colleagues in a town hall meeting. "I like to boil things down to pretty basics and things that are memorable," she said, "so our pillars are going to be the four E's: . . . Engage, Exchange, Educate, and Empower." She planned to enlist diplomats to highlight America's good works abroad; to develop a rapid-response capacity to counter terrorist propaganda; to "forward-deploy regional SWAT teams who can look at the big picture"; to expand exchange programs; to

promote language learning both at home and abroad; and to enlist "citizen ambassadors" to "share their unique American stories
with appropriate audiences around the world."

And then Hughes sallied out bravely into the Arab world, introducing herself to carefully screened audiences in Egypt, Turkey, and Saudi Arabia. "My most important title is Mom," she
said. And, "I'm the granddaughter of a Pennsylvania coal miner
and a Kentucky railroad engineer." She talked about American
values: "We are a country that has freedom of religion, but that
does not mean freedom from religion, although people are also
free not to have faith in America, but many, many Americans like
me feel that our faith and our family are really the most important
things in our lives." She marveled at the bonds that united people
of different faiths and backgrounds: "It's amazing as I look out on
your faces and I realize that you're all unique individuals and yet
I think if I was sitting on a college campus anywhere in my country, the United States of America, I would hear almost the same
answers I just heard—that I would hear young people that
wanted to be successful and help their country." And then, having woven these strands of connection, she took questions.

Hughes's listeners were invariably polite; this was scarcely
"the Arab street." But few seemed inclined to join her celebration
of multicultural harmony. "As representatives of your country call
for and fight for respecting human rights, how can you face questions, directed at you, about violating human rights in Guantánamo and Abu Ghraib by the American army?" asked a student in
Cairo. In other forums, Hughes was confronted more directly. At
a meeting in Saudi Arabia with forty journalists and civic figures,
she was peppered with angry speeches about American support
for Israel and the invasion of Iraq. When Hughes told a group of
Saudi women that they should be permitted to drive, she was met
not with applause or murmurs of support, but with a rejoinder
that Saudi women were quite happy and needn't be told otherwise by Americans. In Turkey, America's steadiest ally in the Is-

lamic world, listeners denounced America's record abroad as simply indefensible.

Hughes's barnstorming tour of the Middle East, like Charlotte Beers's Shared Values campaign two years earlier, was ridiculed both there and at home. Hughes was another innocent abroad; her "communication" skills were no better suited to defusing the hostility and skepticism of the Arab world than Beers's gifts in marketing had been. Hughes continued to travel to the Middle East, but she kept a much lower profile. She did, indeed, launch some of the initiatives she had described, including the rapid-response unit, the "regional public diplomacy hubs" (the rechristened SWAT teams), and some new education and exchange programs. But both she and public diplomacy itself largely disappeared from view after the fiasco of "my most important title is Mom."

I interviewed Hughes in late 2006, and she cheerily agreed—indeed, insisted—that all her comments be on the record. When I asked her what she had found to be the most serious obstacles to explaining U.S. policy in the Middle East, she listed four, in order: Israel-Palestine, detainee abuse, Iraq, and the difficulty of obtaining visas. And like Beers, she had come to recognize how very different the world looked from the Middle East—that it wasn't simply a matter of countering propaganda. Whenever she returned from the Middle East, she said, she made a point of telling both the president and the secretary of state that "to the extent that we can be seen visibly helping the Palestinian people to achieve their state and to achieve a better life and to end some of the humiliation that they experience on a daily basis, that is the single most important thing we could do around the world to create and foster a more favorable impression of America." In one of her first White House meetings after taking her new job, she had, she said, raised the issue of the treatment of detainees. "It was a little bit of the elephant in the room," as she put it delicately. Explaining to the world that "we are a country of law and justice and that . . . we do respect our international obligations" was, she conceded, a "big challenge." And she had told Bush and Rice that too.

Hughes stepped down in the fall of 2007. After six years of public diplomacy, America was feared, loathed, and misunderstood across the globe as never before. According to surveys conducted by the Pew Charitable Trusts, between 2002 and 2007 favorable views of the United States fell from 61 to 29 percent in Indonesia, from 30 to 9 percent in Turkey, and even from 60 to 30 percent in Germany. Hughes's exit was generally greeted with a combination of derision and relief. She was ill suited to the job, of course. But it probably wouldn't have mattered if the president had instead appointed an Arab-American with a good grasp of Middle Eastern realities. Our credibility was gone; we had never been less able to persuade others of our good intentions.

Eleven elections were held in Middle Eastern nations in 2005. In 2006, the number was two—the fiasco in the Palestinian Authority at the beginning of the year, and a more gratifying ballot in Yemen at the end. Backlash, rather than progress, was the rule. President Bush himself was undaunted. In an interview with *The Wall Street Journal* in September 2006, he continued to insist that Iraq was "the first real test" of our commitment to "the ideological struggle" pitting "reformers against tyrants." He was still hopeful about Egypt—if not about Mubarak, then about Gamal—and the reform-minded economic ministers. But Bush's rhetoric seemed increasingly divorced from reality. When Condoleezza Rice returned to Cairo in January 2007, she declared that the United States had "an important strategic relationship" with Egypt, but said nothing at all, at least publicly, about democracy. She had taken to describing the region as split between "mainstream states," including the Gulf nations, and "extremists"—a formulation with which the elder George Bush would have been perfectly comfortable. The new dispensation, a *Washington Post* editorial observed, "betrays President Bush's Freedom Agenda, giving a free pass to dictators who support the new geopolitical cause."

This was no time for hosannas to the march of liberty. Freedom House, which keeps a global scorecard of democracy, reported that 2006 had been a year of "freedom stagnation" as well as "pushback." The group described a "glacial change of peace in the Middle East." Lebanon's "Cedar Revolution," a tremendous source of hope a year before, had been thwarted by the growth of Hezbollah and the refusal of Syria to relinquish its influence over the country. And when Israel responded to provocations by Hezbollah with a massive bombardment of the country, all hope for democratic progress was lost.

The Bush administration, defying pleas from its allies, declined to press Israel to call an early halt to the attack or the subsequent ground invasion. Rice, in fact, went so far as to characterize the violence as "the birth pangs of a new Middle East"—an expression that sparked fury across the region. Perhaps she really did believe that democracy could be promoted by missiles and tanks. The war in Lebanon turned the U.S. image in the Islamic world a darker shade of black. A poll of citizens in Rice's "mainstream" states in early 2007 found that only 12 percent had favorable views of America, while two thirds insisted that democracy was not the real U.S. objective in the Arab world. Another poll sampling attitudes in Egypt, Morocco, Pakistan, and Indonesia found that 79 percent of respondents believed that the real U.S. objective was to "weaken and divide the Islamic world." In Egypt, the most anti-American of the four countries, eight in ten believed that attacks on American troops in Iraq and Afghanistan constituted justified resistance.

In the Islamic world, the United States was increasingly seen as the friend not only of Israel—an alliance we would not sacrifice even if it brought hatred down upon us—but also of the authoritarian states of the region. The president's second inaugural address had been intended to signal that this would no longer be so; but it was so. Egypt was one case; Pakistan was another. President Pervez Musharraf had gained power in a military coup, and he continued to wear his uniform and to exercise military powers. But President Bush had treated Musharraf as a close and trusted ally in the war on terrorism after the latter had denounced the 9/11 attacks. Since that time the United States had given the regime more than $10 billion, much of it to be used in the fight against the Taliban. And yet the Musharraf regime had allowed the Taliban to set up headquarters in the Federally Administered Tribal Areas along the border with Afghanistan; after being bloodied in an attempted incursion, the Pakistani army had even accepted a sort of nonaggression pact. In fact, as diplomats and area scholars noted, the Pakistani army and intelligence service had long drawn on the tribal areas to harass both Afghanistan and India, and had helped organize both the Taliban and home-grown Islamist extremists. Secular political parties were not allowed to operate in the tribal zone, thus leaving those areas wholly under the sway of the mullahs. Musharraf's failure to decisively break that pattern had fostered extremism inside Pakistan and had helped keep much of Afghanistan ungovernable.

The army, which had remained the ultimate source of power in Pakistan even during periods of civilian rule, had seen fit to quietly encourage Islamist parties as a counter to the secular opposition, both marginalizing the secularists and presenting a threat that would gain Washington's attention—much as Hosni Mubarak had done in Egypt. And as in Egypt, it worked. Musharraf's autocratic rule had made him profoundly unpopular at home, but the White House, convinced that the only alternative was Islamic radicalism, declined to push him. In fact, Islamists had never gained more than 14 percent of the vote in legislative elections, but the ever-present fear that Pakistan's nuclear arsenal could fall into the hands of terrorists gave Musharraf a trump card he scarcely even needed to brandish. His critics argued that the only way to drain the Islamist swamp was to open up the tribal areas to nonextremist influences and, more broadly, to remove the clamps from the nation's political life; but Musharraf refused, and the White House went along.

And then, in March 2007, Musharraf began to make an open mockery of the Freedom Agenda. He fired Chief Justice Iftikhar Chaudry, who had ruled against the government in a number of key cases. In the ensuing weeks, thousands of lawyers and democracy activists took to the streets, braving police attacks to defend Pakistan's constitution—precisely the kind of secular opposition that Musharraf had claimed did not exist. Here was the middle force, neither autocratic nor theocratic, that the Bush administration had sought all across the region and had rarely found, and yet the White House remained mute in the midst of the crackdown. Embassy officials didn't want to see a great ally "humiliated." And American diplomats never understood the depth of Pakistani feeling on either Musharraf or the judges.

Musharraf was ultimately forced to restore Chaudry to his position, but in early November, fearing a ruling that might prevent him from serving another term as president and ignoring entreaties from Washington, the general declared emergency rule. He dissolved the Supreme Court and arrested thousands of lawyers, journalists, and opposition activists. The White House once again trod lightly. President Bush urged Musharraf to surrender his military post and to schedule elections "as soon as possible," but issued no threats.

Perhaps Musharraf really did have the White House over a barrel, but the administration had gotten itself into this compromising position. Michael Gerson, the former speechwriter, recalled in *The Washington Post* that in the years after 9/11, there had been "a significant push at the White House"—presumably from him, among others—"to expand democracy-promotion efforts in Pakistan, to encourage party-building, modern electoral

systems and the rule of law." The effort, he wrote, "got little trac-
tion." The aid package to Pakistan was never used for political
leverage. Of the $10 billion officially declared—more was fun-
neled through secret programs—$6 billion went to the military
for what it claimed were antiterrorist efforts, $1.6 billion went to
buy American weapons, and only about $1 billion was spent on
governance and humanitarian assistance. Musharraf had used
the money largely to shore up his rule rather than to enlist in the
war on terror, and to buy warplanes he could use against India
should the occasion arise.

President Bush did in fact press Musharraf to step down as
general and permit his archrival, Benazir Bhutto, to return from
exile and contest elections. Under intense domestic pressure as
well, Musharraf ultimately complied. Then in December 2007,
Bhutto was assassinated, apparently by Islamic extremists. The
Pakistani people turned overwhelmingly against Musharraf. Yet
the Bush administration continued to treat him as the key to the
country's future. Nowhere else had the imperative of the war on
terror so plainly trumped the imperative of democratic promotion. *The Economist* observed that the administration had permitted Musharraf to trample on his people's liberties owing to "the
pre-eminent importance of 'stability' in the world's most dangerous place." That justification had been proved hollow. "It is time
to impress upon him and the generals still propping him up," the
editors wrote, "that democracy is not the alternative to stability. It
is Pakistan's only hope." Indeed, in February 2008, Musharraf's
party was overwhelmingly defeated in a parliamentary election.
And in a striking sign of the appeal of secular democratic principles, Pakistan's Islamist parties performed almost as poorly as the
Musharraf bloc had done.

Pakistan and Afghanistan were stitched together at the chest
like very unhappy Siamese twins. The Taliban had fled across the
border in the face of American attack, destabilizing Pakistan, and
then had used their mountain fastness to launch attacks on

Afghanistan. The only secure way to conquer terrorism in the region was through democratization in Pakistan and nation-building in Afghanistan, and neither had happened. President Bush had not, of course, believed in nation-building back in 2001. Barnett Rubin, one of the foremost experts on Afghanistan, says that he was invited to a White House meeting on September 22, 2001, in which he urged a crash program of state-building once the Taliban were driven from Afghanistan. But he was told that counterterrorism would have to take precedence. And so the White House had declined to support the initial efforts by the UN to build the country's shattered institutions; had refused to let a NATO force operate beyond the confines of Kabul; and later, when Afghanistan's opium production exploded, threatening to reduce the country to a narco-state, had supported crop destruction but refused to pay for programs to give farmers a meaningful alternative.

Afghanistan, once the administration's one unadulterated success in the war on terror, deteriorated from year to year. As the Taliban regenerated itself in the Pakistani tribal regions, larger chunks of Afghanistan became ungovernable. Suicide attacks occurred even inside Kabul. In many areas, development work had ground to a halt for lack of security. Tensions between the United States and its NATO partners increased, as European militaries declined to take the battle to the Taliban. In late November 2007, *The New York Times* carried a front-page story that began as follows: "Deeply concerned about the prospect of failure in Afghanistan, the Bush administration and NATO have begun three top-to-bottom reviews of the entire mission . . ." It was a little late.

By late 2007, the Freedom Agenda had disappeared into the war on terror. Whenever there was a choice to be made, President Bush, who had warned the world's dictators that "success in our relations will require the decent treatment of their own people," had backed away in the face of fears over national security—even in cases where our security might have been better served by requiring that decent treatment. The cold war calculus had come back with a vengeance. Ronald Reagan, the president George Bush most admired, had begun with very much the same mentality, but over time had come to accept, if grudgingly, the wisdom of demanding democratic reform even from our cold war allies. The Bush White House, in its second term, had moved in the opposite direction—from splendid pronouncements to realist arrangements. Of course, the cold war had been waning in Reagan's era, while the war on terror was waxing in Bush's. Nevertheless, the atmosphere of chastened naïveté bore a passing resemblance to the Carter administration—not a comparison Bush would find flattering.

President Bush's rhetoric remained majestic—indeed, transcendent. In July 2007 he explained that his belief in democracy promotion had less to do with "political science" than with religious faith: "I do believe there is an Almighty, and I believe a gift of that Almighty to all is freedom. And I will tell you that is a principle that no one can tell me doesn't exist." And yet by that time the policy itself was effectively dead. Thomas Carothers observed that of the forty-five nations that Freedom House counted as "not free," "the Bush administration maintains friendly, unchallenging relations with the governments of more than half." Looking around the world, Carothers found that Bush had seriously pushed for democracy in no country save Egypt, while "outside of the Middle East it is difficult to find evidence of any major positive U.S. impact on the state of democracy." The view that the Bush administration had embarked on an "all-out democracy crusade" was, he concluded, "an illusion."

7

Mubarak's Egypt

The Dark Arts of "Liberal Autocracy"

In March 2007, the people of Egypt went to the polls to vote on a package of constitutional amendments submitted by the regime of President Hosni Mubarak. Or rather, they didn't go to the polls. Egypt's opposition parties had united around a call to boycott the vote, and the streets and polling places of Cairo were empty that day. Reports from around the country showed equal apathy, save among voters paid and bused in by supporters of the regime. The official tally put the turnout at 27 percent. Egyptians are so profoundly cynical about their country's politics that no election in Egypt in recent memory had attracted much more than 10 to 15 percent of the country's voters; civic groups who canvassed polling stations offered estimates of 2 to 8 percent.

The referendum nonevent was the kind of political ritual that had become increasingly common in Egypt in the period since the Bush administration had begun demanding evidence of reform from the Mubarak regime. The regime, fearful of defying its most important ally, would kick the machinery of representative government into gear in a manner meant to imply genuine commitment, but which the Egyptian people themselves recognized as hollow. Opposition parties, civic activists, journalists, and the like, taking advantage of a public sphere far more open than in years past, would denounce the empty exercise; the regime would recoil in a spasm of outraged virtue, often breaking up protests and throwing demonstrators and political opponents in jail; the Americans would emit a mild bleat of protest; and the exercise would unfold to general public cynicism and disgust. This was democracy as Egypt knew it.

The regime's approach to constitutional reform reflected both its recognition of the need to mollify an increasingly restive public and its unwillingness to make the kind of concessions the public demanded. When Mubarak had responded to pressure from both the Bush administration and domestic activists by agreeing to run in a contested race for president in 2005, he had found himself for the first time in need of a platform, and so had vaguely promised to reform the constitution. The president's aides let it be known that some unspecified loosening of strictures was being contemplated. There was talk in the media that Mubarak, who had already served for a quarter of a century, might agree to limit the presidency to two terms; to change an absurdly onerous licensing system that made it all but impossible for new political parties to gain approval; and perhaps to fashion a new antiterrorism law that would take the place of the state of emergency under which Egyptians had lived for the last fifty years.

But when the drafting committee of the ruling National Democratic Party submitted the proposals, the reforms turned out to be either cosmetic or rhetorical. Archaic language establishing a "socialist democratic system" of economic relations, for example, had been rewritten to specify a system "based on freedom of economic action." The Americans, it was thought, or imagined, would be pleased. The essential theme of the change was the consolidation, not the diminution, of executive power. Article 88, which had stipulated that elections be held "under the supervision of members of the judiciary authority," now granted that control instead to "a higher commission marked by independence and impartiality." Since no such bodies had been known to exist in Egypt, this was apparently intended to undermine the autonomy of judges, whose impartiality had proved embarrassing to the regime in earlier elections. The new antiterrorism law allowed the state to set aside civil liberties enumerated elsewhere in the constitution in the pursuit of suspected terrorists. And a previously innocuous article establishing political parties now included a stipulation that "any political activity or political parties shall not be based on any religious background or foundation"— a transparent attempt to marginalize the Muslim Brotherhood, Mubarak's most popular and well-organized opponent. Human Rights Watch deemed the entire package the biggest step backward on civil liberties since Mubarak had taken power.

I was in Egypt when the amendments were submitted to the Parliament and then to the public. Opposition legislators had walked out rather than debate proposals on which they had not been consulted, and which were certain in advance to be adopted without significant change. I went to NDP headquarters to speak to Mohammed Kamel, a young party leader who had played a key role on the drafting committee. Kamel, a professor of political science, had studied in the United States and served as the regime's designated explainer for the American media. He was an informal figure, in the American style; we sat at a little round table in front of his desk. I had been told, I said, that the entire reform process had been controlled by the ruling party. Kamel bridled. "There was a big debate among the society at large," he said. "Every member of Parliament filled out a form with his own suggestions for reform."

In fact, none of Egypt's many prominent civil liberties organizations had been given the chance to address the drafting committee. If they had, they would have said that the country didn't need to change its constitution but urgently needed to alter some laws, including the one that made prospective political parties jump through impossible hoops. When I asked Kamel about the parties law, he pointed out that Egypt had spent twenty years debating economic reform. Things happened slowly. "I'm not saying

it's going to take us twenty years or so, as it did with economic reform, but it's going to take us some time before we reach consensus on the kind of democracy that we want to have in Egypt.
We're dealing with very tough questions." Term limits? There had
been an internal debate, Kamel explained. "Some people say, in a
country like Egypt you actually need to give more time to the
president to implement his program, his vision, and maybe also
it's wise to allow a person to serve more because he will have
more experience." I did not point out that President Mubarak
had yet to articulate a program after twenty-five years. Kamel
thanked me very graciously for coming by, and as we walked to
the elevator he told me how much he had enjoyed the time he
had spent at the Wharton Business School.

There was talk of confrontation in the days before the vote.
Press conferences and demonstrations were to be staged. One of
the Muslim Brotherhood legislators told me that he would be out
in the street telling his constituents to stay away rather than cast
a no vote that election officials might simply throw out. But the
day was quiet: even the most modest protest in recent weeks had
been met with overwhelming force, and often with beatings and
arrests, and perhaps activists had decided that noncooperation
was the wisest policy. In the ensuing days, opposition and civil-
society groups unanimously declared the referendum a sham.
But State Department spokesman Sean McCormack, eager to
find something praiseworthy in the process, suggested to re-
porters that "over the arc of time, when you are able to at some
point look back at events in Egypt and the political changes under way there, you will see . . . a general trend toward greater political reform, greater political openness." Condoleezza Rice tried
to calm the outrage provoked by this agonized blessing by conceding that she found it "disappointing" that Mubarak hadn't
done better.

Egypt is neither a hermetically sealed state nor a free one, neither a benevolent dictatorship nor an "illiberal democracy." Daniel Brumberg, a scholar at Georgetown University, has coined the term "liberal autocracy" to describe countries such as Egypt. Such regimes, Brumberg writes, "temper authoritarianism with pluralism. They are liberal in the sense that their leaders not only tolerate but promote a measure of political openness in civil society, in the press, and even in the electoral system in their own country . . . But they are autocratic in that their rulers always retain the upper hand." Political participation serves a strategic rather than a democratic function: "to give opposition groups a way to blow off steam." The system perpetually holds out the fruits of change without ever permitting them to be consumed. These regimes, as Thomas Carothers had pointed out, had not temporarily stalled on the path to democracy or modernization. Liberal autocracy was a self-perpetuating condition. And the longer such states "depend on weak political parties and impotent legislatures," Brumberg observes, "the more difficult it becomes to move from state-managed liberalization to genuine democratization."

Although the Bush administration now likes to sort Arab states into the "moderate" and "extremist" camps, from the point of view of Arab citizens it is more meaningfully divided between outright autocracies like Saudi Arabia, Syria, and Iran, and more or less liberal ones, like Egypt, Morocco, and Jordan. The region has no real democracies, save Israel, and never has. Is Islam, as is often alleged, inhospitable to democracy? If so, how to explain the burgeoning democracies in Indonesia, the world's largest Islamic state, and elsewhere in the Muslim-dominated regions of Asia, and in Africa? The problem seems specific to the Arab world, which, as the Arab Human Development Report vividly illustrated, lacks virtually all of the social and economic conditions that Seymour Martin Lipset and others considered the prerequisites for democratic development, and which later scholars saw as, at least, powerful correlates. The Arab world has high levels of poverty amid great wealth, dismal rates of literacy and higher education, no prior experience with democracy, and very little exposure to the Western political tradition. And in almost all Arab countries the state apparatus is both omnipresent and shambolic. In the Middle East, the East Asian model of benevolent despotism that Fareed Zakaria and others celebrated looks every bit as unlikely as democracy.

And yet Egyptians do not have to look back so very far to recall a time when they lived under liberal and constitutional principles, if not under democracy. Indeed, the country's secular reformers see themselves, with reason, as the legatees of a tolerant and cosmopolitan culture. Mohammad Ali, an Albanian soldier, had ousted Egypt's Ottoman rulers in the mid-nineteenth century and put the country on the path to modernization. His successor, Khedive Ismail, planned out Cairo's axial boulevards on the pattern of Baron Nicolas Haussmann's Paris; the constitution of 1882 established an elected parliament. British control put an end to liberal developments, but in the years after World War I, Egyptian intellectuals repudiated imperial rule and ordinary citizens enjoyed the heady and terrifying experience of taking on British soldiers in the streets. Egypt gained its independence in 1922, though Great Britain continued to exercise ultimate authority for the next thirty years. Egypt functioned as a constitutional monarchy, with a progressive constitution guaranteeing individual rights and a legislature dominated by the liberal Wafd Party.

Cairo's liberal intellectuals, and for that matter its doyennes, speak of this golden era with a kind of desperate nostalgia, for it provides the one solid foundation they have for an imagined future. "Everything flourished in those three decades," says Osama al-Ghazali Harb, one of the country's leading democracy activists: "politics, civil society, film, theater, art, literature." Harb then ticked off a list of the Egyptian film stars, the singers, the artists, the businessmen of the day who commanded the Arab world. Cairo was a global crossroads; you can still find the remnants of this life in the city's architectural potpourri, variously Ottoman, Alhambra, Art Deco, Italianate, and English Tudor. This is the turbulent and exhilarating interval rendered in Naguib Mahfouz's splendid *Palace Walk* trilogy of novels.

But it was also an era of liberal failure. The intelligentsia never sank deep roots with the rural or even urban masses, and watched with dismay as the rival Muslim Brotherhood used the organizing power of the mosque to gain a genuine national following. And the reluctance of Parliament to stand up to the English, or to the equivocating King Fuad, tarnished the Wafd's nationalist credentials. The secular liberals proved helpless to respond when the Free Officers, led by Gamal Abdel Nasser, overthrew Egypt's feckless playboy ruler, King Farouk, in 1952. Capitalizing on the disgust of ordinary Egyptians with the dominance of a tiny, Europeanized elite—including the political elite—Nasser expropriated the wealth of the ruling class and established the kind of state-dominated socialism then very much in vogue among emerging nations in Africa and Asia. He made himself a heroic figure in Egypt and across the Arab world by championing the cause of Arab nationalism and railing against the West and against Israel. Nasser understood that the Egyptian people would rally to the banner of socialism and nationalism as they would not to democracy. He summarily abrogated the constitution and clamped a lid on all political debate; and the café intellectuals of Cairo fell silent or joined the revolution.

Anwar Sadat, the military officer who succeeded Nasser upon the latter's death in 1970, aspired to move Egypt into the Western orbit both politically and economically. He tentatively loosened the stranglehold over political expression and permitted multiparty elections. The Wafd came back to life—but feebly. Democracy in Egypt remained a hothouse plant. A pious man who had joined the Muslim Brotherhood at an early age, Sadat cultivated Islamist forces as Nasser had not, bringing religion into the public sphere, rewriting textbooks, and the like. After years of repression, the Brotherhood enjoyed a renaissance. But Sadat also wanted to make peace with Israel; and his brave decision in 1979 to sign the Camp David Accords discredited him with the religious faction. In 1981, he was assassinated by radical Islamists—the forerunners of today's jihadist militants.

Sadat's vice president, Hosni Mubarak, became Egypt's third military dictator. An air force officer with no apparent interest in or talent for political leadership, Mubarak made no attempt to emulate either Nasser's revolutionary charisma or Sadat's liberal reformism. A status quo leader who surrounded himself with apparatchiks and cronies, he restored the emergency law that Nasser had first imposed in 1956. When Egypt's professional associations, known as "syndicates," threatened to became alternative centers of power, he scuttled planned elections. He made no attempt to dismantle Egypt's Soviet-style command economy, even after the Berlin wall fell, ensuring that the country's economy was as vibrant as East Germany's. Egyptians became so cynical and disaffected that sometimes as few as 5 percent voted. As the other founding nations of the "Nonaligned Movement"— India, Indonesia, Brazil, Mexico—began to develop both solid democracies and complex economies, Egypt, along with the rest of the Arab world, slipped into stagnation.

The regime's diminishing credibility became increasingly patent. In the 2000 legislative election, supervised for the first time by Egypt's respected judges, the NDP took only 39 percent of the seats. The ruling party retained its majority only by luring back dozens of candidates who ran and won as independents. The fiasco provided an opening for Mubarak's second son, Gamal, a thirty-seven-year-old banker who had been living in London. Gamal swept into the NDP with a mighty Anglo-American broom. He spoke of Tony Blair's rehabilitated Labour Party, and of the Clinton-Blair "third way." He established a Policies Committee, which included both the wealthy young businessmen who formed his own circle and several of Egypt's bona fide democracy advocates. He persuaded his father to dump the socialist functionaries in several key economic ministries and instead appoint market-oriented technocrats. Gamal himself knew very well how to talk to Americans. The regime "used to be so defensive," says Amy Hawthorne, an expert on democracy and elections in the Middle East. "Mubarak always said, 'We already have democracy.' Gamal had a different message: 'We realize we have to change.' He would overwhelm you with papers and documents and reports. It made it very difficult for the U.S. to say, 'Get moving on reform.'"

Gamal was not, it turned out, the Tony Blair of Egypt. "Everything went well for almost a year," says Hala Mustafa, editor of the quarterly *Democracy Review*, who agreed to join the Policies Committee. "I had the freedom to speak my opinions." And then suddenly she didn't. Mustafa began to be hounded by security officials, and was warned not to get out of line; anonymous denunciations appeared in the press. One of her colleagues, Osama Harb, said that he realized the committee "was only a frame for presenting Gamal Mubarak." Even one of Gamal's closest allies, Hossam Badrawi, a doctor who runs one of the city's leading private hospitals, concedes that while they made real progress in appointing economic reformers, "we did not succeed on the political level, the security level, the human rights level, the education or public health level." That's pretty much everything. Reform could operate only along a path of least resistance, which in effect meant the development of a moderately robust private-sector economy alongside the moribund state-controlled one. But reforms that challenged the existing alignment of political power went nowhere.

Every once in a while the regime would reach out to crush one of its critics, as an object lesson to others. In June of 2000, Saad Eddin Ibrahim, the best known of Egypt's activists for democracy and human rights, had the temerity to suggest, during the television coverage of the funeral of Syrian dictator Hafez al-Assad, that Mubarak might be clearing the way for Gamal just as Assad had for his son, Bashir. (What Ibrahim recalled saying was "If you serve as head of state long enough, naturally you regard the state as yours, so you want to bequeath it to your son.") He then repeated the thought in a widely reprinted newspaper column. He was promptly arrested and jailed, along with twenty-seven employees of his organization, the Ibn Khaldun Center for Development Studies. In an outcome that deeply shocked and frightened Egypt's circle of reformers, Ibrahim, despite his high public profile, was sentenced under the emergency laws to seven years in prison. He was ultimately released from jail after threats by Secretary of State Colin Powell to withhold promised funds from Egypt. In March 2003, Ibrahim and his associates were acquitted of all charges. But in the meantime, his health had been broken—he still walks with a painful limp—and his center was closed down.

Egypt, in short, looked frozen, with apathy below and paralysis above. And yet catalytic events—shocks from the outside—could shake up even the most intransigent situations and open up cracks that until then had barely been noticed. The sudden collapse of a colonial empire, whether the Hapsburgs or the Soviets, had loosed pent-up political energies. And a series of shocks hit the Arab world in the first years of the new century—the terrorist attacks of 9/11, George Bush's passionate calls for democracy, the Arab Human Development Report, and finally the shocking imagery of Saddam Hussein's downfall. Arab regimes found it harder to ignore their own publics, and most made some sort of gesture in the direction of popular sovereignty. In two small Gulf states, Bahrain and Qatar, monarchs initiated processes to limit their own powers. Jordan held long-delayed parliamentary elections, while Saudi Arabia announced plans to hold municipal elections for the first time. Morocco and Jordan convened panels to examine allegations of current and past human rights abuses, while the Mubarak regime allowed the Egyptian Organization for Human Rights to register as an NGO. Women made real advances in political representation across the region.

The logic of liberal autocracy ensured that the reforms never threatened the regime in question. Emergency laws remained in force, as did all-pervasive security organs, such as Egypt's feared Mukhabarat. Elections generally produced predictable outcomes. But the valves, once opened, were not so easy to close, and especially in Egypt. While the Mubarak regime and the NDP, its political appendage, remained frozen, the civic world of journalism and activism was quickening to life. New periodicals and new civic groups began to spring up in Cairo and other major cities. Egyptians increasingly had access to private television and radio stations (though most offered only mass entertainment) and to the Internet. Bloggers described the events of the day bluntly and fearlessly. The same torpid political parties had orbited slowly around the regime for decades, but now new signs of life begin to appear. One group of younger activists split off from the Muslim Brotherhood to form a political party, while another created a rump version of the old Nasserist party. In 2001, a charismatic young legislator, Ayman Nour, formed a new secular democratic party known as Al Ghad ("Tomorrow").

It was one thing to announce a new party, however, and quite another to get it formally licensed to operate. Egypt's political parties law was designed to stifle any and all forms of opposition. It prohibited the formation of parties opposed to the Camp David Accords or to Sharia (Islamic jurisprudence) or to any of the alleged foundations of the state; parties based on class, ethnic, or geographic lines; and parties too similar to existing ones or ones that had previously been banned. Only two new parties had been formed since the law had gone into effect in 1977, and the government had suspended one of them. The Political Parties Committee rejected all three of the new groupings. Al Ghad was finally approved in 2004 after rewriting its platform three times.

Al Ghad played an important role in the Arab Spring, which in fact began in late 2004. The party faithful wore orange scarves to match the party's orange logo; the urban, progressive, secular Cairenes who flocked to Nour and Al Ghad felt as if they were joining the color revolutions that had swept Eastern Europe and the Balkans. Under pressure from the Bush administration, the Mukhabarat relaxed its vigilance sufficiently to permit the kind of demonstrations heretofore almost unknown in Egypt. Some of the public gatherings called on the state to sever relations with Israel—always a popular cause in Egypt. Others, however, demanded political freedom. Protesters gathering in December 2004 stood silently with gags over their mouths—a gesture more eloquent than any torrent of complaint. The gags bore the single word *kifaya* ("enough"), and the heterogeneous collection of secular leftists and Islamists who had organized the assemblies came to be known by this name. It was all very heady for a people long denied the opportunity to speak their mind.

And then, in January 2005, Mubarak announced that he would stand in Egypt's first contested presidential election. The dictator may have considered a contested but tightly controlled election a sufficient twist of the valve to release domestic pressure. He also may have hoped to prepare a path of legitimate succession for Gamal. But most Egyptian activists assume that the president was trying to appease the Americans. "The people around Gamal could see that they needed to make a break from the past," says Negad al-Borai, a human rights lawyer and democracy proponent. "But the most important part was Bush."

The whole issue of American influence was, of course, deeply fraught. A long history of Western intervention had made Arab publics deeply suspicious of any form of intervention from abroad, even for the most putatively benevolent purpose. And the Bush administration had inflamed this sensitivity to the final degree. And yet, for all that, Washington could still make a difference. First of all, the Mubarak regime could not afford to ignore the country that provided it with $2 billion a year and ensured it a central place in Middle Eastern diplomacy. No country mattered to Mubarak remotely as much as the United States. And many Egyptians who despised the administration and all its works had nevertheless welcomed Bush's pressure—indeed, were thrilled at it.

Some were even prepared to accept American help. When advocacy groups tried to raise money in order to train election monitors, they found that local businessmen were loath to risk their relation with the regime by financing so subversive an activity. And so the advocacy groups turned to American bodies such as the NDI and IRI—though some left-leaning or traditionally nationalist NGOs refused to take American money. Several civic leaders held a press conference in which they argued that if the Egyptian government could take $2 billion a year from the United States, they could accept a few hundred thousand dollars in the name of democracy. "We were denounced as American spies," recalls al-Borai. But they went ahead. Americans would thus play the same modest but crucial role they had in the Philippines and Chile in the 1980s, and in Latin America and Eastern European in the ensuing years—or so it was hoped.

The election, which began in mid-August and lasted three weeks, pitted Mubarak against opponents from the traditional parties, few of whom had much of a following; one of the more eccentric advocated the return of the fez. But Mubarak would also have to run against Ayman Nour, a new kind of politician— a well-educated forty-year-old former journalist and secular reformer with no compromising ties to the regime. Nour enjoyed support in the same urban, Westernized circles as other liberal democrats did, but by virtue of having established a political party, and thanks to his own bold and charismatic style, he posed a novel threat to the regime. Mubarak had no obvious heir save

Gamal, who officially eschewed personal ambition. Nour was the kind of figure who just might be able to fill that vacuum. And he obviously unnerved the regime. Nour was jailed in January, announced his candidacy from prison, and was then freed in mid-March after intense American pressure. The incident only enhanced his standing, for Egyptians assumed that the charges had been trumped up for political reasons.

Mubarak did conduct a sort of election campaign. Egyptians enjoyed the novelty of their stiff, dignified leader actually asking them for their votes. The president's team of advisers came up with the slogan "Mubarak 2005: Leadership and Crossing to the Future." And the incumbent had a platform as well—a genuine novelty, since in years past he had seemed to represent no principle higher than the preservation of the status quo. Instructed by Gamal and his circle, the president promised "reform." He would reduce unemployment and improve health care. And he would amend the constitution to open up the political system. Egypt's state-run media, which included virtually all television and radio and *Al Ahram*, the country's largest newspaper, offered fawning coverage of the president and grudging or caustic coverage of his rivals (though opposition newspapers were scarcely less biased in the opposite direction). In the end, despite the unprecedented nature of the contest, most Egyptians turned their back on the whole exercise, as they had long done. Observers estimated that only about 10 percent of voters turned out. (The government pegged the number at about 30 percent.) Mubarak won 70 percent of the vote; Nour finished first among the opponents, with slightly less than 8 percent of the vote. Three months later, he was convicted of the original charges laid against him and sentenced to five years in prison.

The parliamentary elections proved far less amenable to state control. Prior to the 2000 election, the regime had agreed to permit Egypt's judges to oversee the actual balloting. Now, since Egypt had far more ballot boxes than judges, the vote was to be held in three separate stages at the end of November and the beginning of December. The first stage passed with so little incident that the American NGOs who had trained election workers recommended that the United States publicly praise the regime. The results, however, plainly qualified as one of Huntington's "stunning elections": while the secular democratic parties won only a handful of seats, candidates from the Muslim Brotherhood, running as independents—the Brotherhood had never been permitted to form a party of its own—won almost every seat they contested. The regime had counted on the Islamists to serve as a counterweight to secular groupings such as Al Ghad, whom they feared far more, and so had released many of the Brothers from jail before the election and had allowed them to campaign with little interference. But Gamal and his circle of elite, Westernized advisers were so divorced from the life of the street that they wildly overestimated the popularity of the NDP, and failed to recognize the deep roots that the Brotherhood had sunk into Egyptian society over the years.

The second round of polling was a very different story. The police, as well as the hired thugs they typically used as proxies, blocked off access to polling places in pro-Brotherhood neighborhoods and beat up voters, judges, and independent monitors. Riot police reportedly barred women wearing the *niqab*—the full veil—from entering polling places. A gang of twenty men wielding machetes, clubs, and guns was said to have attacked Brotherhood organizers in a village in the Nile Delta. More than seven hundred members of the organization were arrested. The NDP, meanwhile, was widely reported to have paid off voters and brought them to the polling places. The American-trained monitors had been unable to stem the abuse, but they had served as witnesses to it. The state, as one of them put it bluntly, was "sacrificing all attempts to appear serious at democratization rather than lose power to the opposition."

And yet the regime was still failing. The Brotherhood won 76 of the 110 seats they contested. (Of the 445 seats in the People's Assembly, 308 were determined in the first two rounds.) How could this be? Essam El-Erian, one of the Brotherhood's leading strategists, explained to the English-language *Al-Ahram Weekly* that the organization had twenty-five thousand volunteers knocking on doors and getting out the vote. The Islamists were highly professional: They showed up at polling places with laptops; the NDP, with stacks of paper. And while supporters of the secular parties drifted away when the police shut down the polls, the Islamists' voters waited for hours. And finally, as Ibrahim Eissa, one of Egypt's leading columnists, wrote, the Brotherhood, unlike the NDP, had not nominated "corrupt candidates, bank robbers, those who steal the daily bread of the people or state security investigation officers who torture citizens."

After the second round, the association of judges threatened to boycott the voting unless security forces were curbed. Instead, in the third round, the security forces pulled out all the stops. Police and their hired hands opened fire on voters, killing eleven (all, apparently, Brotherhood supporters). There were riots in the streets of major cities; television crews captured scenes of old women in full veils scaling ladders to get to voting booths whose front entrances had been blocked by police. Party officials openly stuffed ballot boxes in full view of judges and monitors. The regime did succeed in holding the number of additional seats won by Brotherhood candidates to twelve, rather than the twenty-five or so that had been predicted. But by the end, NDP candidates had won only 32 percent of the seats they had contested despite rampant cheating, while the Brotherhood, in the face of overwhelming obstacles up to and including murder, had taken well over half. The NDP retained power only by its usual expedient of luring independents—but not those affiliated with the Brotherhood—back into the fold after the election.

The election had been a fiasco for everyone save the Brotherhood. Neither the judges stationed at the ballot boxes nor the five thousand monitors located outside had been able to prevent the most blatant abuses. On the other hand, as Amy Hawthorne, a veteran of Middle East reform efforts, points out, the monitors "set a precedent, which is that, after years and years of the Egyptian government doing everything it could to delegitimize these groups, all of a sudden here they are, allowed to monitor, and they're on the front pages of the state paper every day." It was the regime, not the civic activists, who had been delegitimized. With the world watching, Mubarak and his security apparatus had been forced to resort to the most brutal tactics in order to preserve their power and defy the will of the Egyptian people.

But did that matter? The regime had always depended on apathy more than popularity. The Egyptian people did not take to the streets to protest the theft of the election. They were inured to contemptuous mistreatment. It would scarcely be surprising if 3,500 years of absolutism, stretching from the pharaohs to the Abbasids to the Mamluks to the French and British, had habituated Egypt's rural masses to stoical resignation. And the overwhelming majority of Egyptians, unlike the people of Serbia or the Ukraine, were poorly educated, economically marginal peasants. But democratic movements in the third world typically depended on urbanites and the middle class, not the yeomanry. What was striking about Egypt was the quiescence of the middle class. Egypt's lawyers had not followed the lead of its judges and taken to the streets to protest the subverting of civil liberties, as they would in Pakistan eighteen months later. For all the ferment of newspapers and human rights groups, democracy seemed to be a hothouse growth in Egypt. "Advocates of democracy," wrote Marina Ottaway, a Middle East expert at the Carnegie Endowment for International Peace, "move in a small world, somewhat isolated from their own societies. They congregate in their NGOs and their progressive think tanks and write commentaries for domestic and pan-Arab newspapers. They reach across borders to like-minded people in other Arab states but do not attempt to reach down into their own countries."

And when the Bush administration released the pressure, signaling to the regime that it would accept the election even with all its abuses, that small band of democracy activists were left looking like naifs, or even toadies. They felt betrayed by the Bush administration, and terribly exposed. Few were more exposed than Saad Eddin Ibrahim, who had courageously returned to public activism after his release from jail. Ibrahim had made himself a highly controversial figure inside Egypt by his open support for the Bush administration's Freedom Agenda and even for the war in Iraq. But he was no American stooge: a puckish character with a grizzled goatee, Ibrahim kept a picture of Dick Cheney on one side of his office and of Sheikh Hassan Nasrallah, the leader of Hezbollah, on the other.

Ibrahim had been using American and European funds to train election monitors since 1995. After he had emerged from jail and rebuilt his organization, he had joined with al-Borai and others in the monitoring effort for the 2005 elections. Listening to Condoleezza Rice's brave words in Cairo that summer, Ibrahim had been torn between hope and skepticism. And then the worst had come, and his friends in the White House had said nothing. Invited to speak at a conservative symposium on democracy in January 2006, he said flatly that he and his colleagues, heroes to this audience, felt abandoned. Afterward, John Hannah, one of Cheney's top aides, approached Ibrahim and asked if he would speak to the vice president. Ibrahim, of course, agreed. At the meeting, he recalls, Cheney said, "We won't betray the cause of democracy in the Middle East, but we are assessing what we should do after Hamas." Ibrahim, a battered and gimpy old warrior, didn't hide his skepticism. Cheney said, "How can we prove it to you?"

"Mubarak made six pledges during the campaign," Ibrahim

shot back. "Go to him and say, 'Mr. President, help us help you. You know the foreign aid package barely squeaked through Congress last year; we can't guarantee that it will pass this year unless you engage in serious reform. Why don't you promise to honor three of those pledges in 2006, and the other three in 2007?'" Cheney said that he thought this was a fine idea, and insisted that they meet again the next time Ibrahim was in town. Ibrahim left thinking, "He really means it."

Ibrahim didn't return to Washington until September 2006. By then, between the mayhem in Iraq, the intransigence in Iran, and the vicious war in Lebanon pitting Israel against Hezbollah, the Middle East was looking like a powder keg. Ibrahim called Hannah to say that he was ready to take Cheney up on his offer. "I'm sorry, Professor," Ibrahim recalls being told, "we cannot carry on with what we agreed to. You see the situation in Lebanon; we need every ally we have in the region." Ibrahim went right outside and recounted the conversation to a reporter from *The Washington Post*. But his weary sense of irony did not quite trump his bitter disappointment. "It could have all worked," he laments. "It was my agony that it didn't."

With the 2005 parliamentary election, the Muslim Brotherhood became Egypt's opposition party. Of course, it wasn't a political party at all, but rather a grassroots religious association. But the Brotherhood had filled a vacuum. The ruling party, with no meaningful political program, served as a vehicle for personal advancement. The traditional Nasserist and socialist opposition parties were played out, while the new, democracy-oriented groupings appealed only to a narrow elite. The Brotherhood, meanwhile, was a true national organization with explicit, if vague, principles and a broad following among the country's urban and small-town middle and working class. Millions of Egyptians fed up with the frozen status quo found in the Brotherhood a meaningful alternative and a means of expressing their disgust. Secular activists explained away the strong showing by arguing that the Islamists had won the "protest" vote; but only the Brotherhood's supporters had been willing to face organized violence in order to cast a ballot.

The Brotherhood is a very diverse organization with both reactionary and relatively progressive elements. At least when talking to a Westerner, the group's Cairo-based leaders sound less like staunch Islamists than shrewd and circumspect politicos. Abdel Aboul El Al-Foutouh, a hospital administrator who serves on the Brotherhood's policy-making body, the Guidance Board, says, "The Brotherhood is not a religious party; it's a political party which depends on our understanding of Sharia. Of the fourteen in the Guidance Bureau, only one is a sheik; and even *he* is political." The Brothers demonstrated their acute sensitivity to political reality throughout the electoral period. In order to avoid provoking a confrontation with the regime, the group's leaders fielded candidates in only a third of the districts; provincial leaders were instructed to reduce the number of aspirants to an acceptable figure. And when the Brotherhood held a press conference four days after the election to introduce their new legislators, a reporter asked Mohammed Akef, the supreme guide, if they would be prepared to talk to the Americans. Akef answered, "Yes, but they should forward the request to the Egyptian Foreign Ministry." He was saying both that the Brotherhood was open to dialogue with outsiders, and that it had nothing to hide from the regime.

Many of the new legislators were well-educated technocrats drawn from the ranks of the professional syndicates—teachers, engineers, doctors, lawyers. Those I spoke to were already well known and respected in their neighborhoods. Gamal Hanafy, an attorney who represented an old working-class district in Cairo, said that he had become known in his constituency both as a civil servant and as a volunteer for the Brotherhood. "I've always stayed in touch through my work with families and children, and with the problems of the people," he said. "Our activities in the streets, which had nothing to do with winning the election, attracted people to us." When I asked Hanafy what the big campaign issues had been, he said, "Political consciousness is not so high, so when people vote, they vote for the person based on reputation. When you're a member of the Muslim Brotherhood, that gives you an advantage, because people know that the Brotherhood has integrity, that you won't steal their money. They have that Islamic source that other people don't have." Rampant public corruption, Hanafy said, was a recurrent issue. Otherwise, voters wanted basic services and resources—a sports club for kids, a cultural center for adults, better health care, connections to gas mains.

Once in office, the Brotherhood steered clear of the Egyptian equivalent of "wedge issues"—matters of personal behavior, popular culture, dress. The only exception came in late 2006, when Farouk Hosni, Egypt's minister of culture, criticized the growing popularity of the headscarf and the veil. Leading NDP members in Parliament, including the speaker of the People's Assembly, assailed the remarks as an insult to religion and to Egyptian womanhood, though Hosni was himself a member of the party. This startling injection of personal views into political debate was widely seen as a sign that the ruling party was trying to trump the Brotherhood as defender of the faith. And the Brotherhood responded by joining the attack on Hosni. But it was an issue they had not sought, and otherwise were sedulous to avoid.

Indeed, the Brotherhood bloc took Parliament a great deal more seriously than the ruling party did. The entire eighty-eight-person contingent moved into a hotel in Cairo in order to be able to work and live together while the People's Assembly was in session. Merely showing up changed the dynamic of this somnolent body, since NDP lawmakers had to attend as well, lest they be outvoted. The Brothers formed a "parliamentary kitchen" with committees on various subjects; the committees, in turn, organized seminars to which outside experts were regularly invited.

The Islamists formed a coalition with other opposition legislators and with sympathetic members of the NDP, to protest the extension of emergency rule. They stood in solidarity with judges who were protesting growing infringements on their autonomy; hundreds of protesters, including some of the Brotherhood's major figures, were arrested during several weeks of demonstrations in central Cairo. In a long posting on the website Middle East Report, Joshua Stacher, a scholar affiliated with the American University of Cairo, and Samer Shehata, a professor at Georgetown, concluded that "Brotherhood MPs are attempting to transform the Egyptian parliament into a real legislative body, as well as an institution that represents citizens and a mechanism that keeps government accountable."

In a way, the Brotherhood was blinking in a bright sunshine into which it had only just emerged, and from which some of its members were still inclined to withdraw. The Ikhwan Muslimiya, as it is known in Arabic, was founded in 1928 by Hasan al-Banna, a charismatic figure who opposed the rise of secular Islamic states such as Turkey. Al-Banna hoped to revitalize the spirit of Islam among the *umma*, the worldwide body of believers, and ultimately to reinstitute the rule of Sharia. The Brotherhood was an evangelizing body; but al-Banna also created a paramilitary wing, like Mussolini's brownshirts. During the forties, when Egyptians fought to free themselves from British rule, Ikhwan operatives engaged in a campaign of bombings and assassinations. The organization was banned in 1948; soon afterward, a member of the group assassinated Egypt's prime minister. Al-Banna denounced the deed but was himself murdered, apparently by government security forces. And when a Brotherhood plot to assassinate President Gamal Abdel Nasser miscarried, most of the leading Brotherhood figures were jailed and tortured.

The Brotherhood never entirely escaped the taint of its violent early days. In 1965, the most prominent of its jailed leaders, Sayyid Qutb, produced a tract, translated in English as *Signposts*, that rejected al-Banna's faith in the merits of instruction and moral example. Islamic regimes that failed to establish Sharia were apostates, Qutb declared, and thus no better than the infidels themselves. Egypt was, of course, just such a state. *Signposts* was read as a call to revolution. Qutb was charged with treason and hanged the following year, making him a martyr throughout the Middle East. Among his disciples were the radical Islamists who conspired to murder Sadat in 1981—including Ayman Zawahiri, now Al Qaeda's second in command. *Signposts* is now considered the founding manifesto of jihadism, and Qutb remains a heroic figure for many ordinary Egyptians. But the Brotherhood has sought from the outset to distance itself from his theories. One of his jailmates, Hasan Hudaybi, who had replaced al-Banna as supreme guide, wrote a counterpolemic titled *Preachers, Not Judges* in order to reassert the Brotherhood's commitment to peace and open debate. And during their long underground period, the Brotherhood followed a path of grassroots organizing and political quietism.

At the same time, Egypt's military leadership has increasingly sought the legitimating mantle of Islam. Anwar Sadat amended Article 2 of the Constitution to stipulate that Sharia was the "main source" of the nation's laws. And Hosni Mubarak, though himself a more secular figure, found the appeal to religion equally effective. Both figures quietly sought accommodations with the Islamists. Over time, Egypt's secular classes thus came to view the Brothers not as religious radicals but rather as a silent ally of the state—and thus as an essentially reactionary force. Many of Cairo's secular activists believe that for all the appearances of brutal repression, some kind of deep game persists between the regime and the Brotherhood. Others fear that the Brotherhood, perhaps in collaboration with the military, will try to establish an authoritarian theocracy, as in Sudan.

But as the Brotherhood has stepped out from the shadows, Mubarak has treated it as a very serious threat. The regime has increasingly made the Islamists, not the secularists, the focus of its repressive mechanism. First, of course, came the brutal crackdown during the 2005 elections. Then there were the mass arrests during the judges' campaign. And starting in early 2007, when top Brotherhood officials began talking about publishing a platform and seeking to form a party, security forces began arresting key figures across the country and seizing the assets of businessmen thought to provide the bulk of the group's funding. A few days after I arrived in Cairo in March 2007, a text message sent by Ibrahim Hudaybi, the grandson of the former supreme guide, beeped into my cell phone: "Mahmoud Ghozlan, MB Guide Bureau, is being arrested NOW."

The message had been sent at 2:30 a.m. That was typical. Dozens of police officers, deployed as if for a dangerous terrorist, had rousted Ghozlan from bed in the middle of the night. (Egyptians derisively referred to such raids as the "dawn visit.") He and six others arrested at the same time were accused of having joined a banned group, organizing demonstrations—illegal under the emergency laws—and threatening national unity. In some cases the charges were so flimsy that judges dismissed them and released the prisoners. The regime was then able to use the emergency laws to rearrest the figures and bring them before a military tribunal. Military judges could be counted on to try the accused, to find them guilty, and to hand down a long sentence.

The Mubarak regime went to great lengths to delegitimize the Brotherhood. President Mubarak called the group "a threat to our national security." Hossam Badrawi, the would-be NDP reformer, insisted to me that Egypt should no more allow the Brotherhood to form a political party than Germany should grant such rights to a Nazi Party. Mohammed Kamel, the policy-maker who sought to justify the constitutional reforms, told me that the Brothers are "fundamentalist in their ideology." He added, with a show of intellectual dispassion—Kamel is a political scientist, after all—"I'm not saying necessarily that they're terrorists; they want to establish a religious state based on their interpretation of the Koran and the Sharia."

And the Bush administration, crucially, had chosen to accept this narrative. After her speech at the American University of Cairo, a questioner had asked Condoleezza Rice about the Brotherhood. "We have not engaged the Muslim Brotherhood," she said flatly, "and . . . we won't." In fact, American diplomats had been in regular contact with Brotherhood officials over the years; Rice was declaring—in fact, making—a new policy, designed to mollify the regime at a time when the Bush administration was asking much of it. Then the Hamas victory in the Palestinian Territories had "clarified" our policy toward Islamists in general. In early 2007, after many of its leaders were arrested by security forces on the flimsiest of charges, the Brotherhood openly appealed to President Bush to intervene as he had on behalf of Ayman Nour. But the White House once again remained silent.

One former Bush administration official with a role in Middle Eastern policy insisted that there was "a battle under way for the soul of Islam," a battle which pitted the largely secular reformers whom the administration worked with against the fundamentalists. "The Muslim Brotherhood," this figure asserted, "holds seventh-century views on issues like women and other religions and their right to practice." Of course the White House was quite comfortable with the Wahhabi theocrats who ruled Saudi Arabia, and regularly lauded the democratic bona fides of the Shiite dogmatists who controlled the government of Iraq. What put the Muslim Brotherhood beyond the pale was that Hosni Mubarak had declared them his sworn enemy. We would throw our support behind the feeble secular forces, but not behind the Islamists, who actually commanded the loyalty of millions of Egyptians.

And in any case, the Brotherhood, or at least important elements of it, didn't seem remotely committed to a seventh-century reality. Ibrahim Hudaybi, who had sent me the late-night text message, had recently completed his master's degree in political science at the American University of Cairo. He volunteered for an interfaith group called Bridges. "I'm not always a Muslim Brotherhood member," he said to me. "Sometimes I'm a business consultant, sometimes I'm a football fan." Hudaybi was a pious young man, but he distinguished between "personal issues" like dress and family life, for which Sharia prescribed specific answers, and "social issues," which have to do with civil law, which he said must be determined politically rather than theologically. In any case, he said, "According to Islam, you are not allowed to impose your views on anyone." His mentor, a moderate party leader named Khairat el-Shater who had published a piece titled "No Need to Be Afraid of Us" in the Manchester *Guardian*, had been seized in the wave of arrests earlier that year. Hudaybi said that his worst nightmare was a scenario like that of Algeria in the early nineties, when Islamists had ultimately been provoked into a spasm of violence—though he hastened to add that the Brotherhood would never abandon the path of peace and politics.

Hudaybi arranged an interview for me with Muhammad Habib, the deputy supreme guide, and agreed to serve as interpreter. We met in the Brotherhood's central office, a dingy warren of rooms in a converted apartment. Habib was a former geology professor in his sixties who, like much of the group's leadership, had been in and out of jail. He described the Muslim Brotherhood agenda in strictly political terms: "Ending the state of emergency we are living in, freedom of launching political parties, freedom of speech, journalists saying whatever they want, freedom of peaceful demonstrations, having real judicial independence, having free and fair elections that manifest the people's will."

All this was easy enough to say. The Brotherhood has a history of offering pleasing but evasive answers to hard questions, and three scholars at the Carnegie Endowment had recently published a kind of open letter asking Islamists, and especially the

Brotherhood, to clarify their views on a number of these topics. They asked, "How would the Brotherhood determine when laws are in keeping with the general goals of the Sharia? If a law is adopted through democratic procedures that the Brotherhood feels violates the Islamic Sharia, will the movement restrict itself to the arts of democratic persuasion to change the result?" Habib answered these questions directly. In the case of laws touching on religious matters, he said, the parliament "could go to religious scholars and hear their opinion, but they are only advisory opinions. Parliament is not obligated to listen to these opinions." And should the legislature pass an "un-Islamic" law? "The People's Assembly has the absolute right in that situation," he said, "as long as it is elected in a free and fair election which manifests the people's will. And if any person disagrees, he can go to the constitutional court to decide whether the law is constitutional or not."

Mohammed Kamel warned me that while some Brotherhood leaders "pay lip service to democracy, women's rights and so on," the grass roots are deeply reactionary. "Lip service" hardly seemed to do justice to the depth of the convictions I had heard, but the allegation certainly sounded plausible. One night I drove out to the far northeastern edge of Cairo—a trip that took an hour and a half through the city's insane traffic—to meet with Magdy Ashour, a Brotherhood parliamentarian who, unlike many of his colleagues, was an electrician with a technical diploma. The neighborhood he represented, al-Nozha, turned out to be a squalid quarter of shattered buildings and dusty lanes. Ashour had established himself in what seemed to be the only substantial structure in the area, a half-completed apartment building; I walked through plaster dust and exposed wiring to reach his office. Ashour hurried in from the evening prayers. He was a solemn, square-jawed forty-one-year-old with short hair and unfashionable glasses, a brown suit and brown tie. He had, he said, grown up in the neighborhood and as a young man had often given the Friday sermon at the local mosque. He had joined the Brotherhood when he was twenty-three. He represented, in short, a very different wing of the organization from that of worldly young people like Ibrahim Hudaybi.

I asked Ashour if the recent spate of arrests had him worried, and he said that he did, indeed, fear that the state might be seeking an "open confrontation" with the Brotherhood. Mightn't that provoke the group's supporters to violence? Ashour answered by citing an aphorism he attributed to Hasan al-Banna: "Be like trees among the people: They strike you with stones, and you shower them with blessings." I had apparently touched on a deep core of conviction, for Ashour now embarked on a brief oration: "We would like to change the idea people have of us in the West," he said, "because when people hear the name Muslim Brotherhood, they think of terrorism and suicide bombings. We want to establish the perception of an Islamic group cooperating with other groups, concerned about human rights. We do not want a country like Iran, which thinks that it is ruling with a divine mandate. We want a government based on civil law with an Islamic source of law-making." If Magdy Ashour was a theocrat—much less a terrorist—he was a very crafty one.

Ashour confirmed what Gamal Hanafy and others had said to me, that few voters knew or cared much about political issues such as constitutional reform. He agreed to let me sit by his side one evening as he met with constituents. None of the dozen or so petitioners who were ushered into the tiny, bare cell of his office asked about the political situation, and none had any complaints about cultural or moral issues. There were the heartrending stories of people abused by the powerful, like the profoundly palsied young man confined to a wheelchair who sold odds and ends from a kiosk under a bridge and who had been thrown into the street, along with his meager goods, when a road-improvement project came through. (Ashour promised to go with him to the police station the following morning.) Mostly, though, people wanted help getting jobs. One ancient gentleman with a white turban and walking stick wandered in as if from the Old Testament. He was accompanied by his daughter and three-year-old granddaughter. His daughter had no husband, the patriarch explained, and needed a job. Ashour explained that since the woman had a business degree, she might find work in a private school.

The old man shook his head. "She must have a government job," he said. "She has three girls. I am too old to take care of her. She needs security." Ashour later explained to me that while a private job might pay ninety dollars a month and a public one only thirty-five dollars, the government job would carry a guaranteed fifteen-dollar pension, which felt like insurance against destitution. Only a government job was considered real; Ashour himself had worked as the superintendent for electric infrastructure for a portion of Cairo. Nasser had caught the bug of socialism half a century earlier, and the government continued to dominate the economy and to sap the energies needed for private initiative. Egypt's arthritic economy and its deeply corrupt public administration were much more salient problems for Ashour than was, say, debauchery on TV.

The Brotherhood is an international, pan-Islamic organization, but it has no Comintern, no central apparatus. In the less autocratic of the liberal autocracies, including Morocco and Yemen, Islamist parties enjoy a more or less equal status with secular parties, running for office under their own name and working with both the opposition and the ruling group. Leaders of Morocco's Islamist Justice and Development Party are chosen in open elections, while an internal quota system ensures a significant role for women. Jordan's Islamic Action Front is widely considered that country's most internally democratic and transparent political body. Many of these parties show evidence of generational cleavages, with young moderates squaring off against older conservatives.

This is one side of political Islam; another is Hamas, the Muslim Brotherhood affiliate in the Palestinian territories. For many years, Hamas, like Egypt's Muslim Brotherhood, operated as a quietist religious body, but in the 1990s it evolved into a fighting force fully prepared to use terrorism tactics against Israel. And few Islamists are prepared to criticize, much less repudiate, Hamas. Doing so, in fact, would only discredit them among voters. While the Brotherhood's views of Islamic law have been tempered over the years by harsh criticism from secular opponents of the regime, and by the political imperative of broadening the group's appeal, no such dynamic operates in the case of Israel, which people throughout the Arab world view as illegitimate and unjust. None of the Brotherhood figures I spoke with accepted Israel's right to exist as a matter of principle, or opposed terrorist attacks against it.

When I asked if the Brotherhood, should it take power, would be willing to recognize Israel, Muhammad Habib said, "We think that Israel is an aggressor state that has raped the land of the Arab people and Palestine. With all the massacres and the killing taking place, we should not speak about the hunter before speaking about the hunted."

I asked Habib if he approved of the killing of Israeli civilians in the name of Palestinian resistance. He said, "With the continuous crackdown and ongoing war launched by the Israeli army, which does not distinguish between civilians and non-civilians, you cannot speak about the Palestinians disregarding Israeli citizens."

Suicide bombers?

"If Israel stops its brutal attacks against the Palestinian people and the settlements are dismantled, this will never happen."

"Is that the answer to my question?"

"I think that Hamas is doing this as a reaction to the attacks of the Israeli army. If Israel refrains from attacking civilians, then of course Hamas should refrain from attacking civilians."

This was, of course, the final nail in the coffin so far as the Brotherhood's standing in official Washington went. Democracy promotion in the Bush White House was largely the property of neoconservatives such as Elliott Abrams, Michael Gerson, and Liz Cheney, for whom Israel was the supreme red line. Brotherhood officials, who knew nothing of such people and in any case had no interest in courting them, transgressed that line without a second thought.

In fact, the more worldly among the Brothers understand that Israel is a test just as Qutb is a test; they understand as well that the Western audience matters even if it doesn't vote. I heard the most nuanced view from Essam el-Erian, a clinical pathologist who is the head of the Brotherhood's political committee, a witty character who kept the television in his office tuned into the news and had a thick stack of daily papers piled up before him. El-Erian joked that with Mauritania having just completed a peaceful electoral transfer of power, Israel could no longer be considered the only democracy in the broader Middle East.

"Look," el-Erian said, without the vehemence the subject provoked in almost everyone else, "this is a historical and ideological and religious crisis. It cannot be solved in a few years. Every part in this conflict can be put forth for dialogue." El-Erian's own view was that "history shows that no Jewish state lasts more than sixty or seventy years." I said that I didn't find that a terribly reassuring lesson to have drawn from history. But el-Erian wished to distinguish between his ultimate expectations—and wishes—and his understanding of political reality. "Egypt is a state and Israel is a state," he said. "These two states are living together."

Like virtually all of his colleagues, el-Erian also urged me not to get too hung up on this or any other question of what the Brotherhood might do in some unimaginably remote future in which the regime had somehow relinquished its grip on power. "We can solve the problem of our society," he said, "to have democratic reform respected by Europeans and Americans, whatever happens to the Palestinians."

The Muslim Brotherhood is a peculiar, hybrid entity. It's technically a banned organization, though it operates openly. It constitutes far and away the largest source of political opposition in Egypt, and yet it has never been permitted to form a political party. Morocco's Justice and Development Party (PJD), by contrast, has operated as an autonomous political party since 1998, when the regime opened political participation to Islamist groups. The party accepts the king's title as commander of the faithful and acknowledges the supremacy of the monarchy. It has consciously molded itself into a party that can win votes even from religious moderates. The PJD supported a largely secular rewriting of Morocco's Family Code in 2003, and has refrained from, for example, campaigning to ban alcohol. The party leader, Saad Eddin al-Othmani, has compared the PJD to a European Christian Democratic Party, and makes a point of sharply distinguishing between political and religious sources of legitimacy. The ruling Islamist party in Turkey, known as the AKP, provides a yet more heartening example of the effects of political competition on Islamic parties. The AKP is firmly committed to democracy and economic modernization, and enjoys the strong support of both the Bush administration and European governments.

The Mubarak regime has invested a great deal in discrediting the Brotherhood as a legitimate political force, in the eyes both of Westerners and of secular Egyptians. The chief goal of the constitutional reform seems to have been prohibiting the Brotherhood from forming a political party in the foreseeable future. The fact that the amendment generated so little protest from either secular reformers or Western governments suggests that the regime has succeeded in making its case. But by going quietly off to jail, protesting abuses peacefully, and raising the level of lawmaking, the Brotherhood has refused to collaborate in its own diminishment, and instead has generally set an example of discipline and stoicism. A few prominent secular reformers have even put aside their longtime suspicions: Saad Eddin Ibrahim says that the time he spent talking with the Islamists in jail, and their performance in Parliament, has persuaded him that they are a positive force in Egypt.

In September 2007, the Brotherhood produced a draft platform—and it was not the document that the group's secular and Western backers had hoped for. Here the regime had every right to take credit. Important moderate figures such as Essam el-Erian were languishing in jail. The constant harassment and repression had only reinforced ancient habits of secrecy and opacity. Muhammad Habib insisted in an interview that the document had been produced after broad consultation within the group. An alternative story had it that various more liberal drafts had been circulated and then quashed by conservative leaders outside of Cairo, at which point a more regressive version had been quickly assembled, with no input either from progressives such as Al-Foutouh or from members of the parliamentary bloc. In any case, it sounded more like the NDP than like a political party—which the Brotherhood, of course, was not.

The draft platform, contrary to what Habib had told me, foresaw a council of clerics, elected from the faculty at conservative al-Azhar University, who would review legislation; their judgment would be binding on matters touching on Sharia, though otherwise merely advisory. This proposal, which had never before appeared in Brotherhood policy documents, was quickly seized on as proof that the group favored Iranian-style theocracy. The platform explicitly prohibited either women or members of the Coptic Christian minority from serving as Egypt's president. And despite its 128-page length, the draft platform was virtually silent on the relationship between the Brotherhood as a religious body and as an organ of political advocacy. There seemed not even to be the aspiration to compete on an equal footing with other political parties.

The publication of the draft platform was a fiasco for the Brotherhood. Egypt's state-run newspapers had a field day, citing the most reactionary passages as proof that the religious obscurantists had shown their true colors. Editorial commentary throughout the Middle East was highly critical. Human rights organizations and democracy activists, including some who had been sympathetic to the Brotherhood, were equally vehement. Scholars of the Middle East, such as Amr Hamzawy, one of the authors of the Carnegie paper, were discouraged: "The return to a focus on Sharia in the platform has led to positions fundamentally at odds with the civil nature of the state and full citizenship rights regardless of religious affiliation," he wrote.

But it wasn't only outsiders who were disgusted at the outcome of the deliberations; so were the moderates, the political pragmatists, and above all the younger generation within the Brotherhood. Over the previous year, young people, both men and women, had experienced a political coming-of-age amid the raucous demonstrations and the police paddy wagons. A secular leftist who called himself Ala Sayf wrote on his website of "this new breed of Islamists that reads blogs, watches al-Jazeera, sings *sha'bi* [popular] songs, talks about intense love stories and chants 'down with Mubarak.'" Some of the younger members had started up blogs of their own. And these blogs became a source of intense criticism of the draft platform. This in turn led to harsh rebukes from older members, and stubborn reassertions of the right to criticize. Such open discussion, not to mention such intellectual vigor, would have been unthinkable inside the NDP.

And the Brotherhood leaders felt the heat. Habib and others began to stipulate that the document was only a draft, that it was far from final. Habib sat for an interview on the Brotherhood's highly professional and unbuttoned English-language website, known as Ikhwanweb, in which he declared, despite the language of the document, that the judgment of the Religious Council was to be "advisory, not binding on any authority." As Amr Hamzawy observed, while the platform itself implied "a sense of regression," as the Islamists sought to keep hold of core constituencies, the ensuing brouhaha proved that "we are looking at a very dynamic movement" that airs "a plurality of opinions in an open way."

Amr Hamzawy and his coauthors, Marina Ottaway and Nathan J. Brown, put the matter plainly in another study on political Islam: "It would, of course, be much more reassuring, much more desirable, if the major political actors in the Middle East were secular organizations with impeccable liberal credentials and a clear track record of democratic politics. But liberal organizations capable of mobilizing large constituencies simply do not exist in Arab countries today. As a result, Islamist groups will remain the most important opposition force for the foreseeable future, whether or not secular Arabs and Western governments like it." What the authors ask of the Islamists themselves is that they confront the contradictions and the "gray areas" within their own agendas, and resolve them in ways consistent with the rise of a liberal civic order. What they ask of Western powers, and above all the United States, is that they recognize the important distinctions among and within Islamic movements, and support progressive, forward-thinking forces. The outcome of this internal battle for the soul of political Islam, they conclude, "will determine the future of political reform in many countries."

"Like it or not" offers a rather weak incentive for action. But there is also a more affirmative reason for engaging with Islamist groups. The real alternative to groups such as the Brotherhood is not, after all, secular reform, but religious extremism. The mod-

ern Brotherhood was born out of a split with the first generation
of jihadists; and it is the Islamists who present the most convinc-
ing alternate path for the alienated young people who become the
shock troops of fundamentalism. The Islamists have a credibility
no outsider, and certainly not the United States, could duplicate.
One scholar has likened relationships between political Islam
and extremism to that of the European left in the fifties and sixties with communism. We made the pragmatic decision to support the democratic left as a counterweight to the totalitarian left,
and it was a wise decision.

Think of the following contrast: the brutality of Egyptian prisons turned Ayman Zawahiri into a committed terrorist. On the
other hand, Muhammad Habib, who was jailed in 1981, in 1995
(for five years), and again in 2001, says that prison taught him
patience and afforded him time for spiritual reflection. "Because
it was a harsh experience," he says, "I became more determined
to face authoritarianism and tyranny." Turning to violence, he says,
was unimaginable. "The organization," he explained, "has immunity against violence and extremism through our education and our
texts." Ayman Zawahiri attacks the Brotherhood to this day with
the savage vitriol reserved for competitors for hearts and minds.

But the Brotherhood probably exaggerates that immunity.
How long will the next generation, primed by the Internet and
satellite news, put up with repression and paralysis? How long
before Ibrahim Hudaybi's nightmare of the Algerian scenario becomes reality? Would it really be so surprising if the Egyptian
people went from stoicism to confrontation? Is it so hard to think
of precedents? It may not be an act of realism but rather of
naïveté to once again put all our chips on "moderate" dictators
such as Hosni Mubarak. "The Faustian bargains of the pre-9/11
era have returned," writes Shadi Hamid, a Washington-based student of Middle East politics, "and, just as before, the risks of realist realignment are many."

The United States does not need to embrace the Muslim Brotherhood (nor does the Brotherhood need to be embraced by the United States). It does, however, need to acknowledge the group's centrality, its relevance, to Egypt's political future. Doing so would send a message to the Mubarak regime that it could no longer use the threat of political Islam as a bogey in the face of demands for reform. More important, it would send a message to the Arab street. Whether it is fair or not, our refusal to deal with Hamas and Hezbollah has made publics in the Islamic world dismiss the whole idea of democracy promotion. It has reinforced the belief that, for American policy-makers, Israel outweighs everything. An acknowledgment of the Brotherhood would show that the United States is willing to accept groups whose views on Israel and the Middle East it does not share. And to the Egyptian people it would send the message that the United States will not permit the Mubarak regime to decide who is and is not a legitimate player. Finally, it would make good the president's claim that Americans do not seek to "impose" or "export" democracy, but rather to nurture the shoots that poke up from local turf.

The Brothers, of course, scarcely need the support of the White House in order to enhance their popularity in Egypt— quite the contrary. They are not looking for American approval, and they are deeply suspicious of American designs in the world. At the same time, they are, like people all over the world, very curious about America itself. After the line of petitioners in Magdy Ashour's office cleared out, and I prepared to take my leave, he asked if he could pose some questions of his own. "I've heard," he said, "that even George Bush's mother thinks he's an idiot. Is that true?" And "Why did George Bush say that America is going on a Christian crusade against the Muslim people?" And, finally, "Is it true that the Jews control and manipulate the U.S. economy?" These are, alas, the kinds of questions—with the possible exception of the first—that people all over the Middle East ask.

Then Ashour said that he was thinking about visiting America. I asked how he could afford such an expensive journey, and he explained that the Brotherhood has offered each legislator one free trip anywhere in the world—a remarkable program for an organization said to be bent on returning Egypt to the Middle Ages. "I would," Ashour said, "like to see for myself."

8

Mali and the Feeble Democracies of Africa

Sometimes You *Can* Eat Dignity

On March 22, 1991, Moussa Traoré, the general who had ruled Mali since overthrowing his predecessor twenty-three years earlier, ordered his security forces to attack protesters who had taken to the streets to demand political freedom. Before the day was done, more than three hundred students and workers had been killed, many of them burned alive when a heavily occupied building was set aflame.

Mali is not a violent country; citizens were profoundly shocked and outraged by the massacre. The military decided to move against its leader. Four days later—these dates are graven in the country's collective memory—Amadou Toumani Touré, the head of Mali's commando unit, along with the chief of Traoré's personal security detail, informed the president that a mob, bent on mayhem, was surging up the hill from downtown Bamako. Traoré understood the coded language of the coup, and left without a struggle. This was not an unfamiliar script in Africa, but the next stage was: the officers joined with civic leaders to form an interim civilian government, which Touré agreed to head only until a president could be elected. Fourteen months later, he stepped aside in favor of Mali's first elected president, Alpha Oumar Konaré, an archaeologist and museum director—who in turn stepped aside after serving two terms.

Mali was considered such a political success story that in 1999, when then secretary of state Madeleine Albright was assembling the core group of the Community of Democracies, a sort of United Nations General Assembly for the world's democratic states, this woefully impoverished and landlocked nation was the first African country invited to join. (South Africa, Ghana, and Benin came on board soon thereafter.) The Community of Democracies has met every two years since 2001 on a different continent. The first meeting was in Warsaw, the next in Seoul, the third in Santiago—and the fourth, in November 2007, in Bamako. This constituted a sort of democratic benediction of Mali, and of Africa, almost half of whose 47 states were deemed sufficiently democratic to be invited to participate in the event. (Overall, 120 of the world's states were invited.)

Mali represented a relatively new type of state: the feeble democracy. This was something different from the Potemkin state that Larry Diamond had called the "electoral democracy," and Fareed Zakaria the "illiberal democracy." In Mali, a functioning democracy presided over crushing poverty—a phenomenon that would have seemed baffling to modernization theorists. And yet there were now so many such states that they could no longer be treated as the exception to some rule. Of the twenty-two countries at the bottom of the UNDP Human Development Index, characterized by "low human development," eight were deemed sufficiently democratic to be invited to Bamako. According to the annual Freedom House rankings, three of those bottom-dwelling countries are "free" and twelve "partly free." Though deeply impoverished democracies exist in Asia and Latin America, all of Africa's democracies are poor, and all twenty-two of those nations at the bottom of the Human Development Index are located in Africa. Mali was unusual only in the extreme disparity of its political and economic standing. Freedom House rated Mali as more democratic than India, while the UN listed it four slots above the bottom (which is two better than the year before).

᾿ Democracy in Mali has plainly not "delivered": After sixteen years, virtually the entire country still functions at the subsistence level. Yet that hasn't discredited democracy itself. No matter how critical they are of the regime, many Malians still speak with great pride of the events of 1991. In 2001, in the midst of a recession, 70 percent of respondents to a poll rejected the idea of a return to one-party rule. How had democracy, and faith in democracy, persisted? Malians themselves tend to resort to historical and cultural explanations. One often hears how the nobles of the Empire of Mali met in 1236 to draw up a sort of Magna Carta whose first article read, "The human person is sacred and inviolable." Mali is a nation-state in the European sense. "The nation already existed before the state was created," as Seydou Sessoúma, the president's spokesman, puts it. "The communities learned for centuries to spend time with each other, to mingle." And over the centuries the country's chief ethnic groups—Ful, Bambara, Songhoi—gained and lost control over the various kingdoms of West Africa. This is said to have introduced the principle of orderly, or at least inevitable, succession.

Malians often speak of *cousinage*, a word used throughout the larger region that conveys the idea of consanguinity across different ethnic groups. *Cousinage* establishes a neighborly, jokey relationship among groups otherwise separated from one another by language, tradition, and often livelihood, and thus blunts sharp edges. Mali is a notably calm country, and Bamako a calm and peaceable capital. Security is so light that when my taxi driver accidentally pulled into the courtyard of the president's administrative headquarters—a shooting offense on much of the continent—the watchman on duty barely bestirred himself from his guardhouse to ask that we park outside. Malians celebrate ancient tribal combat, but not modern warfare. The only statue of a soldier in Bamako's many traffic circles was put up by the

French after World War I. The other *ronds-points* feature elephants or hippos.

For all the discontent that comes of dismal public services and chronic unemployment, a striking politesse seems to govern daily transactions. If you plan to pass a car on the road, the driver in front will turn on his left blinker light until it is safe to pass, at which point he will switch to the right. One almost never witnesses the browbeating that all over Africa reminds the little man that he is at the whim of the big. Nor is there much bowing and scraping to be seen. A surprising sense of equality, or perhaps of essential human dignity, seems to reign: I was delighted to find that the guy who came to fix the air conditioner in my hotel room, or the watchman on duty outside the house of an official I was interviewing, expected to shake my hand.

And despite deep frustration over the lack of opportunity, especially among the mass of urban youth, even the humblest citizens seem proud of Mali's democracy, and feel that it has brought them very real benefits. One afternoon I spoke to a group of village elders in the Dogon region east of Bamako. After we had talked about the harvest, and the local town council, and the price of crops, I asked a man who had been sitting quietly all the while what he thought democracy was about. The man's name was Amaguimé Dolo. He pondered for a moment. "In earlier times," he said, "you couldn't go and speak to a man in an office."

"Because you were afraid?"

"Yes, because we were afraid. A peasant would not have the opportunity to speak to a functionary. Now you can go and speak as you wish. Democracy has erased the fear and given free expression to everyone. So I think democracy is a good thing."

Perhaps, in a strange inversion of modernization theory, Mali is democratic not despite its poverty but because of it. Neither Aristotle nor Lipset would have predicted that a country consisting almost wholly of the poor would form a democratic republic, but perhaps *cousinage* flourishes best in a place where scarcely anyone leaves home or undergoes a drastic change in status. Mali's *rentier* class is relatively small. The "ins" are not that much better off than the "outs." What's more, Mali has been spared the "resource curse." Most African nations endowed with sizable deposits of oil, including Nigeria, Angola, and Sudan, have descended into tyranny or anarchy, or oscillated between them. The same is true of countries with great mineral wealth, such as the Democratic Republic of the Congo. The state becomes a prize to capture, and politics the deadly business of securing one's grip. Democracy has proven to be almost impossible to maintain in such a setting. Mali, by contrast, has no source of concentrated wealth at all. Though the country is quite corrupt, the state is a prize of far more modest value. And in the unforgiving climate of the Sahel, wealth itself is understood as transitory. As Ibrahim Ag Youssef, a scholar and former UNDP consultant, notes, "The only valid insurance is provided by how much one has invested in people, the least investment being respect for the poor and guarding oneself from being haughty."

So culture matters; but so do politics, and political choices. The decision of Amadou Toumani Touré (or ATT, as he is called), to abjure the power he might easily have chosen to hold was virtually unprecedented in African history. What came next was no less important. In the summer of 1991, the interim government called a constitutional convention, which drew up a highly progressive constitution with extensive guarantees of political and press freedom. The constitution requires the public funding of political parties; it also stipulates, remarkably, that anyone who applies for a license to operate an FM radio station can go ahead and provisionally operate one if they don't hear back from the state within three weeks. In November of that year, the government convened a Convention on Trade and Industry that drew up new rules for the transition from a socialist to a market-oriented economy.

President Konaré, who had gained stature by publishing a weekly that called for democratic reform during the period of protests, was elected president in 1992 in a ballot generally considered to be honest. Konaré, though much admired abroad, was scarcely a heroic figure. His privatization of Mali's state-run industries was widely denounced as a Russian-style fire sale to cronies. He allowed corruption within the government to fester. He used state-run media to glorify his own reign. The parliamentary elections of 1997 were so grossly rigged that the constitutional court, whose investigation, I was told, turned up 117 types of fraud, ordered a new ballot, which the opposition then boycotted. (This was, however, the first instance on the continent of a court overturning an election and ordering a new one.) Thereafter, the principal opposition party refused to recognize the legitimacy of Konaré's rule; its members would not even address Konaré as "President." Mali's schools were so dreadful that students remained more or less permanently on strike.

And yet, for all that, Konaré handled the precious legacy he had been given with real care. When he was first elected, he included several opposition members in his cabinet, explaining that it was his "deepest conviction that democracy does not work well without an opposition." And he rarely used the fullest extent of his powers. The greatest threat Konaré faced was a rebellion by the nomadic Touareg people of the north, which had been simmering since 1989. By 1994, the rebels threatened to take their patch of desert and secede. "Everyone recommended to Konaré to seek a military solution," says Gaoussou Dramo, then one of the president's chief aides. "He was the only one resisting; he said, 'I'm going to reinforce security, but I'm not going to war.'" Konaré reached an intriguing solution with the rebels: Rather than grant them the autonomy they sought, and which both Traoré and ATT had promised to offer, he drew up a decentralization plan that would, at least in theory, push power down from Bamako to 703 local "communes" nationwide. The rebellion abated, and Konaré established a new system of local government, with mayors and town councils.

ATT had, in the meantime, enhanced his considerable popularity by running a foundation that focused on Mali's youth. He won a hard-fought presidential election in 2002. ATT is a smallish, muscular, energetic man. He is a pragmatist and problemsolver with little interest in either ideology or high-flown rhetoric. He has run and served as an independent, and has roped all but the most prickly or adversarial of the country's parties into a "consensus," which can be counted on to support his initiatives. There is, in fact, very little difference of opinion in political circles over issues of development or investment; Tiébilé Dramé, a sharp critic who leads one of the few opposition parties that has refused to join the consensus, cites as his chief policy critique the president's failure to capitalize on Mali's diaspora, which supplies more capital than all sources of foreign aid combined. ATT presides over a hybrid economy whose planning bureaucrats still issue five-year plans projecting galloping growth rates—though the impetus is supposed to come from the private sector. He has focused much of his economic effort on building the roads and bridges and power lines his country so desperately lacks.

ATT has preserved the peace by hewing to his predecessor's soft line on the Touaregs, who have increasingly been infiltrated by religious extremists from Algeria and elsewhere. He quietly welcomes the small squads of American Special Forces troops who run dragnets through the north, looking for Al Qaeda supporters. This costs him no political support, since Malians seem to prefer having Americans skulking around than, say, Libyans. He is, however, widely criticized for trying to muddle through a genuine threat to Mali's future. Mohammad Mahmoud, a Touareg activist in Bamako, warns that even in major urban areas such as

Timbuktu, the government is steadily losing ground to the foreign fundamentalists, known as Salafists, who build health clinics and madrasas and who teach that Islam is no respecter of national boundaries. Mahmoud says that his pleas to the regime to provide social services in the region to counter the Salafist threat have fallen on deaf ears, while the regime looks to handpicked leaders with no local following.

Critics such as Tiébilé Dramé insist that ATT is far less popular than he appears, and has had to depend on electoral fraud to succeed. The 2007 election, in which the president was returned to power, was indeed marked by widespread fraud: the president of Mali's constitutional court concluded that election officials had falsified tallies and expelled monitors from opposition parties from polling places. Yet just as Konaré modeled democratic behavior by imposing limits on his own authority, so ATT has been willing to shine a bright light on the doings of the state. While serving as interim president he had visited Canada and had been much impressed by its highly independent auditor's office. He hadn't had the time to establish such a position in Mali, and Konaré had been quite content to make do with a toothless office under his own control. But almost as soon as he returned to power, ATT pushed for a Canadian-style auditor-general. When parliament objected, the president threatened it with dissolution, an act permitted under Mali's constitution. The law passed, and Mali now has an auditor-general—a Malian who worked for Ernst & Young in Paris—who operates independently of the president and of parliament, who is empowered to bring potential criminal cases to the attorney general, and who each year issues a report exposing the failures of the public fisc. The 2006 report, which was distributed to donors and released to the press, showed that $1.8 billion, about one tenth of the national budget, had been lost, wasted, or stolen. The report pointed directly to failures in specific departments; much of the Agriculture Ministry in a major provincial city wound up behind bars.

Adam Thiam, the office's spokesman, says, "I think ATT had no idea how powerful an independent auditor could be." International donors have said that they will reduce assistance unless the office's recommendations, which include both systematic reform and criminal prosecution, are instituted. Mali will thus have imposed stricter standards of financial probity on itself than apply to almost any other country in Africa. Thiam himself says that he wonders if the office won't do more harm than good. But, he says, "the government has done nothing to strangle us. They could have cut our budget, they could have blocked investigations, they could have seized on whatever mistakes we made. But they haven't."

Mali thus has both a culture that makes democracy possible and a political leader committed to the principles of democratic rule. But in between the bedrock of values and the superstructure of presidential behavior lies the whole world of political institutions and practices. Democracies become "consolidated" only when democratic principles infuse these institutions and practices. Mali has, for example, more than one hundred political parties. But the parties are not membership bodies, as in the West, but simply vehicles whereby an individual can fund his political ambitions. Few have platforms or even policies; few exist beyond the confines of Bamako. And they cease to function once the candidate in question is elected. Elections bear almost no relation to the business of governing. The consequence, as one official of a Western democracy-promotion body explained to me, is that "people have no confidence in the process; they treat the whole thing as a kind of drama." Voter turnout averages 20 to 30 percent, and is lowest in big cities, where voters are not being marshaled to the polls by the village chief.

Tierno Diallo, a consultant on local governance with whom I traveled to eastern Mali, explained his country's predicament as a crisis of authority. "There are three levels to our society," Diallo observed as we drove through the blazing heat across the bleached landscape near Mali's border with Burkina Faso. "At the political level, the colonial system completely replaced the old authority of the chief. At the religious level, the system pretty much left traditional authorities alone. But the problem lies at the socio-economic level, the level of relations between people and state structures. The problem is one of representation. Who represents the interests of the people? The political parties just fight among themselves, and the politicians lose interest as soon as they get elected. There's no party which represents workers, or teachers, or farmers. When we had a crisis over the price of cotton a few years ago, no one said a word in parliament; no one proposed any kind of solution."

This deep problem of representation is scarcely peculiar to Mali. In *Democratic Experiments in Africa*, Bratton and van de Walle note that few parties operate outside of the capital and major cities; parties are "differentiated less by ideology or programmatic concerns than by the narrow interests of clientelist networks, typically organized around an individual." This is what is known as the "neopatrimonial" pattern—the pattern of big man and dependent client, rather than of elected representative and constituent. The big man, as Tierno Diallo puts it, says, "You've got a problem; come to me. I'll help you." But systematic problems never evoke systematic solutions—save whatever comes down from above.

Mali's national political institutions are weak. But national politics is not the only avenue of representation. The decentralization process that Konaré fostered sparked great hopes in Mali—in the Touareg region, but elsewhere, too. Decisions about local needs, whether for schools or health care or road repair, would no longer be made by the prefect and subprefect, who represented the central government, but by mayors and town councils, in collaboration with federal ministries. Moreover, each commune would retain about three quarters of its local tax revenue for its own purposes. The euphoria didn't last long, as it became clear that the funds available to localities would be very modest—normally about $25,000 to $50,000 a year. And, inevitably, the old neopatrimonial patterns intruded on the new relationship between local and central government. As Diallo, who advises localities on these issues, says, "You can have a plan, you can write it out chapter by chapter, but the ministries are going to give money only to the ones which are in their interest to back. What does it mean to say that you have the right to make these decisions at the local level if you don't have the resources?"

Certainly there was no getting around the modesty of the enterprise. I went with Diallo to Sanga, the capital of the famed Dogon region, 450 miles or so east of Bamako. The mayor, Daniel Guerro, a middle-aged gentleman who was principal of the middle school in Sanga, explained to me that he was responsible for fifty-six villages with a population of twenty-four thousand spread out over eight hundred square kilometers—most of it arid scrub. He and his twenty-three counselors had about $35,000 at their disposal. That was scarcely enough money for even modest development projects; and the government in Bamako lacked the funds to supply the commune's needs. Only a few villages have health clinics. And while President Konaré had decreed a decade earlier that every village would have a school, the Sanga commune had only thirteen elementary schools and six middle schools. Still, school attendance was increasing, especially among girls, who traditionally did not go to school at all. "It's progressing," said Mayor Guerro. "Before, people thought the woman is only for marriage and preparing meals. But today it has changed a lot."

I went out into the fields behind the town and talked to three women who were cultivating an onion patch. We stood under a big spreading tree; a baby wrapped in a blanket lay on the ground near us, and the women took turns mothering it. The men, they explained, harvested the millet, while women engaged in *marechage*—the cultivation of crops in raised beds that can be immersed in water. None of the women had been to school, though they insisted that all of their children—including the girls—attended school, which may have owed to the fact that they lived in the village beside the commune's biggest town. Amadamo Dolo, a voluble woman in a bright yellow dress, said, "We regret that we didn't get to go to school as kids, so now we work hard so we can afford to send our children to school. We don't want them to have to work the fields the way we do." But she and the others knew of children who had gotten diplomas from middle school—the terminal academic stage, so far as they knew—and yet had not been able to find jobs.

I had been told that women voted in much larger numbers than men, and indeed, all three women had voted in the recent elections for the commune council. I asked how they had decided whom to vote for. Did their husbands tell them? Absolutely not, said Amadamo. "We didn't know who to vote for, so we formed a little group, and after the fourth prayer of the day we met and talked about it right under this tree where we're standing now."

"How did you decide who to choose?"

"We voted for the candidate who tilled the ground like we do, because we thought he could help the peasants."

I asked how they had learned about politics. I had heard a great deal about Mali's network of private radio stations, which reach 89 percent of the country's population. But no, the radio was on only when they were out in the fields. Dogal Temé, a younger woman in a white dress, said she had learned about the national elections from television. I asked how that had happened. "I often watch, but I don't speak French," she said. (The women spoke Dogon, which was in turn translated into French for me.) "But I watch with one of the schoolchildren, and she explains what the president is talking about, what his objectives are."

"What do you think of ATT?"

"I like him. He is good for women."

"In what way?"

"He has made Caesarean operations available for free." This was true, as I was later told. The women had also seen ATT, who spends much of his time in the countryside, and had been impressed by his fine words and very modest command of Dogon. I asked if the word *democracy* meant anything to them. "We know it is something good, and good for the people," said Amadou. "But I don't really know any more about it."

I walked between the onion patches and the millet into Sanga Ogoli, the quarter of the village farthest from the town and its bustling market. A Dogon village looks like a mud-walled phalanx until you get close enough to see where the outer wall has been pierced by alleyways, which wind toward the center. At the heart of Sanga Ogoli was a plaza with an odd layer-cake structure called *la case à palabre*—"discussion house." The *case*, made of alternating bands of earth and straw, is about eight feet thick, with a four-foot clearance above the ground, the whole structure being supported by thick stone columns. The men sit either beneath the *case* or on its shady side; women may only observe from a distance. The reason the *case* is so low to the ground, I was later told, is that, having observed that people rise to their full height when they become agitated, the Dogon designed a conversational space that forces participants to remain seated. Here, too, one sees the cultural origins of Mali's civilized discourse.

It was here that I spoke to the village elders, who were sitting in the dirt in the shade of the *case*. I asked what sort of issues they looked to the local government to resolve. "You see the road to Sanga, which is so bad," said Tonio Dolo, an old gentleman in a white prayer cap to whom the others deferred. (In fact, the twenty-eight-mile drive on the shattered dirt path from the main road to the top of the Dogon plateau had taken almost two hours.) "When it becomes even worse, we speak to the mayor, and ask him to go to the government to fix it."

"And does he act on your concerns?"

"He almost always does what he can; when he doesn't act, we understand that many things are not in his power."

I asked if they felt that life had gotten better since the time of Moussa Traoré.

"Democracy has made things better," said Tonio. "Before, if you went into the market without your ID, the soldiers would take your motorcycle away from you. You had to give it to them; you had no choice. Now it's not like that; the soldiers are much more relaxed."

I asked if the economy had gotten better, but no one seemed to think so. They lived hand-to-mouth now, as they did then.

It was true, in fact, that the ancient pre-Islamic patterns of Dogon village life remained largely intact. The village chief still owned the best land, and the farmers still gave him a portion of their harvest. But much had changed. Tourism in the Dogon region had created new opportunities. The status of women was finally beginning to rise: one of the men said that he now understood that he had been mistreating women and, after some resistance, had come to welcome new practices such as the education of girls. But for both the men and the women I talked to, democracy, or politics, had some value independent of whether it spurred development. The women voted, and talked and thought about their vote; the old men no longer felt quite so helpless before anyone in a uniform or a tie. Even humble people could make choices—and could hope that the choices mattered. It wasn't very much, but it seemed to matter to them.

Bania Touré, a government official who in 1999 was serving as political attaché in Mali's embassy in Washington, notes proudly that Mali was the second country the United States invited to join the Community of Democracies—after Poland and before India, Chile, South Korea, and the Czech Republic. The American organizers of the body aren't quite so sure about the sequence, but there's no question that Mali was the first African country asked to join. Nelson Mandela was then president of South Africa, which would have been the logical representative of the continent, but Mandela was skittish about the organization. South Africa identified with its revolutionary brethren, a group very much including Cuba and China, more than it did with the democratic West and its African allies, some of whom had supported the apartheid regime. Though Konaré and much of Mali's governing elite had been trained behind the iron curtain, they were delighted to be recognized as democratic icons. At the community's initial meeting in Warsaw, Mali put itself forward as the site of the first African meeting.

The Bush administration had initially treated the Community of Democracies (CoD) with the same studied neglect it accorded all the Clinton administration's legacies. But a democracy-promoting administration could scarcely ignore the world's only conclave of democratic states; and Condoleezza Rice had attended the meeting in Santiago, Chile, in 2005. Rice was expected to come to Bamako as well; so, it was said, would Bernard Kouchner, France's dynamic and glamorous new foreign minister. The announcement by the U.S. State Department that owing to the press of business, and so on, Rice would be sending John Negroponte, her number two, set off a domino effect that toppled not only Kouchner but every other foreign minister in the world, right down to that of Mali's yet more humble neighbor Niger. This was a big disappointment, not only for Mali but for the American NGOs that remained in many ways the driving force of the CoD. It was, to be fair, a lot harder to get to Bamako than it was to Lisbon, the site of the next meeting, and it was not nearly as much fun to stay there.

The fourth ministerial conference of the Community of Democracies convened in mid-November in Bamako's International Convention Center, a complex of stupendous white meeting halls set in a vast plaza—the Martian aesthetic that is China's signal architectural contribution to Africa. The opening ceremony included much dancing and singing, and speeches by Mali's foreign minister and by ATT, who cited both the covenant of the nobles of 1236 and the 2003 law establishing the auditor-general's office as a sign of Mali's unswerving commitment to democratic principles. In between came remarks by a number of luminaries, including both John Negroponte and John Danilovich, head of the Millennium Challenge Corporation, which had recently made a $461 million grant to Mali. This was a remarkably candid acknowledgment of the American role in both founding the CoD and driving it forward.

The Bush administration had done its bit to poison the well, insisting that both Afghanistan and Iraq be included—and not merely as "observers" like Nigeria or Egypt, but as full members. (In any event, neither country sent a delegation.) This directive sent a clear message that Washington would demand an exemption for its own clients from the moderately rigorous standards applied to everyone else. Otherwise, however, the United States played a very modest role. In the closed meetings in which national delegations hammered out the "Bamako Declaration," the American representative sat silent (even as the Egyptian, though only an observer, lodged one objection after another to clauses laying out the obligations of democracies). A Canadian diplomat noted with some surprise that the United States had recruited Canada to join its Asia Pacific Democracy Forum so as to avoid the (correct) impression that Washington had called it into being. He took it as a small but telling sign that the Bush administration had finally come to recognize that democracy ought not be promoted as an American brand.

The theme of the conference was one of piercing relevance to Mali and to Africa—"Democracy, Development, and Poverty Reduction." The premise was not only that democratic states had to produce prosperity for their citizens but that, in fact, they would do so far more reliably than would autocratic ones. Each of the

CoD conferences had concluded with a final statement laying out a set of principles and recommendations; the Bamako Declaration asserted that "democracies have embedded institutional advantages incontestably favorable to sustainable development." This was so because such states "provide political incentives for governments to respond to the needs and demands of the people, allow for more informed and extensive policy dialogue, are more adaptable, and create necessary checks and balances on government power." In order for democracies to work effectively, the declaration went on, states needed "well functioning political parties," "checks and balances in government," and "an effective, efficient and responsive public sector." States needed to decentralize power and confront corruption, respect human rights treaties, develop independent governance audits, welcome domestic and international election observers, and carve out a space for civil society.

The example of places like Mali proved that even the poorest countries could become, and remain, democratic; but these places scarcely demonstrated that democracy provided more tangible benefits than other forms of government. A number of Latin American states, including Venezuela, Bolivia, Peru, and Argentina, had suffered severe losses of credibility when democratic regimes had failed to lift citizens out of poverty; the first three had reverted, to one degree or another, to populist dictatorships. And Asia was full of fast-growing autocracies—not just tiny Singapore, but midsize Vietnam and giant China, too. In Taiwan and South Korea, democracy had arrived only after a middle class developed under an authoritarian regime began to demand political rights—precisely according to the dictates of modernization theory.

In *The Democracy Advantage*, a 2005 study for the Council on Foreign Relations, Morton H. Halperin, Joseph T. Siegle, and Michael M. Weinstein take on the theory that autocracy is an economically rational choice for poor countries. Comparing democratic and autocratic nations with per capita incomes below $2,000, they find that economic growth rates from 1960 to 2001 were virtually identical. This hardly demonstrated a "democracy advantage," but the authors argue that since some of the worst dictatorships fail to report economic data, the figures for this group were artificially inflated. More persuasively, they look to social indicators rather than merely economic ones, writing, "Citizens of democracies live longer, healthier and more productive lives, on average, than those in autocracies." Thus citizens of Ghana live much longer than those in Guinea; a far larger fraction of children go to school in the Philippines than in Indonesia (which only in the last few years has made an abrupt transition to democracy). For this reason, the authors point out, democracies significantly outperform economically comparable autocracies on the UNDP Human Development Index.

This is so for the reasons that the Bamako Declaration spells out, and for some others as well. The authors note that politicians in democracies must respond to the wishes of voters, and to the civic groups that champion the interests of citizens; checks and balances "avoid the devastating consequences of radical policy choices made by an exclusive set of individuals"; limited government allows private initiative to flourish; the free marketplace of ideas increases the likelihood that sound policies will be adopted and that sound practices will filter down through the state apparatus; transparency in public behavior leads to greater accountability.

The theory of the democratic advantage, though, raises several concerns. First, the line separating wobbly democracies from wobbly autocracies can be quite blurry. The authors of *The Democracy Advantage* describe Angola as an uncertain democracy and the Democratic Republic of the Congo as a despotic state. These two states have more or less flipped categories since the book was written—but with little noticeable effect on economic prospects. In fact, both are effectively kleptocracies. In Angola, a tiny political and business elite controls the immense wealth and power that come from the country's exploding oil industry, virtually none of which has trickled down to towns and villages still prostrated by a decade of savage civil war. The DRC now has a democratically elected government, but it is powerless before— indeed, a participant in—the violent scramble for mineral and agrarian resources that pits ethnic militias against one another, and against the national army. How much does it matter that the Congolese, unlike the Angolans, have chosen their president through an internationally supervised election, that they sport an obstreperous press and clashing political parties? Not at all, to the desperate and hapless peasants who flee deeper and deeper into the forests of North Kivu to escape marauding bands.

The authors also dismiss China and the East Asian "tigers" as a giant aberration, or point to the number of democratic attributes these authoritarian states evince, as if they succeed because they are democratic despite themselves. This is too easy. The success of the "Confucian" countries also demonstrates that certain cultures—and not just the Northern European ones built around what Max Weber called a Protestant ethic—are well adapted to succeed in a market system, just as peaceful and cohesive cultures such as that of Mali make democracy easier to adopt and to sustain.

Finally, democracies now vastly outnumber autocracies (eighty-nine to fifty, with fifty-four "partly free" nations in between, according to the 2003 Freedom House survey cited in *The Democracy Advantage*). Non-democracies constitute a dwindling set, at least outside the Middle East. That being so, the distinction between the two groups matters less than the differences among democracies. How democratic do you have to be before the "advantage" kicks in? And which democratic attributes weigh more heavily than the others? Halperin and his coauthors point to studies showing the relative importance of "accountability institutions," as well as press freedom and the protection of property and other economic rights.

If democracies really do have "embedded institutional advantages" with regard to development, as the Bamako Declaration maintains, then the central question is "How can we deepen fledgling or brittle democracies so as to advance the cause of development?" And this was indeed the chief subject of both the Bamako Declaration and the CoD conference. One roundtable discussion featured Joseph Siegle, the development economist who had done the research for *The Democracy Advantage*. Siegle laid out his case, which of course encountered little resistance in this setting, and then an oddly charming discussion ensued. The experience of trying to harness democratic institutions for economic development gave everyone in the room a common foundation—as if they were all, say, model train fanciers.

The Lithuanian vice minister of foreign affairs said that in his experience the key issue was connecting growth to poverty reduction, and that this in turn required broad public engagement—so that, for example, the public would demand a more honest and effective civil service. The Tanzanian talked about the difficulty of balancing long-term needs with the imperative to validate democracy by showing quick improvements. The state secretary of Mongolia, speaking excellent French, spoke of how his country had used the UN's Millennium Development Goals to guide the painful transition from Marxist dogma to democracy and free markets. The South African said, "Democracy by itself is not enough. We need to find the economic formula which will lead not only to growth but to shared growth"—which her country had not yet managed to do. The problem was not one of political organization, she said, but of "human capital development." The South Korean, intriguingly, criticized the argument for the "Asian values" that Singapore prime minister Lee Kwan Yew and others had long pushed—the claim that collectivist Confucian values offer an alternate paradigm to democratic individualism. South Korea's experience, he said, proved the opposite, for his country had taken off economically only after democratic rule replaced dictatorship. But, he added modestly, "I'm not sure if our case can be applied to other states."

Talking to delegates and to representatives of NGOs, one felt a generalized mood of hopefulness. There was more democracy in more places, including places where democracy wasn't supposed to take root. I asked Paul Graham, head of the South Africa–based Institute for Democracy, if he worried that the current wave of democratization on the continent would turn out to be a flash in the pan. "There is a general sense of moving forward," he said. Democracy was becoming the norm in virtually every region in Africa, save the Horn, where Somalia, Eritrea, and Ethiopia seemed determined to starve and bludgeon one another into submission. Even countries such as Rwanda and Uganda constituted more or less benevolent dictatorships. More and more leaders eschewed "ideological tub-thumping." Economic growth was also becoming normal—though largely owing to the rising price of commodities and the burgeoning role of China.

At the same time, Graham said, "Do parliaments have the capacity and the will to operate independently? Almost nowhere." The same was true of electoral commissions. Only a few countries had developed a thriving enough private sector that leaders felt they had an alternative to clinging to power, and that elites felt that they could look to the marketplace rather than to the levers of state. And African countries remained "such tough places for the middle class," Graham said, that brain drain felt irreversible. Democracy was expanding rather than deepening.

Even the expansion looked far from inevitable. The year before, Nigeria had staged a presidential election so transparently fraudulent that it had been stricken from the list of participants at the conference and reduced to "observer" status. Two months after the conference, Kenya, one of the most stable and respected states in Africa, would plunge into chaos and bloodshed after President Mwai Kibaki apparently changed vote tallies rather than accept defeat in his reelection bid. Kenya suddenly regressed into tribal warfare, with Kibaki's Kikuyu supporters and the Luo backers of his rival, Raila Odinga, slaughtering one another in the streets. The mayhem seemed to vindicate the conventional view that Africa just wasn't ready for democracy. And yet only a few years earlier, the two men had joined together, despite tribal affiliations, to oust a deeply unpopular and corrupt regime. And in countries including Senegal, Ghana, and Zambia, incumbents had stepped down after losing elections. Democracy could work, and often did work, in Africa, but leaders who betrayed democratic promises provoked much more volatile passions in Africa than in regions not so desperate and impoverished.

Democracy was no mere façade in Africa; but neither was it a miracle cure. In real life, the relationship between democracy and development was indirect and complex; they were joined not by a transmission belt but by a confusing tangle of wires. Culture mattered, and so did history. The gaudiest democratic institutions, like elections, often made the least difference with regard to development and poverty reduction, while the ones that really mattered, like the regard for law and legal authority, evolved the most slowly. Look at Mali: here was a country with one of the more vibrant democracies on the continent, and at sixteen years old one of the relative veterans; and yet it still lagged behind Chad and the DRC on the UN Human Development Index.

You could argue, in fact, that history and geography had conspired to ensure Mali's impoverishment. The empire of Mali lay at the heart of the great trade route linking North Africa, with its salt and spices, to the Atlantic, with its slaves and cola nuts. Then the European powers replaced the desert caravans with the Atlantic trade route. With no outlet to the sea, no resources, and endless swaths of arid terrain, Mali became a sparsely settled land of subsistence farmers and herders.

It's also true that the authoritarian socialism Mali practiced for the first two decades after the French left made a bad situation even worse. The country experienced negative growth in eight of ten years during the 1980s. Its already humble exports shriveled. Despite an ancient tradition of textile design and manufacture—you can see the samples in the national museum—Mali now exports cotton, but no finished cloth. It exports mangoes, but not, for example, mango jam. Most farmers grow millet or sorghum, and use whatever revenue they earn to buy essentials. Mali has made some strides since Moussa Touré was toppled, in regard both to economic growth and to such social indicators as immunization and the education of girls, but the progress has been painfully slow.

After the session on democracy and development, I spoke to one of the panelists, Guy Darlan, an elegant and eloquent World Bank official from the Central African Republic. Mali was stuck in place, he said. "On education, they're doing all the right things: they're training teachers, they're increasing access for girls. They're trying so hard, it's almost disarming to see the poor results." Mali ranked dead last in the world in every educational category save number of children per classroom, where Chad was even worse. Mali has the lowest rate of school attendance and graduation in Africa—a stupefying achievement, given how many African countries have seen their school systems upended by war. But Mali is so big and so sparsely populated that most villages can draw on only their own resources; the children can't go to school in the next village over. At the same time, the population was still growing at 3 percent a year, wiping out whatever gains the country made. Population growth also increased pressure on the land, while desertification reduced the stock of arable property. The lack of access to the sea doomed the export economy. It was "the curse of geography," said Darlan, compounded by the curse of demography. Of course there was plenty of human error to go around. "It's remarkable how effective they are in establishing the formal institutions," Darlan said, "but there's never enough substance to them." But he was not really inclined to find fault. "Maybe it's too early," he reflected. "Maybe we're being impatient. At least the Malian people don't seem to be getting impatient about democracy."

Perhaps democracies really do have "embedded institutional advantages" with regard to development, and thus more democracy would produce more development. But the relationship is so slow and indirect that it doesn't *feel* very true. And this in turn opens the way for competing claims, though you don't hear much about them in Bamako. The most compelling among the alternatives is China. Over the last three decades, China has grown at an astounding 9 percent a year without benefit of democracy. And its citizens have largely accepted the trade-off. To autocratic regimes everywhere, China holds out the promise of keeping citizens satisfied, or at least complacent, without having to cede any political authority.

While China does not promote its brand of authoritarian capitalism as explicitly as the United States promotes democracy, it has becoming increasingly aggressive about offering an alternative to the Western model—and above all, in Africa. China has become a major investor in Africa's oil states, including Sudan, Nigeria, and Angola, and such mineral-rich states as Zambia and the Democratic Republic of the Congo. China is now the chief trading partner, and chief investor, in many African counties. And it supplies aid and investment on terms very different from the West. China pays a premium to lock up guaranteed access to resources, and then expects the recipient government to use much of that revenue to hire Chinese construction firms to build immense infrastructure projects.

China is officially agnostic about the choices its beneficiaries make. Indeed, China's Africa Policy, published in 2006, offers "a new type of strategic partnership" that "respects African countries' independent choice of the road of development." Unlike Western donors, China makes no demands about transparency, honesty, or democratic engagement. But its typical pattern of investment concentrates vast wealth and power in the hands of elites, and then supports a top-down, heavily engineered program of economic development. This model of development has worked miracles in China, but there is good reason to fear that it will not work nearly so well in ill-governed, corrupt, fractious African countries. Yet as China's growing political influence in Angola, Sudan, Zimbabwe, and elsewhere proves, it's a model that elites—and above all, autocratic elites—find highly appealing.

The other chief rival to the "democracy advantage" theory is an explanatory rather than a political one. Both third world intellectuals and many Western economists of leftist bent mock demands for democratic reform as a species of neocolonialism or an excuse for inaction. In *The End of Poverty*, the development economist Jeffrey Sachs argues that since many African countries already are democratic, democracy can scarcely be the secret to development. "The links from democracy to economic performance are relatively weak," he insists. Similarly, countries that score well on indices of good governance grow only slightly faster than equally poor countries with bad governance. "Africa's governance is poor because Africa is poor," Sachs asserts. As incomes rise, corruption will drop and overall governance will improve. Democratization and governance are dependent variables of poverty, not the other way around. The real source of Africa's ongoing failure, Sachs believes, is disadvantageous geography and ecology, compounded by poor infrastructure. And the solution is therefore more development assistance much more thoughtfully targeted. Sachs goes around Africa telling elites that the problem has nothing to do with their behavior and everything to do with the behavior of donors—another very appealing, if very different, message.

The experience of Mali demonstrated that even in the poorest country—perhaps especially in the poorest country—a democratic regime could attain sufficient *political* legitimacy to flourish even in the face of economic and developmental stagnation. Indeed, the authors of *The Democracy Advantage* observe that only 5 percent of democracies collapsed as a result of three or more consecutive years of economic contraction, and of those, 60 percent returned to democracy within several years. At the same time, democracy will come to seem an increasingly hollow achievement if it does not bring prosperity in its wake. But principles of democracy and good governance must seep deeply into a nation's institutions before, for example, citizens demand, and the state supplies, a more responsive and professional civil service or a more autonomous and incorruptible judiciary. Even then the relation between democracy and development will seem perilously indirect. And many countries now have a highly attractive alternative in the form of China. What, then, can outsiders who believe in democracy and in "the democratic advantage" do to encourage and sustain states such as Mali?

The most pertinent answer had come, of all places, from the Bush administration, in the form of the Millennium Challenge Corporation. In the fall of 2005, Mali had been identified as a country eligible for an MCC grant. Over the next year, according to Bania Touré, the former political attaché in Washington, who now heads the agency overseeing the program, government officials consulted with civic groups and the private sector to come up with appropriate projects. Touré says that they examined eleven projects that had gone unfunded in years past. They looked for investments that would most effectively promote growth. In the end, after conversations with MCC officials, they decided on three: the renovation of the airport in Bamako, the establishment of an industrial park not far from the airport, and a plan to irrigate sixteen thousand hectares of land. The airport project had been sitting in a drawer for eight to ten years; it was too big for any donor to undertake. And donors generally shied away from bringing new land under cultivation, as opposed to programs to increase yield on existing land. The three projects together came to $460.8 million—a huge sum in a country whose annual budget was $19 billion.

Touré explained that the airport and the industrial park were linked. Mali exports only unfinished products, which cannot travel economically by air. And since the country has no access to the sea, its exports must move by road or rail to Dakar, nine hundred miles away—an extremely expensive and wasteful process. Mali can't change its geography, but the airport would become useful for freight handling if Mali began to export more high-value finished products. That was where the industrial park came in. Local entrepreneurs could bottle mango jam, or manufacture textiles, in the new facilities near the airport. It would then make economic sense, in turn, to upgrade the airport for freight as well as for passengers. The government of Mali projected that the investments would produce fifty thousand new jobs. The agricultural project, which cost $234 million, would increase the amount of land under irrigation in Mali by 20 percent, and was expected to affect forty thousand farmers and their dependents. The project was also meant to dovetail with Mali's long-term poverty-reduction plan, which foresaw the improvement of small-scale farms and the establishment of legal mechanisms for secure title to agricultural property.

Touré was also delighted that, as he put it, "The way it's set up, you have no choice—you have to promote transparency." His agency would put out all the contracts for construction and would choose the entrepreneurs—but an American firm would inspect the contracts to make sure that no one was enriching their cousin. This was an altogether new idea in Mali, where, as in much of the third world, using a government position to favor friends and relatives is so routine as barely even to count as corruption. "And since the procurement process doesn't create a lot of suspicion," he added, "the process can move much faster." That was the theory, anyway—nothing existed yet.

The American role in Mali was, of course, nothing like the

American role in Egypt. Feeble democracies presented very different problems from liberal autocracies. The politics were relatively easy; the difficult thing was to find ways of supporting such frail states that increased their autonomy and self-reliance, while also of course making inroads on poverty. NDI was working with legislators to try to make the parliament more effective, and to somehow connect politics with legislation. The Pentagon had given USAID $2 million to create livelihoods among Touareg youth, and thus, in effect, outbid the Salafists. The only problem was finding some useful way to spend the money, since the north had no natural resources and no obvious source of employment. They had tried marketing camel cheese; the product appeared, however, to be an acquired taste.

The MCC held out the possibility of change on a vastly greater scale. It was a hopeful model, but it looked more like a hypothesis. The Bush administration, which was prepared to threaten a constitutional crisis over funding for the war in Iraq, had surrendered when Congress took a meat-ax to its requests for foreign aid. Even the modest sums for the MCC were being taken from other aid programs, and there was a real danger either that promises the MCC had made would have to be postponed or that money would be doled out on an annual basis rather than through the five-year guarantees that allowed recipients to commit themselves to ambitious plans. There was no way to sustain the feeble democracies without spending significantly more money than we had in the past, and here, as elsewhere, the Bush administration was largely failing the test.

9

Democracy Promotion
in the Post-Post-9/11 World

The post-9/11 era is drawing to a close. Until now, the foreign policy of the United States has been governed by the reaction the terrorist attacks produced in George W. Bush and his team. American behavior toward the world would have looked very different—more classically "realist," in all probability—had the attacks never occurred. Our behavior would probably also have been very different—more internationalist and less bellicose—had Al Gore been declared president in 2000. But this event happened to this administration, and so we have the "war on terror," the war in Iraq, and the doctrines laid out in the National Security Strategy of 2002 and President Bush's second inaugural address. All that will necessarily shape and constrain the choices of whoever succeeds George Bush. But he or she will make a new set of choices—a post-post-9/11 strategy.

Where, in this thinking, will the Freedom Agenda fit? Where should it fit? It is an article of faith among current and former Bush administration officials that democracy promotion, with whatever modifications may be introduced, will remain a fixed element of our policy. Liberty at home now depends on liberty abroad, and so any president will do whatever he or she can to promote democracy. But that assumes a great deal: both that the formulation is true, and that, whether true or not, the president's self-defeating policies have not deeply curbed both the national appetite and the national capacity to promote democracy.

The boldness of President Bush's assertions and actions sent deep currents coursing through the academies, think tanks, and publications where foreign policy theory is debated. In Bush's first term, when the war on terror seemed to have carried the day, the "forward-leaning" neoconservative paradigm was celebrated in books by major scholars of international relations, including John Lewis Gaddis, Walter Russell Mead, and Robert Kagan. In the second term, the failures of this policy were brutally anatomized in works not just by liberals but by mainstream and even conservative figures, including Francis Fukuyama, Andrew Bacevich, and John Hulsman, and by former Bush administration officials, including Richard Haass of the State Department and Flynt Leverett of the NSC. Neoconservative foreign policy was, in effect, discredited by virtue of having been put into practice. The Freedom Agenda, which the president had presented as a central element of his worldview, may well be in jeopardy of being discarded along with the rest.

Indeed, Bush's reckless behavior and self-righteous rhetoric have inflamed opinion at home as they have abroad. One class of critics now explains Bush-era policy, very much including the Freedom Agenda, as merely a particularly blunt expression of the long-standing American drive for global dominance. In 2007, Tony Smith, who in *America's Mission* offered an extensive and highly nuanced history of democracy promotion, produced a drastically different account in his flavorsomely titled *A Pact with the Devil: Washington's Bid for World Supremacy and the Betrayal of the American Promise*. Smith argues that centrist Democrats such as Madeleine Albright who favor a strong military and an interventionist policy in the Balkans have become "indistinguishable" from the neoconservatives who made the case for war in Iraq: both advocate a "progressive imperialism" whose goal is to promote "human rights and democratic government among peoples who resisted American hegemony." Andrew Bacevich, a military historian, writes that if Americans insist on promoting democracy in the Middle East, we should no longer "bamboozle ourselves with claims of righteousness which few believe," but rather acknowledge our actual goal: "to keep the world safe for our economy and open to our cultural assault."

Prolonged exposure to George Bush has blinded some critics with rage—just as at one time it blinded others with hero worship—and led them retrospectively to recast the American narrative in the darkest possible terms. But there is a more serious and measured case against the promotion of democracy—or any other founding American principle, for that matter. The realists of the 1950s entertained few of the doubts about the merits of American democracy that one finds today on the left, but they considered the Wilsonian ambition to spread democracy across the globe a grave mistake, as well as an act of hubris. Hans Morgenthau ridiculed this "missionary" impulse, whether expressed through diplomacy or foreign aid. George Kennan insisted that, far from representing a universal aspiration, the system of democratic government was suited to the distinctive history and values of the Anglo-Saxon world. He scoffed at those who dreamed of the democratic conversion of Russia or of other outposts of despotism.

The scholar and essayist William Pfaff laid out the case for a neo-Kennanite policy in *The New York Review of Books* in early 2007. "It is something like a national heresy to argue that the United States does not have a unique moral status and role to play in the history of nations, and therefore in the affairs of the contemporary world," Pfaff writes. "In fact it does not." Pfaff traces this sense of divine election back to the nation's origins. He argues, as Kennan did, that the cold war proponents of "rollback" sought to unleash this deeply arrogant self-conception on the world. The fall of the Berlin wall removed the restraints of prudence, and entranced policy-makers of both sides with a vi-

sion of endless intervention on behalf of democracy and free markets. In Pfaff's view, George Bush updated and reinterpreted this
tradition of providentialism for the post-9/11 age. The administration proposed to replace the centuries-long balance-of-power
system, in which states acknowledged one another's inevitably
conflicting interests and unequal capacities, with a coalition of
democracies led by Washington. Bush thus demanded that the
world fall in behind American leadership. And to the surprise of
all those sharing his delusions, the world resisted, sometimes
subtly and sometimes violently.

Pfaff notes that in *Around the Cragged Hill*, Kennan's memoirs of his old age, the diplomat and scholar asserted that democracy would arise only among a people who fully understood it and
who would do whatever was needed to bring it about. Kennan
went on to acknowledge that many autocracies were unstable.
But, he insisted, "We are not their keepers. We never will be." We
should leave such peoples "to be governed or misgoverned as
habit and tradition may dictate," asking rather that their ruling
regimes observe "the minimum standards of civilized diplomatic
intercourse." Pfaff thus recommends, as Kennan had, a "nonin-
terventionist" policy that presumes that "nations are responsible
for themselves," and avoids the cataclysmic mistakes of crusading
America—Vietnam as well as Iraq—by adopting a policy that
"emphasizes pragmatic and empirical judgment of the interests
and needs of this nation and of others." In effect, Pfaff presents
the elegant version of the claim George Bush advanced in the
2000 campaign when he said, "I'm not so sure the role of the
United States is to go around the world and say, 'This is the way
it's gotta be.'"

Noninterventionism is not isolationism, but rather a policy of
prudence, modesty, watchfulness. It would ward off the worst at
the expense of forgoing the best. But Pfaff would have us forgo a
great deal. He asks us, astonishingly, to accept Kennan's archaic
and at times very unsavory views about culture and democracy.

Kennan expressed a seigneurial contempt for the mass of men, whether at home or abroad; chafed against the very idea of democratic accountability; and in the late thirties started in on a book recommending that Americans adopt a more authoritarian model of government that would, among other things, restrict suffrage. The naïveté of the faith in the universal aspiration to democracy seems much preferable to such Tory cynicism. Worse still, are we really prepared to leave citizens in autocracies to be governed as "habit and tradition" dictate? Is authoritarianism a quaint species of folk culture?

Classic realism of this sort bids us forgo something else as well: the focus on the rights of the individual rather than the prerogatives of the state. We are to accept that nations are responsible for themselves rather than thinking that regimes are responsible to the citizens from whom their legitimacy arises. It's none of our business if some states ignore or trample popular will or the public good—to each his own habits and traditions. This is not just reactionary but archaic. The recognition that individual rights may supersede those of the state is now enshrined in international law. The principle goes back at least to the UN Declaration of Human Rights, and is recognized as well in documents such as the Helsinki Declaration. The UN itself, founded as a club of states, has come to be defined, as Kofi Annan put it, "by a new, more profound awareness of the sanctity, and dignity of every human life." The organization has formally endorsed this principle by accepting, first, a right of access of humanitarian organizations to beleaguered individuals, and then, the right of humanitarian intervention, or "the responsibility to protect." Pfaff himself accepts such intervention when it is "relatively simple to deal with," but notes that humanitarian crises "are often the current manifestation of intractable historical grievances." The wish to do nothing thus happily coincides with our own helplessness.

Realist nonintervention thus depends on a willed indifference to the fate of others. This isn't just morally unacceptable; in a world where we can no longer seal our borders against the consequences of state failure halfway across the world, it's self-defeating, not to mention impossible. But if we are to intervene in the hopes of making life better for people elsewhere in the world, ought it be in the name of democracy? In a recent tract, *Ethical Realism*, Anatol Lieven and John Hulsman, also great admirers of the strategic thinkers of the 1950s, insist that policy-makers on both sides have fallen prey to "democratism," a "messianic commitment" to spread democracy across the globe. In fact, they say, "the beliefs that democracy can be easily spread, that it can be combined with free market reform, and that it will lead to countries becoming peaceful and pro-American" is a delusion born of ideology and of a specious analogy to the experience of Eastern Europe after the end of the cold war. What's more, they observe, the very act of promoting democracy provokes a nationalist backlash, above all among citizens of the Arab world. "Preaching democracy and freedom at them," the authors write, "will be useless if they associate the adoption of Western-style democracy with national humiliation and the sacrifice of vital national interests."

But Lieven and Hulsman seek to practice an "ethical" realism, and so instead of pursuing a "Democratic Peace" that they predict will be neither democratic nor peaceful, they propose that we seek to spread a "Great Capitalist Peace." Marketplace values, they suggest, are far more widely accepted than democratic ones, while prosperity is a surer hedge against aggression than democracy is. They propose trade reform to help developing nations, a focus on good governance rather than on individual rights, and a huge increase in foreign aid directed toward strategically important countries such as Pakistan. (Africa loses out.) The fact that Lieven is a journalist of the left who regards the United States in terms not so different from those of Tony Smith, while Hulsman is a conservative who supported the war in Iraq, speaks volumes about the bipartisan disillusionment with the Bush administration's Wilsonianism of the right.

Realist noninterventionism has become broadly unpalatable, but the argument for less-than-democracy or other-than-democracy has gained many adherents as a result of the failures of the Freedom Agenda. It offers a kind of fallback position for those who are uncomfortable with the language of democracy as well as with the stark calculus of traditional realism. Autocratic regimes themselves are far more receptive to the message of "good governance," "the rule of law," and "modernization." And those who believe that democracy will be solidly founded only when regimes have passed through the long period of gestation while institutions become mature also believe that we should focus on governance and institution-building.

In 2006, the Princeton Project on National Security, which brought together almost every major national security expert from the moderate left to the moderate right, issued a report titled "Forging a World of Liberty Under Law." The authors write, "Democracy is the best instrument that humans have devised for ensuring individual liberty over the long term, but only when it exists within a framework of order established by law . . . Elections remain important as a long-term goal, but a grand strategy of forging a world of liberty under law means broadening our approach by bolstering the many elements that underpin a stable and sustainable democratic government and by countering the multiple ills that may destroy it."

Why not, then, seek to spread the free market, the rule of law, human rights—instead of *democracy*, a word that has been almost fatally tainted? Well, what would that mean? Does it mean that we will help train judges and prosecutors and policemen and jail wardens, but not political parties? That we will not exert diplomatic pressure to ensure that elections are transparent—or that they occur at all? Will we protest when prisoners are abused but not when newspapers are shut down? Where, in short, is the barrier between democracy and its many constituent elements?

The authors of "Forging a World of Liberty Under Law" write that rather than use the divisive language of democracy, we should seek to nurture "Popular, Accountable and Rights-regarding government." They characterize these regimes as follows:

> PAR governments are more transparent, due to the checks and balances that naturally result from pluralist, participatory systems. They are more effective, because accountability reduces corruption and increases competence. And they are more trustworthy, because they are constrained by the laws governing their behavior toward their own citizens. Further, PAR governments provide many more opportunities for their citizens to achieve their goals through ordinary political processes and to make better lives for themselves through economic opportunity.

These are, of course, the central attributes of democracy. The only thing gained by the change in terminology is the clear recognition that stable democracies rest upon strong institutions, and not simply on the outcome of elections. But we know that.

If there is any meaningful debate here at all, it is not really about one thing as opposed to another, but rather one set of things before another: rule of law/economic development/marketplace reform before elections. But elections can be the crucial catalyst for those broader, slower changes, as in the "color revolutions" of the former Soviet Union and the Balkans. And how do you respond, as Thomas Carothers asked in response to Fareed Zakaria, when people say that they want elections even though the state is not "ready" for them? Do you tell them to wait? You can't, of course. And you shouldn't. Even desperately poor people sometimes care very much about representation.

The "participation explosion" that Gabriel Almond and Sidney Verba observed forty-five years ago is vastly more powerful and widespread today. And yes, that demand for voice can be, and is, stoked by illiberal democrats and even genocidal maniacs. So is religious belief; the problem lies not with the belief but with the political mechanisms by which it is manipulated. Democracy promotion offers a means, however limited, by which outsiders can help shape those mechanisms for the purpose of authentic representation rather than exploitation.

Democracy promotion is not only something we should do but also something we should be seen doing. Of all the candidates for president of either party, the one who spoke most often of democracy, and of what our democracy means to the world, is Barack Obama. Unlike any of his rivals, Obama was raised outside of the continental United States, in Hawaii and Indonesia; his father was Kenyan, and much of his family remained there. Obama is acutely aware of what America looks like from the outside—both the resentments it engenders and the profound sense of hope it raises. In a speech delivered in Washington in August 2007, he observed that United States senators typically see "the desperate faces" of Darfur or Baghdad from the height of a helicopter. He added: "And it makes you stop and wonder: when those faces look up at an American helicopter, do they feel hope or do they feel hate?" Obama believes not only that our well-being depends on the well-being of ordinary third-world citizens—as George Bush and Condoleezza Rice do—but that it also depends on what those children thought as they gazed up at an American helicopter. Those children had to feel that their well-being mattered to us.

Obama believes that the spread of democracy is in our power as well as our interest. He (along with John McCain, among others) cosponsored the 2005 ADVANCE Democracy Act (which never became law), which instructed U.S. diplomats and officials "to use all instruments of United States influence to support, promote, and strengthen democratic principles, practices, and values in foreign countries." But Obama also thinks that the Bush administration has lost sight of the daily reality of the people they proposed to help. In a conversation just before his Washington speech, Obama pointed out to me that FDR hadn't even included voting in his famous 1942 "Four Freedoms" speech. "People want freedom from fear, they want freedom from want. To some degree those are the foundational freedoms. We have to be focused on what are the aspirations of the people in those countries. Once those aspirations are met, it opens up space for the kind of democratic regime that we want."

Obama doesn't favor subordinating democracy to other considerations; in fact, he says that we should be demanding free and fair elections as one of the conditions of our continued aid to Pakistan. Rather, he proposes enmeshing democracy assistance in a larger system of aid. In his speech, he went on to say, "We do need to stand for democracy. And I will. But democracy is about more than a ballot box . . . I will focus our support on helping nations build independent judicial systems, honest police forces, and financial systems that are transparent and accountable. Freedom must also mean freedom from want, not freedom lost to an empty stomach. So I will make poverty reduction a key part of helping other nations reduce anarchy." Obama proposed doubling foreign aid, and vowed to establish a $2 billion fund to promote free access to secular education. He said that he would radically increase our capacity to engage in nation-building to prevent frail states from failing altogether. He would stop using public diplomacy simply as a means to prop up White House policy, and would open up "America Houses" all over the Islamic world. He would restore our ties with multilateral institutions. And above all, he would show the children looking up at the helicopter that the United States held itself to the highest democratic standards. "We will," Obama said, "again set an example for the world that the law is not subject to the whims of stubborn rulers, and that justice is not arbitrary."

We must set an example; this is where democracy promotion begins. During the 1960s we understood—or at least the "cold war liberals" did—that civil rights legislation helped us win the war of ideas by showing that democracy could better serve marginalized peoples than communism did. We understood that we had to live our ideas. And now? The president who has placed the promotion of democracy at the very core of his foreign policy, at least rhetorically, has behaved with more contempt for the liberties of citizens and noncitizens alike, with less transparency in his deliberations, with a greater readiness to manipulate public opinion, and with less respect for his domestic opposition or for public opinion abroad than almost any of his predecessors.

Nothing any successor administration does with respect to promoting our ideals will matter so long as we appear to be unwilling to apply those ideals to ourselves. And the fact that we are now engaged in a "war on terror" will not be seen as an excuse for the suspension of traditional American liberties, but rather as a test of our commitment to them. It is precisely because torture might possibly produce useful information, and precisely because catching thousands of Muslim men in a legal dragnet might possibly turn up a potential terrorist or two, that we must make, and be seen to make, the choice to forgo such tactics. Thomas Carothers writes of the need for a policy of "decontamination," starting with how we behave at home. The next president, while remaining resolute in such lethal settings as Afghanistan, will have to openly forswear Bush-era tactics, and very publicly act to change them. Of course, it takes much longer to regain a reputation than it does to lose it; we will operate under a very dark cloud of suspicion for a long time to come.

But decontamination is also a matter of rhetoric. It is profoundly discrediting to say that we will judge our relationships with foreign leaders on their progress in democracy so long as other considerations, whether of regional security or trade, dictate otherwise. It is reckless to speak of the spread of democracy in transcendent and theological terms, especially at a time when much of the world is recoiling from what it sees as an American crusade. It is pointlessly alienating and self-righteous to describe the promotion of democracy as a peculiarly American faith and policy—as President Bush did in his second inaugural—when so many Western governments and NGOs are deeply involved in the endeavor. The next president must not abandon the language of democracy or retreat into the kind of hard-shell realism that George Bush the candidate proposed in 2000. But he or she could be more honest, more modest, more generous. As Michael McFaul and Francis Fukuyama suggest in a recent policy brief, "Acting in concrete ways to support human rights and democracy groups around the world, while speaking more modestly about American goals, might serve both our interests and ideals better."

McFaul and Fukuyama, and Carothers too, suggest that we uncouple democracy promotion from the war on terror. While it's true that the terrorist attacks showed how vulnerable we are to the internal political culture of remote countries, the constant linkage of the two policies inevitably implies that we consider regime change and military force instruments of democracy promotion. Our most discredited policies thus taint our most supposedly idealistic one. What's more, so long as those ideals are subsumed into our power, we guarantee the nationalist backlash of which Lieven and Hulsman warn. And our hypocrisy will seem patent. "The Bush Administration," as Carothers writes, "has fallen into the habit of using democracy promotion as a cover for U.S. efforts to change or shape political outcomes in other countries for the sake of U.S. security interests with little real regard for whether the effect on the other country is in fact pro-democratic." We should rather acknowledge the truth, which is, as Carothers writes, that "the United States balances its interest in democracy against its other interests and often struggles to match its actions to its ideals."

We need equally to find a less strident and breast-beating way to talk about ourselves. The Bush administration has tried to use public diplomacy as a branch of democracy promotion, as if we will win converts by repeating often enough and loudly enough what a noble enterprise is America. This has not worked, and will not work. And the era when America can broadcast its virtues into a void has ended. Local and satellite media, the Internet, podcasts, and so on will largely drown out the American voice. If public diplomacy means arguing our side against their side, we will lose. But it can also mean giving people abroad access to America and to American life. We need to be giving out far more scholarships to young people, and eliminating the humiliations now attendant upon obtaining a visa and passing through our customs checks. And Barack Obama is right that we need to open, or rather reopen, "America Houses," where people can go and read books and magazines and access websites—and, he suggests, get English lessons and vocational training in a safe and pleasant and uncensored setting (though concerns about terrorism will make some of these facilities as much virtual as actual).

In *The End of Poverty*, Jeffrey Sachs uses medical diagnosis as a metaphor for foreign assistance. He argues that since every country's conditions and needs are different, it's foolish and dangerous to insist that each take the same neoliberal medicine, slashing government spending and deregulating the economy. The same may be said of democracy promotion; both the Clinton and Bush administrations were inclined to apply the same formula everywhere, though the two forms of treatment were quite different. Democracy promotion needs less ideology and more of the fine-grained analysis that realists such as Pfaff consider the ground-work of diplomacy. At the very least, we should begin by thinking about distinct classes of countries. Stable and essentially popular autocracies like Russia and China are very different from the profoundly unpopular autocracies of the Middle East, which are in turn very different from the fledgling and often brittle democracies of Africa, Asia, and Latin America. Each presents its own problems and possibilities.

Democracy promotion is scarcely a meaningful policy toward self-confidently authoritarian regimes. We had little ability to shape Russia's political culture in the midst of the cold war. Then we enjoyed a period of influence when Russia's empire and economy collapsed—though even then we turned out to have less capacity to alter domestic events than we imagined. Now that the price of oil and natural gas has made Russia a new, if very different, kind of continental empire, the country is once again all but impervious to outside influence over internal affairs; reducing our consumption of oil, and that of others, would probably constitute our most effective democracy-promotion policy. China's economic boom produces a similar effect; the country is now confidently exporting its own alternative model in the third world. In Iran, whose coffers are filled with oil billions, American democracy promotion efforts provoked such a backlash that Akbar Ganji, a brave dissident celebrated in the West, publicly implored the U.S. Congress to pass a law prohibiting payment to "individuals or groups opposing the Iranian government."

The recognition that we can do little if anything to shape the politics of such regimes does not mean that the United States should simply abandon the brave figures who challenge those regimes. Karim Sadjadpour, an Iranian expert with the Carnegie Endowment, testified before Congress in late 2007 that while the United States should abandon democracy promotion in Iran, it should continue to speak out against political jailings, the persecution of religious minorities, and the like. He also proposed that the United States fund "objective, professional Persian-language news sources"—as opposed to the highly politicized Voice of America broadcast. In each of these countries, of course, we will continue to face hard choices between advancing our strategic and economic interests on the one hand and protesting human rights abuses on the other.

Impoverished democracies, above all in sub-Saharan Africa, are of course far more amenable to Western help. Few would argue that they shouldn't be helped. But their needs will often seem bottomless. Nations such as Mali or Zambia, or even El Salvador and Nicaragua, force questions about our will to provide economic assistance, the efficacy of that help, and the capacity of the host country to use those resources effectively. We clearly need to spend more money, as Democrats such as Barack Obama argue, and to spend it more wisely. We must also work on building the strength of political parties, on promoting reform in the various aspects of governance and rule of law, on pushing protected markets to open up, on strengthening civil society and the like. We must, as the economist Paul Collier suggests, help countries avoid the "resource trap" by establishing mechanisms to ensure that revenue from oil or copper makes its way to the treasury, and then is used effectively. This is all the work of a generation. And there will be a great deal of backsliding, as the violence in Kenya in December 2007 made painfully clear. Often, there will be little or nothing outsiders can do to ward off catastrophe.

The hardest and most important category is the one in between—be it shaky autocracies like Ethiopia, "liberal autocracies" like Morocco or Jordan, or regressing former democracies like Thailand or Nigeria. And of course this question is most urgent in the Middle East and the Islamic world. And here, also, the Bush administration has left the biggest mess. Should we say that the well is, at least for now, hopelessly poisoned? Flynt Leverett, a former NSC official and a Middle East expert, argues that Bush's democracy policy in the Arab world has "emboldened radicals and weakened moderates," and he pleads for a return to the realism of Bush's father. "While the United States should engage moderate Arab partners more systematically on economic reform and human rights," Leverett concludes, "Washington should drop its insistence on early resort to open electoral processes as a litmus test for 'democratization.'"

Washington has, of course, already done just that, restoring the emphasis on regional stability that Condoleezza Rice publicly renounced in June 2005. The change in policy has done nothing to address the problems outlined in the 2002 Arab Human Development Report. Yet it's true that our ability to shape the internal dynamic of the Arab world is very limited—though not because these states can afford to be indifferent to the U.S. or even because, as the example of Egypt shows, their publics utterly reject an American role. In a study for the Carnegie Endowment, Michele Dunne and Marina Ottaway refer to what Samuel Huntington described as the King's Dilemma: even limited change authorized by the autocratic ruler often emboldens reformers, and thus endangers, rather than secures, his power, as the Shah of Iran learned in the late 1970s. Rulers who resist change are thus acting perfectly rationally. At the same time, however, Arab elites increasingly recognize that they must change in order to keep pace with a globalized economy, and thus satisfy the popular demand for social mobility and economic opportunity. The goal of such regimes, Dunne and Ottaway write, "has not been democratization but modernization."

The Middle East furnishes some slightly more hopeful models, the authors note: in Morocco, the monarchy has made real changes in family law, permitted freer elections, and allowed an Islamic party to operate; an opposition party now functions in Yemen and Algeria. But in every case, the regime has decided how much reform is compatible with retaining an uncontested grip on power. And even where a younger generation, as with Gamal Mubarak in Egypt, has gained some control over the instruments of modernization, hard-liners have retained their monopoly on political and military power. The authors predict "continued political stagnation" rather than risky attempts to offer real political change. Outsiders, they note, have largely accommodated this impulse by focusing on economic and institutional, rather than political, change. The new policy, they argue, "is having very little effect." They conclude by observing that "political reform can never be risk-free: Too much close management perpetuates authoritarianism, and unmanaged processes have unpredictable outcomes."

And so the realists' fear that democracy promotion could endanger stability in the Middle East is scarcely baseless. And there is every reason to expect that regimes will dig in their heels in the face of pressure for real political change. And yet at the same time "modernization only" won't work: Arab regimes must open up if they are to gain real legitimacy in the eyes of their citizens. How, then, to get from here to there? Ideologues such as Natan Sharansky—or George W. Bush—imagined that if you shattered the existing order in the Middle East, a democracy would rise in its place. This fantasy has now been thoroughly chastened. People such as Dunne, Ottaway, and Thomas Carothers, who have extensively studied the political dynamic of the Middle East, recognize that there is no formula for reform, nor even a clear path from autocracy to democracy. Their expectations are suitably modest. But they do not profess nonintervention. As Dunne remarked in congressional testimony in 2006, now that Arab publics have begun demanding change, we must choose between supporting them or not.

Exaggerating our helplessness is at least as great a mistake as exaggerating our capacity. The Bush White House succeeded in pushing Hosni Mubarak further than anyone might have guessed. The mistake was not in the effort but in the failure to rise to Mubarak's challenge, and in the overreaction to the Hamas victory in Palestine. When Congress mandated that American democracy assistance go directly to civil-society groups rather than through Cairo, the regime resisted, and then relented. We should direct more money throughout the Middle East to reform-minded organizations. And we should begin to put conditions on the vast aid we now give as a reward for compliant behavior on regional security issues. Those billions should also be seen as an inducement for better behavior toward the regimes' citizens. Why should we be predicating our aid throughout the world on democratization, marketplace reform, and progress against corruption and yet make no such demands in the Middle East? Some leaders may walk away rather than accept such demands, and then rally citizens by inveighing against "blackmail." It's far less likely that they will then choose to act as regional spoilers: conservative Sunni states are not going to throw in their lot with Iran or Syria.

And we must accept that "moderate Islam" is a meaningful category, and distinguish between those groups willing to play by democratic rules and those who are not. "If we are serious about Middle Eastern democracy," writes Shadi Hadid, a democracy activist and scholar, "then we must accept that it will come with an Islamist flavor." Hadid lists the chief Islamist parties in Egypt, Jordan, Algeria, Kuwait, and, of course, Turkey among the moderates. (The same should be said of mainstream Islamists in Morocco.) Some of these parties, like the Muslim Brotherhood in Egypt, endorse the terrorist tactics of Hamas but have explicitly renounced violence in their own countries; and we should view this latter point as the more salient one. Many of those groups have no desire for help from Westerners, and certainly not from the United States. But we should treat them with respect, encourage them to compete in the political marketplace, and welcome their success, even as we make clear that terrorism is unacceptable everywhere and that Israel's survival is not negotiable (though the terms of Israel's relationship with its neighbors certainly are).

Finally, the neoconservative's simple-minded faith in "liberty" and their antipathy to nation-building, quite apart from matters of equity and justice, has painted us into a corner from which we must escape. If democracy has nothing to do with access to school and clean water and health care, or with knowing that the land you farm is yours and can't be stolen from you through force or fraud, then ordinary people won't put much stock in it. As Barack Obama puts it, we should focus on people's real aspirations—which of course include political freedom and democracy. Why should we seek to advance one set of goods to the exclusion of the other? Though there is still some disagreement about whether, or to what extent, political development must follow a certain sequence—with institutions first and elections only later—no one argues that a democracy can become stable absent basic political, economic, and social institutions. The neocons and the small-government ideologues believed that democratic elections would lead these institutions to generate spontaneously, or that we would do more harm than good in trying to nurture them. That a priori view is another casualty of the Bush era.

If rebuilding failed states, conquering infectious disease, training policemen and parliamentarians, nurturing civil society, and strengthening political parties are all of a piece, then we should reorganize our efforts accordingly. Right now such aid originates in the State Department, the Pentagon, USAID, the Millennium Challenge Corporation, and elsewhere—and this after Condoleezza Rice streamlined the aid bureaucracy. Michael McFaul and Larry Diamond have called for the creation of a cabinet-level Department of International Development and Reconstruction that would consolidate all of these functions. They also suggest that funds for democracy promotion be disbursed largely through NGOs, including the NED and its party-based branches. This not only helps remove the taint of the American brand but also avoids the situation in which State Department diplomats must cultivate good relations with regimes while at the same time financing programs that are bound to discomfit those regimes.

Democracy promotion is, in this sense, a single facet of a larger effort or, perhaps one should say, of an idea of our role in the world. We must take far more responsibility than we have in the past for the well-being of weak, endangered, striving states. We are obliged to do so not only out of moral considerations but, as President Bush and Condoleezza Rice concluded, out of calculations of self-interest. Liberty at home may not depend on liberty abroad, but it surely depends on a sense of hope and possibility abroad. Our powers, of course, are limited: we can't cure what ails the Congo, and we seem unable to banish the political nightmares of Sudan, Somalia, and Zimbabwe. But we must try to make a difference where and when and how we can. We have been trying, in our heartfelt, overbearing, and self-righteous way, since the Philippines. It's true that we haven't succeeded most of the time, but it matters now so much more than it ever has before.

A Note on Sources

This book draws on both academic and journalistic sources. I have listed below the books, reports, scholarly articles, and the like that I read in the course of my research, and that especially inform the historical portions of this book. For the latter 60 percent or so of the book, I also read a wide variety of news accounts and conducted a hundred-odd interviews—with officials of the Bush administration; students of democracy promotion; and activists, politicians, scholars, and ordinary citizens in Egypt and Mali.

Albright, Madeleine. *Madam Secretary*. New York: Miramax Books, 2003.

Almond, Gabriel A., and Sidney Verba. *The Civic Culture: Political Attitudes and Democracy in Five Nations*. Newbury Park, Calif.: Sage Publications, 1989.

Bacevich, Andrew J. *The New American Militarism: How Americans Are Seduced by War*. Oxford: Oxford University Press, 2005.

Beinart, Peter. *The Good Fight: Why Liberals—and Only Liberals—Can Win the War on Terror and Make America Great Again*. New York: HarperCollins, 2006.

Brands, H. W. *Woodrow Wilson*. New York: Times Books, 2003.

Bratton, Michael, and Nicolas van de Walle. *Democratic Experiments in Africa: Regime Transitions in Comparative Perspective*. Cambridge: Cambridge University Press, 1997.

Brown, Nathan J., Amr Hamzawy, and Marina Ottaway. "Islamist Movements and the Democratic Process in the Arab World: Exploring the Gray Zone." Carnegie Endowment, Democracy and the Rule of Law Program, March 2006.

Brumberg, Daniel. "Islam Is Not the Solution (or the Problem)," *The Washington Quarterly* (Winter 2005–2006).

Carothers, Thomas. "The Backlash Against Democracy Promotion," *Foreign Affairs* (March/April 2006).

————. *Critical Mission: Essays on Democracy Promotion.* Washington, D.C.: Carnegie Endowment for International Peace, 2004.

————. *In the Name of Democracy: U.S. Policy Toward Latin America in the Reagan Years.* Berkeley: University of California Press, 1991.

————, ed. *Promoting the Rule of Law Abroad: In Search of Knowledge.* Washington, D.C.: Carnegie Endowment for International Peace, 2006.

————. "U.S. Democracy Promotion During and After Bush," Carnegie Endowment for International Peace, September 2007.

Carothers, Thomas, and Marina Ottaway, eds. *Uncharted Journey: Promoting Democracy in the Middle East.* Washington, D.C.: Carnegie Endowment for International Peace, 2005.

Carter, Jimmy. *Keeping Faith: Memoirs of a President.* New York: Bantam Books, 1987.

"Changing Minds, Winning Peace: A New Strategic Direction for U.S. Public Diplomacy in the Arab and Muslim World." Report of the Advisory Group on Public Diplomacy in the Arab and Muslim World, October 1, 2003.

China's African Policy, January 2006.

Collier, Paul. *The Bottom Billion: Why the Poorest Countries Are Failing and What Can Be Done About It.* Oxford: Oxford University Press, 2007.

Dahl, Robert A. *Polyarchy: Participation and Opposition.* New Haven, Conn.: Yale University Press, 1971.

"Democracy, Development and Poverty Reduction," Community of Democracies, 2007 Bamako Ministerial Consensus.

DeYoung, Karen. *Soldier: The Life of Colin Powell.* New York: Alfred A. Knopf, 2004.

Diamond, Larry, ed. *Democracy in Developing Countries: Latin America.* Boulder, Colo.: Lynne Rienner Publishers, 1999.

Dunne, Michele. "Evaluating Egyptian Reform." Carnegie Endowment, Democracy and Rule of Law Project, no. 66, January 2006.

"Forging a World of Liberty Under Law: U.S. National Security in the 21st Century." Final Report of the Princeton Project on National Security, September 27, 2006.

Friend, Theodore. *Between Two Empires: The Ordeal of the Philippines, 1929–1946.* New Haven, Conn.: Yale University Press, 1965.

Fukuyama, Francis. *America at the Crossroads: Democracy, Power, and the Neoconservative Legacy.* New Haven, Conn.: Yale University Press, 2006.

Fukuyama, Francis, and Michael McFaul. "Should Democracy Be Promoted?" The Stanley Foundation, June 2007.

Gaddis, John Lewis. *Strategies of Containment: A Critical Appraisal of American National Security Policy During the Cold War.* Oxford: Oxford University Press, 2005.

————. *Surprise, Security, and the American Experience.* Cambridge, Mass.: Harvard University Press, 2004.

Gerson, Michael J. *Heroic Conservatism: Why Republicans Need to Embrace America's Ideals (And Why They Deserve to Fail If They Don't)*. New York: HarperOne, 2007.

Gleeck, Lewis E. *American Institutions in the Philippines, 1898–1941*. Manila: Manila Conservation Society, 1976.

Goldgeier, James M., and Michael McFaul. *Power and Purpose: U.S. Policy Toward Russia After the Cold War*. Washington, D.C.: Brookings Institution Press, 2003.

Halperin, Morton H., Joseph T. Siegle, and Michael M. Weinstein. *The Democracy Advantage: How Democracies Promote Prosperity and Peace*. New York: Routledge, 2005.

Hamid, Shadi. "Engaging Political Islam to Promote Democracy." Progressive Policy Institute, June 2007.

Hamzawy, Amr, Marina Ottaway, and Nathan J. Brown. "What Islamists Need to Be Clear About." Carnegie Endowment, Democracy and Rule of Law Program, February 2007.

Huntington, Samuel P. "The Clash of Civilizations," *Foreign Affairs* (Summer 1993).

———. *Political Order in Changing Societies*. New Haven, Conn.: Yale University Press, 1968.

———. *The Third Wave: Democratization in the Late Twentieth Century*. Norman: University of Oklahoma Press, 1993.

Jessup, Philip C. *Elihu Root*. New York: Dodd, Mead and Company, 1938.

Kagan, Robert. *Of Paradise and Power*. New York: Alfred A. Knopf, 2003.

Kaplan, Robert. "The Coming Anarchy," *The Atlantic Monthly*, February 1996.

———. "Was Democracy Just a Moment?" *The Atlantic Monthly*, December 1997.

Karnow, Stanley. *In Our Image: America's Empire in the Philippines*. New York: Random House, 1989.

Kennan, George F. *American Diplomacy*. Chicago: University of Chicago Press, 1984.

Kirkpatrick, Jeane. "Dictatorships and Double Standards," *Commentary*, November 1979.

Leiken, Robert S., and Steven Brooke. "The Moderate Muslim Brotherhood," *Foreign Affairs* (March/April 2007).

Lieven, Anatol, and John Hulsman. *Ethical Realism: A Vision for America's Role in the World*. New York: Pantheon, 2006.

Lipset, Seymour Martin. *Political Man: The Social Bases of Politics*. Baltimore, Md.: Johns Hopkins University Press, 1981.

Lukacs, John. *George Kennan: A Study of Character*. New Haven, Conn.: Yale University Press, 2007.

McFaul, Michael. "Democracy Promotion as a World Value." *The Washington Quarterly* (Winter 2004–2005).

Malone, David. *Decision-Making in the UN Security Council: The Case of Haiti.* Oxford: Clarendon Press, 1998.

Mann, James. *Rise of the Vulcans: The History of Bush's War Cabinet.* New York: Penguin Books, 2004.

Mansfield, Edward D., and Jack Snyder. *Electing to Fight: Why Emerging Democracies Go to War.* Cambridge, Mass.: MIT Press, 2005.

Marshall, Will, ed. *With All Our Might: A Progressive Strategy for Defeating Jihadism and Defending Liberty.* Lanham, Md.: Rowman and Littlefield Publishers, 2006.

May, Glenn Anthony. *Social Engineering in the Philippines: The Aims, Execution and Impact of American Colonial Policy, 1900–1913.* Westport, Conn.: Greenwood Press, 1980.

Mead, Walter Russell. *Power, Terror, Peace and War: America's Grand Strategy in a World at Risk.* New York: Alfred A. Knopf, 2004.

Moore, Barrington. *Social Origins of Dictatorship and Democracy: Lord and Peasant in the Making of the Modern World.* Boston: Beacon Press, 1993.

Morgenthau, Hans J. *Politics Among Nations: The Struggle for Power and Peace.* New York: Alfred A. Knopf, 1965.

Muñoz, Heraldo, ed. *Democracy Rising: Assessing the Global Challenges.* Boulder, Colo.: Lynne Rienner Publishers, 2005.

Muñoz, Heraldo, and Joseph S. Tulchin. eds. *Latin American Nations in World Politics.* New York: Westview Press, 1996.

O'Donnell, Guillermo. *Transitions from Authoritarian Rule: Comparative Perspectives.* Baltimore, Md.: Johns Hopkins University Press, 1986.

Osgood, Kenneth. *Total Cold War: Eisenhower's Secret Propaganda Battle at Home and Abroad.* Lawrence: University Press of Kansas, 2006.

Ottaway, Marina, and Michele Dunne. "Incumbent Regimes and the 'King's Dilemma' in the Arab World," Carnegie Endowment for International Peace, December 2007.

Packenham, Robert A. *Liberal America and the Third World: Political Development Ideas in Foreign Aid and Social Science.* Princeton, N.J.: Princeton University Press, 1973.

Packer, George. *The Assassin's Gate: America in Iraq.* New York: Farrar, Straus and Giroux, 2005.

Pfaff, William. "Manifest Destiny: A New Direction for America," *The New York Review of Books*, February 15, 2007.

Plattner, Marc F., and João Carlos Espada, eds. *The Democratic Invention.* Baltimore, Md.: Johns Hopkins University Press, 2000.

Piccone, Ted, and Richard Youngs, eds. *Strategies for Democratic Change: Assessing the Global Response.* Washington, D.C.: Democracy Coalition Project, 2006.

Pringle, Henry F. *The Life and Times of William Howard Taft.* New York: Farrar and Rinehart, 1939.

Rice, Condoleezza, "Promoting the National Interest," *Foreign Affairs* (January/February 2000).

Rosen, Gary, ed. *The Right War: The Conservative Debate on Iraq*. Cambridge: Cambridge University Press, 2005.

Rothkopf, David. *Running the World: The Inside Story of the National Security Council and the Architects of American Power*. New York: Public Affairs, 2004.

Sachs, Jeffrey D. *The End of Poverty: Economic Possibilities for Our Time*. New York: Penguin, 2005.

Sharansky, Natan. *The Case for Democracy: The Power of Freedom to Overcome Tyranny and Terror*. New York: Public Affairs, 2004.

Shehata, Samer, and Joshua Stacher. "Boxing in the Brothers." Middle East Report Online, August 9, 2007.

———. "The Brotherhood Goes to Parliament," Middle East Report Online, March 9, 2007.

Smith, Tony. *America's Mission: The United States and the Worldwide Struggle for Democracy in the Twentieth Century*. Princeton, N.J.: Princeton University Press, 1994.

———. *A Pact with the Devil: Washington's Bid for World Supremacy and the Betrayal of the American Promise*. New York: Routledge, 2007.

Soderberg, Nancy. *The Superpower Myth: The Use and Misuse of American Might*. Hoboken, N.J.: John Wiley and Sons, 2005.

Stanley, Peter W. *A Nation in the Making: The Philippines and the United States, 1899–1921*. Cambridge, Mass.: Harvard University Press, 1974.

Talbott, Strobe. *The Russia Hand: A Memoir of Presidential Diplomacy*. New York: Random House, 2002.

Traub, James. *The Best Intentions: Kofi Annan and the UN in the Era of American World Power*. New York: Farrar, Straus and Giroux, 2006.

———. "Downsizing Foreign Policy," *The New York Times Magazine*, January 14, 2001.

UN Development Programme. Arab Human Development Report, 2002.

Wittes, Tamara Coffman, and Sarah E. Yerkes. "What Price Freedom? Assessing the Bush Administration's Freedom Agenda," Saban Center for Middle East Policy at the Brookings Institution Analysis Paper no. 10, September 2006.

Woodward, Bob. *Bush at War*. New York: Simon & Schuster, 2002.

———. *State of Denial: Bush at War, Part III*. New York: Simon & Schuster, 2006.

Worcester, Dean C. *The Philippines Past and Present*. New York: Macmillan, 1914.

Wright, Lawrence. *The Looming Tower: Al Qaeda and the Road to 9/11*. New York: Alfred A. Knopf, 2007.

Yacoubian, Mona. "Engaging Islamists and Promoting Democracy," United States Institute of Peace Special Report 190, August 2007.

Zakaria, Fareed. *The Future of Freedom: Illiberal Democracy at Home and Abroad*. New York: Norton and Company, 2003.

———. "The Rise of Illiberal Democracy," *Foreign Affairs* (November/December 1997).

———. "Why Do They Hate Us?" *Newsweek*, October 15, 2001.

Zoellick, Robert, "A Republican Foreign Policy," *Foreign Affairs* (January/February 2000).

Acknowledgments

Much of what I know about democracy promotion owes to the work of three scholar-practitioners: Larry Diamond, Thomas Carothers, and Michael McFaul. Each of them also read portions of the manuscript, as did Steven Sestanovich, Hala Mustafa, Raphael Ouattara, and Ibrahim Ag-Youssouf. I'm very grateful to all of them. I received invaluable guidance as well from Ken Wollack and Michele Dunne. My account of the early history of democracy promotion leans heavily on Tony Smith's irreplaceable book, *America's Mission*. Philip Zelikow and Steven Krasner, senior Bush administration officials, were kind enough to speak to me at length both during and after their tenure. I could not have navigated Cairo without the help of Lauren Lovelace, nor Mali without Adam Thiam and Tierno Diallo.

My agent, Andrew Wylie, insisted that I write the book that meant the most to me, and cheered me on thereafter. My editor, Eric Chinski, offered, as always, wise counsel and support. Gena Hemshaw helped guide the book, with unfailing tact and charm, from blueprint to drydock to launch. Wah-Ming Chang, my production editor, saved me from error. My mother, Lee Traub, spotted a misused show-off word. All remaining errors are, of course, my own.

Index